Benjamin S. Kleinberg

University of Maryland,
Baltimore County

American Society
in the
Postindustrial Age

Technocracy, Power, and the End of Ideology

Charles E. Merrill Publishing Company
A Bell & Howell Company
Columbus, Ohio

Merrill Sociology Series

Under the editorship of

Richard L. Simpson
University of North Carolina, Chapel Hill

and

Paul E. Mott

Published by Charles E. Merrill Publishing Company
A Bell & Howell Company
Columbus, Ohio 43216

ISBN: 0-675-09034-2

Library of Congress Catalog Card Number: 72-89898

1 2 3 4 5 6 7 8 / 78 77 76 75 74 73

Printed in the United States of America

Contents

To Susan,
and to Allen and Leah,
a generation of beauty and hope

Preface

American society in the late twentieth century is moving into a new stage of history, not only for itself, but as a model of possibility which other advanced industrial nations, from Western Europe to Japan, already appear to be following. As an emerging "postindustrial" society, America today is a study in striking and confusing contrasts, in which growing differentiation of occupations, life styles, and subcultural identities combines and often clashes with the growing integration and centralization of economic and political institutions. This book attempts to analyze those major trends which characterize American society as it moves into the postindustrial age. As a sociological analysis it seeks to describe the social structures and institutions which are central to these developments, and the relation between these institutions and the emerging new "technocratic" class which is so closely connected with them. This structural analysis is accompanied by an examination of the ideas and rationalizations of the new class, and particularly of its social scientists who act both as theorists and proponents of a technocratically managed postindustrial society. In addition, the reaction of other groups in the society affected by postindustrial development is also analyzed. Thus the present work is a simultaneously structural and ideological analysis, and the aim of this dual approach is to provide a rounded picture of a society in rapid and radical transition, a new social type which is as yet only partially understood.

Because the issues involved in this work are not only matters of social theory, but ultimately also questions of public policy, the intention has been to make them understandable to social science students and interested laymen as well as to other scholars. At the same time, a work which seeks to discuss developments that go beyond established theory and to analyze newly emerging social patterns that affect the overall society, necessarily operates on a broad canvas and can be no more than a suggestive beginning. Thus, it is not merely routine to state that the ideas expressed here and their manner of formulation, though benefitting from the advice of those acknowledged below, are finally my own, and that I assume responsibility for any errors or omissions in this presentation.

My first acknowledgment must be to Arthur J. Vidich, Chairman of the Department of Sociology of the New School, for his continuing encouragement and critical insight in helping me through a complex task of analysis while this book was taking its initial shape as a doctoral dissertation. Acknowledgments are also due Deborah Offenbacher and Hans Dreitzel of the New School, for their critical comments on the manuscript; and to Richard Sabatino, Professor of Economics at the University of Rhode Island, for his sympathetic reading of the first chapters of an earlier version. Further thanks are due the Littauer Foundation and its President, Harry Starr, for research support which helped the completion of this work in its original version, and provided background information for its present revision. In addition, acknowledgments are due to my colleague William Rothstein of the University of Maryland Baltimore County, and to Fred Rosenberg of the Nassau-Suffolk Regional Planning Board, for their helpful comments. In particular, acknowledgment and many thanks are due to Richard L. Simpson, for his thorough critical review and perceptive suggestions which helped me to update and revise this work. Thanks are also due Mrs. Laura Justus for her careful typing of manuscript.

Finally, to my wife Susan, my deepest gratitude is owing for her patience and devotion in helping both of us through the writing of this book. As in everything else, she shared in this to the full, giving it the benefit of her good taste and sense of relevance.

B.S.K.

Baltimore, Maryland
1973

Introduction

In the context of the contemporary crisis in American public life and thought, the "end of ideology" and its evolution into a theory of "postindustrial" society should be of interest to all those concerned with where our society, and its social sciences (understood as its organized attempt at self-comprehension), are going. At the very least, this is so because both of the main themes first introduced by this evolving theory have since been incorporated into informed political discussion as well as into the outlook of many social scientists, and are already influential in the shaping of new perspectives on American society.

The "postindustrial society," based on epoch-making developments in technology, social structure, and relations between government and economy, has become widely adapted as a basic term of reference for discussions of the new society into which the United States and several other technologically advanced societies today appear to be evolving. Accompanying this, the notion of "technocratic guidance" of social development has become a major theme in discussions of how direction and purpose are to be established in the highly complex and technical "postindustrial" society of today. These discussions emphasize the displacement of the traditional market economy, the growth in the role of the public sector, and the increasing importance of planning and of conscious orientation toward future societal needs and developmental opportunities on the part of trained administrators and planners in and out of government. Despite much early criticism of the notion of major decision making by technically qualified elites and its impact on the institutions of democratic society, the idea has become increasingly accepted and incorporated into much contemporary writing. At the same time, though the related theme of an "end of ideology" has been widely challenged, particularly with the onset of new ideologically oriented movements in the late 1960s, it has taken deep hold in the intellectual perspective both of active political figures and of influential social scientists. Through them it may well leave its mark on the thinking of at least part of the current generation of politically interested laymen and students, and perhaps beyond.

Understood as an ongoing attempt at explaining the new society both in its own right and in its relation to the institutions of the preceding era, the evolving technocratic theory, first formulated in American social science by the "end-of-ideologists," distinguishes the rapidly emergent present of the post-World War II period from the quickly receding prewar past. It forcefully points up the growing inadequacy of traditional theories of popular democracy and political pluralism, as well as classic economic theories of a self-regulating market economy. In their place, it puts forward a significant new model of a society in which technologically sophisticated administrative coordination within and between giant organizations replaces earlier uncoordinated competitive modes of economic and political control. In the process it stimulates our awareness of the need for a thorough review of the received theories of contemporary American society; at the same time, however, by identifying itself closely with the emerging technocratic orientation in politics and social science, it raises many questions concerning its own biases regarding the changes taking place, and the adequacy of its assessment of their significance.

Other commentators have already competently reviewed the historic setting of the early Cold War which provided the larger political and ideological context for the development of the "end of ideology" theory.[1] Suffice it to say here that it was in the context of the shift by American intellectuals from radical political alienation during the Thirties to a kind of patriotic assimilation during the Fifties that the basic elements of the theory of the "end of ideology" first made their appearance. This theory began from the optimistic premise that the social changes of the 1950s, which included the burgeoning of suburbia and the rapid growth of a defense "R & D" complex, amounted to advanced development and solid progress for American society. Thus for the most part the "end of ideology" theory looked approvingly at the effects of these early postwar changes on established American institutions and values. All of this stood

in very sharp contrast to the position of a handful of social critics like
C. Wright Mills,[2] who registered serious concern for the political and
cultural implications of these developments. What critics like Mills saw
as the growing detachment and alienation of citizens from an increasingly complex and hierarchically organized "mass society," these theorists
viewed as the quiet contentment of masses incorporated into a highly
productive, politically democratic society. Ideology, at least the ideology
of discontent, seemed to have ended; the system had apparently succeeded in living up to its promises. In contrast with Mills' concern about
the concentration of power in a bureaucratic society, the end-of-
ideologists looked upon the greatly expanded administrative apparatus
of major institutions as an instrument of productive efficiency in industry,
and as a means of equalitarian fairness in politics and organizational life.
In their eyes, the basic problems of industrial society had been solved;
the classic poverty of the working classes had been overcome, the economic system had been stabilized, and the welfare of the marginal groups,
of minorities and the residual poor, was administratively insured.

Looking back from the perspective of the troubled and highly ideological 1960s and later, one wonders how leading sociologists could fail
to sense the serious and explosive tensions which lay beneath the surface
of the seemingly placid, unevenly "affluent" society of the preceding
decade. Yet what is in question is not the competence with which these
major figures in American sociology did their work; rather it is the influence of their own ideological perspective on the conduct of their work,
down to the fundamental theoretical conceptions which they employed.
Embracing the overall changes in American institutions of the past generation as a set of positive developments, the end-of-ideologists shaped
a persuasive image of American society as a "welfare state" in which
ideological antagonisms fade away, displaced by the higher, more rational
"sociological consciousness" of industrial and governmental administration. From this base, they proceeded to elaborate a theory of America
as a "postmodern," "postindustrial" society, as it moved into the late
1960s and beyond. In this society, the accustomed modes of decision
making typical of an earlier, simpler small-scale society would no longer
be adequate to coping with the problems of life in a densely populated,
closely interrelated ecological and institutional environment. Increasingly,
an administrative model of decision based on superior technical understanding and information, constituting a higher, more objective and more
comprehensive rationality than the self-interested pluralist bargaining of
the past, would come to supplement and in various ways, displace, the
latter. Not only was this a forecast of the future, it was also a statement
of conviction by these theorists, who emerged increasingly as overt ideologists of a kind of technical-administrative rationality.

It is therefore of interest to contemplate how the work of some of the most sophisticated American sociologists, engaged in developing an explicitly "anti-ideological" theory of the society, has come to have profoundly ideological functions. We propose here to examine the thesis of the "end of ideology" on the two levels at which it functions. We examine the thesis first as a theoretical index of changes in the structure of American society which were largely initiated during the New Deal and World War II eras, and second, as a response to ideological demands on sociological theory made during a postwar generation of extraordinary challenge to the nation's welfare and security. Accordingly, we examine critical structural developments in postwar American society, particularly in their relation to the role of the postindustrial state and its linkages to established and emergent institutional interests, such as the changing corporate economy and the rise of a scientific-industrial research-and-development sector which has in turn contributed to the growth of a "technocratic class." Inasmuch as their theory also functions as an ideology of technocratically managed development, we also examine the politically oriented work of the end-of-ideologists in their roles as "social technocrats." Finally, we examine current ideologies of support and opposition to technocratic government in American society, and conclude with an analysis of prospective developments under conditions of continuing rapid technological change in postindustrial America.

CHAPTER I

The
Thesis
of the
"End of Ideology"

This chapter begins with a brief examination of the "end of ideology" thesis in relation to certain changes in the structure of industrial society in the West during the past century and particularly over the past generation; developments in which the United States has often taken the lead, but is by no means alone. These changes include the emergence of a highly productive society in which government intervention integrates the economy with the political system and helps incorporate the working classes into the polity. Our examination of the thesis points up the emphasis of the end-of-ideology theorists on the continuing political and economic integration of advanced industrial society, as an explanation for the decline of ideological conflict and the rise in its place of a "sociological consciousness." We also observe that, while the "end-of-ideologists" are opposed to extremist or radical ideologies of social change, they stand as proponents of an ideology in their own right, which combines elements of welfare liberalism and moderate socialism in a supposedly nonideological theory of technocratic social development. The assumptions of that ideology are briefly discussed in this chapter, and examined at length later in this work along the lines laid down in this discussion.

Structural Bases of the "End of Ideology"

The concept of the "end of ideology" first came into currency during the mid-1950s, among an influential segment of politically oriented intellectuals.[1] Sociologists, political analysts, economists, politicians, and journalists both in America and Europe asserted that a significant change had occurred in the politics of Western societies as compared with the prewar period. Despite some variations among the reports on this change, at least one common theme could be discerned: the ideological component in the politics of advanced societies had been sharply reduced; issues formerly posed in terms of irreconcilable political values had lost much of their intensity and been reduced to matters of compromise rather than conflicts of ultimate principle. Observers of Western Europe and America alike emphasized the new consensus between the parties of Left and Right on the need for governmental intervention and welfare measures; in a sense, on the government's "right to intervene" in the economy, as well as on the institutionalization of the politics of collective bargaining through various means of representation of workers in the political and economic decision-process. Finally, they cited the disappearance or serious decline of the large-scale extremist parties of the prewar period in most of Northern Europe. In short, the end-of-ideology theorists claimed that on both left and right the classic positions of the nineteenth century had been abandoned because of their theoretical exhaustion and political irrelevance. In place of the divisive dogmas of classic Marxism and classic liberalism, intellectuals and political leaders were arriving at a rough consensus of viewpoint.

The two major American representatives of the end of ideology as a sociological perspective on modern politics have been Daniel Bell and Seymour Lipset. Between them, they have presented most of its major themes.[2] Both Lipset and Bell have published essays which deal explicitly with the question of the end of ideology in the context of collections of articles written mainly during the decade of the 1950s. Bell's "Epilogue," and Lipset's "Personal Postscript," each reflected upon the more general social and political analyses preceding them, and projected what was, from the author's perspective, most suggestive and significant for further analysis. Reporting in his essay on the 1955 Conference of the Congress for Cultural Freedom which met in Milan, Italy, Lipset observed that the intense political debate which might have been expected between the leading European socialists, liberals, and conservatives gathered for the conference did not occur. Instead there was "general agreement" that traditional issues "had declined to comparative insignificance. . . ."[3] What differences remained had dwindled to disagreements over how much government control of the economy was required, with no one seeming to believe that it really made a crucial difference which party held office. In this context, the continued identification of the parties with different class interests no longer signifies intense class struggle, but the parties' acceptance of the same kind of "representation functions" which are served by unions in the interests of workers and by trade associations for business interests.[4] Commenting along the same lines, Bell noted the existence among politically involved intellectuals of a general consensus which included "the acceptance of a welfare State; the desirability of decentralized power; a system of mixed economy and of political pluralism."[5]

Ultimately underlying these changes in ideological outlook are deepgoing structural processes which have produced the economic, political, and social forms of what has sometimes been called the "new society."[6] These are the characteristically modern processes which can be summarized under the headings of industrialization, urbanization, and bureaucratization, often combined under the term "modernization," plus the process of "democratization" which has been characteristic of certain countries in the West.[7] The end-of-ideology thesis focusses on these processes after they have reached a certain critical stage in their development, and relates this achievement to the working out of institutional solutions to some characteristic political-economic problems of earlier industrial society. In approximate historical sequence, the crucial solutions have been, first, the granting of political and industrial "citizenship" to the working class, next, the achievement of a technologically sophisticated, highly productive industrial-capitalist society and, finally, the modification of capitalism by means of the "welfare state."[8] Each of these institutional changes is directly relevant to the end-of-ideology argument; i.e., occurring at different historical stages of industrial capitalism, each has involved the political acquiescence of conservatives who had formerly opposed it, while on the Left each has contributed to the substitution of a program of limited reform for one of full-scale revolution or total state control. In Lipset's view, the resulting displacement of a politics of intense ideological conflict by a politics of gradual reform through "interest-bargaining" is a very significant indicator of basic political-structural changes in the society; in short, it "reflects" nothing less than "the fact that the fundamental political problems of the industrial revolution have been solved."[9]

In this vein, both Bell and Lipset speak of the achievement of a new political economy, in which new social structures and cultural milieux can be identified, and the image by which they characterize the whole is a composite of Affluent Society and Welfare State, representing a politically modified, technologically advanced capitalism. In developmental perspective, a new stage of advanced industrial society has been achieved, one in which new levels of integration within and between the political and economic orders have been achieved, and in which ideological political conflict has sharply subsided. Implicit in this formulation is the notion that while ideological politics is intrinsic to the early stages of industrial capitalist society, its disappearance is promoted by the transition to highly advanced, or "postindustrial" capitalism. Thus, contrary to Marxist predictions, intense ideological conflict, which first emerges in early industrial society and becomes acute with the consolidation of industrialism, is viewed as declining with the achievement of the welfare state, which is characteristic of advanced industrialism, rather than continuing to mount to a final revolutionary explosion. From a "social-system" perspective, both "political citizenship" and the "welfare state" may be viewed as aspects of a trend toward socioeconomic integration of modern large-scale societies; in the one case, the integration of the lower classes into the political system, in the other, the explicit linking of the political with the economic order, breaking down the earlier autonomy of business from government. From this viewpoint, "industrial-democratic" society can be pictured as having achieved fundamental integration as a system, after more than a century of critical social cleavage and conflict within and between its political and economic subsystems.

Both of these perspectives can be further understood by viewing the changes described above as the historical and structural aspects of the process of "modernization," as it applies to advanced industrial society. For the most part, the concept of modernization has to date been used for the study of developmental process in underdeveloped countries. Notably, in such studies the structural achievements of the advanced countries of the West often seem to be pictured as a kind of final goal; the "good society" toward which the underdeveloped countries are striving.[10] However, development does not stop at the achievement of a "modern" or "modernized" society. It goes on, making profound changes in society, changes of a depth and subtlety not previously foreseen, and reflected not merely in the changes of structure indicated by the linked processes of industrialization-urbanization-bureaucratization, but also in the transformations of the style and content of social consciousness, particularly as expressed in political ideologies and cultural value-systems. Indeed, focussing on the contemporary phenomena of political ideology and culture, there is little doubt that a change has occurred in the tenor of political thought under the impact of these structural developments. But whether it is of the type the end-of-ideology theorists describe, or has the significance they ascribe to it, are major questions we intend to investigate here.

To begin this investigation, we will first briefly outline the rather simple developmental model which underlies the end-of-ideology thesis. In this model, the achievement of high economic productivity and of new integrative relationships between the polity and economy of advanced industrial capitalism resolves the crisis of the earlier, conflict-ridden industrialism, and produces a change in the outlook of certain key "ideological groups." This change in the outlook of Western intellectuals and political leaders amounts to a basic acceptance of the functioning of the advanced industrial system, and a tacit agreement to remain within its structural limits ("the rules of the game") in formulating social policy which will secure its stable operation. This means that the opinion leaders of Right and Left respectively cease to introduce into the political arena the earlier intense, fundamentally opposed positions regarding either the maintenance of traditional structures or their drastic modification. The net result is the hypothesized reduction in ideological conflict in the political system, at least so far as the classic issues of domestic politics are concerned. In short, the ideological elites are viewed as the medium through which the newly achieved conditions of productivity and social integration are translated into an increasingly nonideological consciousness in the larger society.

Ideological Orientations of the "End of Ideology"

Insofar as they discuss the new consciousness, the end-of-ideology theorists treat it as a positive kind of political consciousness involving a new type of social awareness, specifically, a "sociological" awareness. Thus, the major corollary to the waning of ideology is the rise of sociology in its place as the most important intellectual perspective for social analysis and policy formation in the state and other major institutions of contemporary society. From the perspective of the end-of-ideologists, the changing nature of social criticism during the 1950s (involving a shift from radical political criticism to broad cultural critiques of the "mass society"), was a significant reflection of "the general trend . . . away from ideology towards sociology."[11] Thus, they viewed the increasing importance of sociology in the practical affairs of Western societies as confirming evidence of a decline of interest in traditional ideologically-concerned political inquiry. According to this argument, the ideological mode of analysis has little relevance for the understanding of the large bureaucratic organizations which are today characteristic of modern industrial society, whether it be capitalist or socialist, and which can best be understood in terms of sociological conceptions of organization, administration, and bureaucracy. Furthermore, the trend of bureaucratization is not limited to the industrial organizations of society, but affects the structures and processes of government and politics as well. Thus, in the eyes of the end-of-ideologists, "politics is seen as changing into administration as the manager and expert take over in government as well as in business."[12]

On a more general level, the rise of the sociological perspective is attributed to the fact that the problems of mass society and its culture are simply too complex to be open to ideological analysis, since this is way of thinking which relies on only a few fundamental beliefs and is theoretically underdeveloped. Ideological thought is portrayed as being inadequate to the task of coping with the richness and diversity of socially complex large-scale society and its various problems. (As Bell puts it, the ideologue is a "terrible simplifier.") In particular, the problem of radical criticism in the early postwar period is that besides having only a "single unifying idea" (the concept of America as a "mass society"), this idea itself suffers from a certain ambiguity and amorphousness, since broad attacks on "the culture" do not point to any specific political "enemy."[13] As of the early 1960s, most of the small band of radicals who attacked the society through its aspect as a "mass culture" were intellectuals who had stubbornly clung to the traditions of the Old Left, trying desperately to maintain standards of radical political criticism with reference" presented many dangers to the future of democracy, including a bureaucratic organization of the society which underlies the new "affluence" presented many dangers to the future of democracy, including a widening gap between those who make or administer policy in the society, and those who are the objects of administration. In particular, the decline of intense political discontent amongst the relatively satisfied "middle masses" tended to reduce interest in the formulation of alternatives to the social status quo. This left the remaining social underclass of the poor and the minority groups stranded without political goals or leadership, in a condition of passive dependence on the welfare bureaucracy. Since this underclass remained essentially quiescent during the Fifties, the radical intellectuals tended to turn from traditional radical criticism emphasizing the economic exploitation of the lower classes, to a broader type of critique involving various cultural aspects of the society: its status-anxiety, its social conformity, the low quality of its communication media and the spread of their influence, etc. The end-of-ideologists, however, took this as testimony to the waning relevance of radical political criticism, since the radical critics seemed no longer capable of making a specifically political criticism of American society, in their new preoccupation with the theme of cultural alienation in the mass society.[14]

Over and above this shift in the focus of radical criticism, it remains that only a small and shrinking circle of intellectuals persisted in some form of radicalism throughout the 1950s. The main drift of ex-radical intellectuals indeed seemed to be increasingly anti-ideological, "skeptical . . . that socialism, by eliminating . . . exploitation, would solve all social questions."[15] Perhaps as the end-of-ideologists argue, these intellectuals were merely responding to the new complexity of American society, in which social problems like those of "school costs, municipal services, the urban sprawl," etc., were being found to be of "piece-meal technology" and thus not amenable to all-embracing radical solutions.[16] Still, in their lack of enthusiasm for sweeping change, there also appears to have been reflected a new satisfaction with the directions of development set by established American institutions. In the postwar period, as Bell observes, "American intellectuals found new virtues in the United States." In his estimation, they were encouraged to do so out of a combination of political principle and self-interest; partly because they admired the country's continuing political and cultural pluralism and its progress toward a "Welfare State," and partly on account of "expanding opportunities for intellectual employment." Moreover, whatever their criticism of the inequities of the domestic scene, they had adopted a Cold War viewpoint in which Soviet Russia appeared as the "principle threat to freedom;" thus they gave relative priority to dealing with the menace of Communism above other problems.[17] Interestingly, in connection with this political-moral (shall we say "ideological"?) revaluation, there occurred a distinctive revaluation in social theory involving the displacement of established analytic themes such as class or interest conflict by specifically sociological concepts such as "status anxiety" and "status politics."[18] Thus the theoretical shift from "class analysis" to an outlook mainly concerned with status ranking and competition and its attendant social anxieties and political consequences paralleled a broad shift in political ideology among American intellectuals and academics from the diffuse populist radicalism of the earlier twentieth century to the redefined "liberal-pluralism" which characterizes the postwar period.

In this context, the end-of-ideologists' own position can perhaps best be understood in terms of a political reaction against earlier radicalisms, domestic and foreign, and a committment instead to the "rules of the game" of postwar liberal politics. Thus with the excesses of the past in mind, the end-of-ideologists adopted a posture of political moderation[19] and sharply criticized the emerging New Left for its easygoing attitude toward revolution as a means to achieving social goals. Already as of the early 1960s Daniel Bell observed that "if the end of ideology has any meaning, it is to ask for the end of rhetoric, and . . . of revolution. . . ."[20] Later, Bell amplified this position and made it explicit that he was not merely describing the end of ideology, but actively urging its demise. In his own words, the "end of ideology" was now "a call for an end to apocalyptic beliefs that refuse to specify the costs and consequences of the changes they envision."[21]

Now it is one thing to factually describe the exhaustion of political ideas which was a hallmark of the quiescent 1950s, but it is another to subscribe to the desirability of such a development. In crossing the line between description and exhortation, Bell employs his "anti-ideological perspective" as a means of deliberate polemic against those ideologies of which he *disapproves*. For, while he broached the end-of-ideology thesis in terms of the current irrelevance of *both* Marxism and laissez-faire liberalism,[22] it was "particularly Marxism" which had lost its right to "claim truth" for its view of the world.[23] In any event, to parallel in this way the decline of traditional liberalism with that of Marxism was at least on the American scene rather misleading; for laissez-faire liberalism had suffered its eclipse as an ideology of real importance in the United States at least by the 1930s, well before the collapse of the traditional-Marxist "Old Left" in the 1950s. Moreover, since the 1930s there had emerged a new kind of statist liberalism, associated at first with the New Deal and then with the Cold War (and later with the peculiar mixture of foreign war and domestic "deal" which for a while went under the heading of the "Great Society"). Yet in the *End of Ideology* Bell never mentions the new liberalism in his comments on the recent exhaustion of political ideas even though it is this variety of liberalism with which the "end-of-ideology" perspective can be most closely identified. Absorbed in describing the demise of extremist ideologies of the past, he does not criticize his own ideological presuppositions as to what he believes is the "vital center"[24] of the new society. In this way, he neglects to examine the viability of the contemporary liberal-pluralist position; instead he tends in his early work as an end-of-ideology theorist simply to assume it and to use it as the point of departure for his own evolving position.

The nature of the connections between the postwar liberal ideology and the end-of-ideology position emerge somewhat more clearly in a subsequent statement by Bell's colleague Seymour Lipset. Pressed to defend his own exposition of the end-of-ideology theme, Lipset quite explicitly asserted that "not only do class conflicts over [various economic and political] issues . . . continue in the absence of *Weltanchauungen,* but . . . the decline of such total ideologies does not mean the end of ideology."[25] Instead, it means commitment to a pragmatic politics of interest bargaining and gradual reformist change, combined with a principled opposition to both unrestrained laissez-faire and total government control. Taken together, these political values, which incorporate basic tenets of modern liberalism, "constitute the component parts of an ideology." Moreover, the new political consensus which has emerged in the West and "which might be best described as 'conservative socialism' has become *the* ideology of the major parties in the developed states of Europe and America."[26] Apparently, despite differences of terminology, there is considerable common ground between Lipset's "conservative socialism" and the "managerial," "welfare" liberalism with which Bell associates him-self.[27] At the least, both seem very serious about respecting the existing "rules of the game" of bargaining among organized collective interests, broadly within the established boundaries of modern corporate capital-ism.[28] Both, however, go beyond any simple commitment to pluralist liberalism in their attempts to take account of and absorb current de-mands for expanded social welfare and security, through government policy processes which they believe will become increasingly technical and administrative in the future. The overlapping of conservative-revisionist socialism and managerial-welfare liberalism expresses a pe-culiar ideological combination of equalitarianism as a political end and centralized bureaucratic organization as a technical means, mixing gov-ernmental acceptance of responsibility for the general welfare with sophisticated managerialism as a practical way of attaining it.[29] Clearly, the end-of-ideology theorists are not merely reporting or analyzing the trends which have led to this wedding of revisionist socialism and con-temporary liberalism, they are actively endorsing its ideological offspring.

If additional evidence is needed that ideology still thrives in this day of its alleged decline, we need seek no further than Bell's book *The End of Ideology*. For example, in his discussion of the newly emergent class of corporate managers, Bell notes that the lack of traditional sanction for their position moves them to create "an ideology to justify their power and prestige," an ideology which also serves as "a social ce-ment."[30] In fact, "in no other capitalist order, . . . has this drive for an ideology been pressed so compulsively."[31] The compulsion to produce a justifying and solidarizing ideology is in part a response to the special need of the "new class" of managers to legitimize their status to others as well as to assure its legitimacy to themselves. The other aspect of this drive to produce a justifying ideology arises in response to the emergence of an economy in which the state is increasingly instrumental in allo-cating resources to group claims. In a politically "managed economy," interest-group politics, operating through the government, tends to re-place the market as the instrument for allocating resources for produc-tion. Thus government intervention encourages pressure groups "each to adopt an ideology which can justify its claims and which can square with some concept of 'national interest'."[32]

Here we have the paradox of the theorists of the "end of ideology" attesting that the formulation and dissemination of ideology has not ceased at all; so that while they claim that radical ideologies are ex-hausted, ideology *per se* is far from ended. How shall we reconcile this with their major theme?

At this point it is useful to adopt an elementary distinction between "particular" ideology and "total" ideology, i.e., the difference between ideology as a mask for narrow, particularistic interests, and ideology as a whole way of thought reflecting an angle of vision which corresponds to the social location of the thinker; simply expressed, the difference between specific interest rationalization and a general perspective on the world, *Weltanschauung*.[33] Clearly when Lipset writes of the end of ideology he means the end of comprehensive, integrative complexes of belief which could provide the members of a given class or subculture with both a theory of society, and a normative framework for its evaluation. Thus, what Lipset is describing is the end of *total* ideology, *Weltanschauung*. However, his singling out of radical leftist or rightist *Weltanschauungen* tells us he is concerned with only certain kinds of total ideology; those which embrace an extremist, or potentially revolutionary, viewpoint, rather than total ideology *per se*.

"Conservative socialism," the ideology which Lipset embraces, is no less a total ideology seeking to inform and organize the crucial institutions of contemporary society than were classic liberalism or Marxism; it can be contrasted with them only in terms of its specific value commitments: to gradual change, through a process of pragmatic interest bargaining whose results are implemented by the agencies of a welfare-oriented central government. Compared to these other ideologies, the professed antitotalitarianism of "conservative socialism" makes it no less comprehensive, or "total," as a perspective on the social order, and on the proper aims of political policy within this order. Moreover, the "agreement on fundamentals" is obviously more than simply a matter of consensus over the routine procedures, the "rules of the game," of interest bargaining. It is a provisional agreement on the present limits and tempo of change, and thus on the very nature of change; a political agreement on the maintenance and gradual improvement of living standards as defined by prevailing concepts of welfare and affluence, within a social context of established interests and institutions which is to be protected from sudden radical upheaval. In short, "conservative" or "revisionist" socialism is a total ideology in its own right whose major commitment is to gradual, nonrevolutionary change sufficient to temporize egalitarian demands without *abruptly* challenging established functional or class hierarchies.[34]

The end-of-ideology thesis as a pointed reaction against revolutionary ideology is even more clearly illustrated in the work of Bell, who tends to directly equate ideology with revolutionary "apocalyptic" belief. With the decline in religious faith in the last century, argues Bell, there was lost a major means of displacing the emotions of popular discontent. Here was where ideology made its historic entrance. For, while the manifest function of ideology is to provide a means for "translating ideas into action," its latent function is the redirection of mass emotion into political action. In place of religion, which had traditionally drained off secular discontent into other-worldly concerns, ideology emerged as an instrument which "fuses these energies and channels them into politics," in short, as an instrument of political mobilization.[35]

According to Bell, it was Marx (as one of the left-wing descendants of the German philosopher Hegel) who in the nineteenth century developed most clearly that conception of ideology which views it as a means of translating ideas into political action. While most of the other left-Hegelians contented themselves with essentially literary activity aimed at promoting secular enlightenment and social reform, Marx strove for revolutionary change which would usher in a new millenium, allegedly basing his vision of revolution in "chiliastic ideas" which could be traced back to the radical Anabaptists of early European history. Thus, in Bell's image, ideology (taking its sharpest expression in classic Marxism) translates ideas into revolutionary action by infusing its followers with belief in their inevitable victory through a revolutionary apocalypse which will sweep away the old order and clear a path for the building of Heaven on Earth.[36]

This interpretation gives us a rather dramatic picture of ideology. It is a portrait of fanatic devotion and dogmatic belief; of passionately held absolutist ideas which simplify reality and promise salvation, through the agency of political action instead of religious worship. In effect, ideology is construed as a kind of secular faith; by stressing its apocalyptic qualities, Bell joins Lipset in defining ideology as revolutionary creed. In the context of the end-of-ideology theory, the concept of ideology thus undergoes a narrowing in accordance with the ideological presuppositions of these theorists. Despite the all-encompassing implications of the phrase "the end of ideology," the focus of theoretical attention is actually trained upon those ideologies whose intention is the fundamental transformation of society, and away from those ideologies whose basic aims are in conformity with the norms of the ongoing system, the frequently cited "rules of the game." In fact, under further examination we will seek to demonstrate that the theory of the "end of ideology" functions only quite selectively as an anti-ideological perspective, and finally supports in its own right the developing ideological position of its authors.[37]

To what extent the end-of-ideology position has since its initial formulation become the basis of a new political ideology may be glimpsed from a recent work on the application of "social intelligence" to public policy making.[38] The editor, Bertram Gross, and his assistant, Michael Springer, speak of a new "politics of relevance" that "eschews rhetoric and traditional ideology," and is "buttressed with candor, flexibility, and empiricism." The practitioners of this politics will be "liberal, secure, and well-disciplined," and they will act as leaders of a new class of intelligence users and producers;" as such, they will constitute the natural vanguard of a movement for a politics of relevance-without-rhetoric. Their political consciousness is to be shaped by a particular kind of social intelligence: information gathered with an eye toward what is "probable" rather than what is "possible."[39] Rejecting the search for the socially optimum possible and its formulation as a standard for political achievement,[40] the new politicians will pursue those "incremental improvements on existing conditions" which are politically practical, feasible, "probable."[41]

Very briefly we may observe here that this politics seems to be essentially a technically updated liberalism seeking to address itself to the new stresses and crises of a complex society in postindustrial transition. Though they confess that "the social order seems to be coming apart at the seams," the theorists of the "new politics" suggest that its practitioners can lead the society away from crisis essentially by employing a political "incrementalism" which strongly resembles the "piece-meal solutions" of traditional liberalism, with the added feature, to be sure, of improved technical intelligence. Apparently, this limitation of political thinking to the consideration of the "probable," as viewed from within a given social context, would involve a kind of conscious self-censorship of political imagination. In a sense, then, this explicitly embodies now an ideology not only of the "end-of-ideology," but also of the end of "Utopia," i.e., the end of political vision that seeks to transcend immediately given existing conditions in formulating its goals. It seems appropriate to inquire whether this might not actually tend to *limit* the application of "social intelligence" to the making of small changes here and there which would merely relieve pressure from one crisis to the next,[42] and to discourage addressing serious contemporary problems as products and symptoms of the *overall* social system, requiring a more comprehensive approach.[43] Much of the present work seeks at least to raise that question, in its relevant contexts.

The Concept of Ideology and the "End of Ideology"

In order to approach the notion of the end of ideology with some perspective, it is useful to first put forward some of the leading themes entailed by the concept of ideology itself and to discuss their contemporary connotations. In its simplest form, an ideology is a more or less integrated set of ideas and values characteristic of a group, put forward to protect or enhance its position in the larger society of which it is a part, and to motivate its members to act in support of these aims.[44] It does this first, by relating its particular interests to the general, or "public interest" ("What's good for GM is good for the nation"); and second, by encouraging the internal unity of the group through appeals to the common interest of its members ("Solidarity forever — the union makes us strong!"). In this definition, ideology is on one side a set of internal appeals for the allegiance of a group's members to the furthering of group interests; on the other it is a complex of external rationalizations and justifications for the interests of the given group. Thus, a persuasively posed ideology may help make group goals acceptable to outsiders and win allies for their achievement.

Potentially, ideology has many functions. In the course of history, ideology has sometimes justified the rule of established elites by appeals to "divine right" or claims that some particular group possessed of special qualities bears a natural responsibility for administering the political or cultural values of the society.[45] On the other hand, ideology has also served to express the discontent of masses who felt excluded from the governance of society or the enjoyment of its productive achievements. Thus, ideology can either represent the interests of groups established in power, or of their critics, seeking changes in particular institutions and sometimes fundamental transformation of the society as a whole.[46] Viewed categorically in relation to the structure of power in any given society, ideology has been employed by established elites (e.g., aristocracies), by critical counter-elites (e.g., emergent middle classes), or by representatives of discontented nonelites. (In the latter instance these representatives themselves sometimes take on the character of an elite group as in the case of leaders of some working-class parties and unions).[47] Thus ideology can be regarded as a consciously shaped cultural instrument, a cognitive-symbolic instrument of group aspirations and group struggles, and a tool of political expression and political conflict.[48] As a political-cultural instrument it incorporates the basic values and assumptions of the groups or strata for which it speaks into their political struggles, sometimes raising these assumptions to considerable refinement in the context of articulated theoretical systems which seek to describe the overall society, its historical tendencies, and the groups' role with respect to both.

It should be noted that while political ideology can be viewed as a political-cultural instrument, it is not synonomous with "political culture." We can define the "political culture" of a society as the entire existing complex of values, beliefs, attitudes, and symbols regarding the structure of political power and its employment in the society. Included in the political culture alongside some very general theories of man and society, are general procedural norms as to how political decisions should be made and by whom, as well as broad substantive values concerning the purposes for which political authority should be used.[49] Thus we would regard the political culture as the overall context of politically relevant cultural meanings and symbols within which the clash of social, ethnic, and economic groups or strata takes place, this conflict being expressed in the form of political ideologies rooted in the social interests and perspectives of the respective groups or strata. A political ideology is a cultural system for political belief and action which is differentiated from the background political culture of the society and explicitly articulates the conflict of interests and values of the given group or stratum as against other groups or strata of the society. The political culture, on the other hand, incorporates both the shared political values and the conflicting ideologies of the groups in the society; thus it may be basically unified when there exists an underlying consensus among these groups, or it may be deeply split by their conflicts, and this will ultimately depend upon the political posture of the various groups in the society.[50] Typically, the established elite will seek to express and encourage political-cultural themes which bind together the greater number of participants in the system around political symbols, slogans, and formulae that serve to encourage a feeling of consensus, of harmony of interests, between the mass and the elite through persuading the former of the appropriateness and legitimacy of rule by the latter. Thus the role of political ideology probably becomes *most* interesting and relevant during periods like the present when the established political culture comes into question and the legitimacy of the rule of the elite is challenged.[51]

One can trace the history of ideology back at least to the ancient civilizations, in which there first emerged stratified communities containing differentiated social groups with distinctive institutions and perspectives, typically using religious symbols to express them. Our interest however, will be in secular ideology, reflecting the conflicts of groups in modern and modernizing societies, typically employing the symbols of nation and class to express political objectives and rally political support. Secular political ideology is historically a recent creation, connected with the rise of urban-industrial societies and the decline of religiously oriented agrarian systems in the West during the past two centuries.[52] The major function of secular ideology in the West has been the articulation of class divisions and conflicts in the society as it approaches and becomes an "industrial system." This has been enhanced by the fact that industrial society, at least as it matured in the West, has been one of formal legal freedom of political expression and representation of differentiated class and occupational interests in the political arena. As such it has historically contributed to and encouraged the ideological articulation of the different interests of major groups in the society. Thus the prospects for the further development or cessation of ideological conflict can ultimately be viewed as a question of the further development of the industrial system.

Some of the functions of ideology go considerably beyond the limits of the simple definition given above. In addition to serving the interests of particular groups or classes, ideology can give a special sense of identity to those individuals who accept it, and it may even confer upon some a sense of importance and mission in history; at the least it will help provide some special meaning to their relationships and activities in the society.[53] Under appropriate circumstances, ideology can make the difference in moving otherwise reluctant individuals to take action toward the realization of group aims, even at considerable risk to themselves. Alternatively, ideology may seek to address the needs of the society as a whole, or at least of broad multiclass or multigroup segments of it, as against the narrower interests and needs of particular groups or individuals. It can do this by encouraging social unity in the face of threats from without, as in nationalistic, patriotic ideology, or by stimulating broad support for needed basic changes in the society, as in some radical or revolutionary ideologies. This kind of ideology corresponds approximately to Karl Mannheim's concept of "total" ideology, involving a broad social perspective in which the overall requirements or structure of the society are explicitly considered, as opposed to the "particular" ideology of groups involved essentially in legitimating their own position or aspirations in the larger society.

Particular ideology is typically the ideology of interest groups like business, labor, farmers, veterans, professionals, which accept the basic structure of the society, but seek to achieve within it relative gains for their own members' particular interests. Total ideology, on the other hand, envisions social goals whose realization involves major impact on crucial institutions of the society, either by requiring significant institutional contributions to the system's defense or expansion, as in war, or demanding broad institutional change for the sake of transforming the system, as in social revolution. Total ideology generally is an ideology either of social movements which seek to rally masses of people to support deep-going change in the structure of the society, or of elites with access to institutions of broad societal scope, like government. Such elites will seek to mobilize the society as a whole, particularly in time of crisis, around their political program. If the crisis is recurrent, or long-term, as for example the political-military confrontation of the Cold War, the program of the power-elite coalition becomes a program for the long-term mobilization of the society around political goals on which these elites find agreement.[54] In brief, total ideology can be viewed as an instrument of large-scale mobilization to implement designs for broad social action, while particular ideology is a tool of relatively limited organization for the sake of specific interests.

Typically, fully developed political ideologies put forward some kind of theory which explains the workings of society and the motivations and goals of the people who constitute it. This is more true of total ideology than of particular ideology (in which the theoretic component is often only implicitly stated). In any case, the ideologist's aim in theorizing about society is not merely abstract or academic; characteristically he will also posit certain values and ideals as standards against which the performance of the society and the behavior of its members are measured. Secular political ideology is a combination of both social theory and social ideals, and it is the interaction of theory and ideals which provides the dynamic by which ideology seeks to influence social action. Accordingly, those ideologies favoring social change will emphasize the disparity between the ideals they espouse and the actual performance of the society, while others, supporting the existing social structure, will try to demonstrate that its institutions accomplish quite adequately the desired ideals emphasized. In this way, the same social reality will be subjected to interpretation in terms of rather different value criteria, leading to different conclusions as to its acceptability. Moreover, the theoretical system which the ideologist employs to provide a model of social reality may itself incorporate his ideological slant, thus orienting him toward a selective perception of society which confirms his own value judgments of it.

Upon a first examination of the work of the end-of-ideologists its ideological aspect may not be immediately apparent. One factor which tends to conceal the ideological bearing of their work is the repeated self-identification with dispassionate scientific analysis, and the sharp contrasting of that kind of analysis with the methods and style of ideological thought. As Bell and Lipset define it, ideology is tantamount to the blatant simplification and distortion of reality for the sake of mobilizing masses for revolutionary action; it is the rhetoric of angry Messianic radicals. Unfortunately this conception of ideology is a rather narrow one, exaggerating a single quality, not so much of ideology *per se*, but of its vulgarized form as a mode of "soapbox" address. By comparison, it will not be difficult for most social thought, including the productions of the end-of-ideologists, to appear ideologically neutral; but this is hardly an adequate yardstick to employ.

In point of fact, ideology can range in theoretical sophistication all the way from the crudest street corner vulgarizations to the most subtle, erudite philosophic and scientific distinctions. Neither manner of expression nor quality of style are foolproof criteria for distinguishing ideology from social science. The critical difference can ultimately only be formulated with respect to their difference in content; ideally, though social science studies valuatively-oriented social behavior, it seeks to be free of valuative bias in interpreting that behavior; ideology, on the other hand, consists in the intimate interweaving of valuative judgments with empirical statements about society. The long, still unresolved debate over whether it is actually possible for social science to be entirely "objective" indicates, however, that this simple distinction can only refer to the ideal-typical poles of a continuum which stretches from "pure" value-free theory to highly value-oriented ideology, rather than to any truly clear-cut dichotomy between the two.

In any particular case, an ideological system may incorporate the most profound and powerful theoretical apparatus, based on carefully interpreted empirical data; while the work of the social scientist may be ideologically slanted, either in its underlying theoretical assumptions or in its overall political intentions. Merely because a social theory is put forward in conjunction with a minimally emotional, "dispassionate style" does not mean that it is "nonideological." Nor can classification as to the predominant bearing of a system of social thought be based *a priori* on the occupational or political identity of the source, on whether his perceived "role" is that of "social scientist," or "ideologist." To be reliable, any test of classification must consist of a substantive analysis of the presence and function of valuative elements in the work at hand. Certainly it cannot rely on the theorist's claims that he has made himself immune from ideological influence by placing himself in a state of noncommitment, disengagement, or "positive alienation," with reference to political movements and programs.[55]

In order to briefly clarify the ideological bearing of the work of the "anti-ideologists," it is helpful to return to our earlier discussion of total ideology. As we indicated there, total ideology has historically associated itself either with elites having access to central social institutions that could be used to mobilize the overall society, or with radical social movements led by "counterelites." Along these lines, it is significant that the end-of-ideologists in the course of their work express, on the one hand, strong condemnation of contemporary radical political movements in the United States and Western Europe, and on the other, emphasize the image of postwar America as a "mobilized" society.[56] Despite prefatory comments as to their ideological noncommitment, their programmatic goal is stated explicitly at points, and is apparent in the overall thrust of their later work; namely, that the technical-managerial methods which were brought into being for purposes of military mobilization during war and cold war should now be extended to other areas of social decision, for purposes of general societal development.[57] In particular, this would mean the extension of technocratic methods into "social program" areas, such as health, education, housing, etc. The continuity with the welfare-planning orientation of New Deal liberalism is clear, except that what the "anti-ideological" social-technocrats envision goes far beyond anything projected by the New Deal in its scope and sophistication; for theirs is the benefit of the experience of techniques of social and economic management and planning developed in the generation since the 1930s.

It is particularly in the course of their recent work as theorists of "postindustrial" society that the end-of-ideologists have produced an ideologically oriented theory, which emphasizes the need for "technocratic guidance" of the society by a combination of expert knowledge and sophisticated intellectual technology placed at the service of central structures of power. Characteristically, this theory tends to play up certain features of current developments which support its technocratic assumptions, and to deemphasize or neutralize others which raise serious questions as to the political consequences of its realization; particularly questions concerning the impact of technocratic planning on the possibility of democratic participation in a highly organized postindustrial society. In observing this, we do not overlook the "liberal-pluralist" assumptions which the end-of-ideologists incorporate into their theoretical work, such as their emphasis on the role of organized interest bargaining in a democratic polity or on voluntary associational life as a significant understructure for pluralist politics. The mixing of these emphases with an enthusiasm for the introduction and diffusion of technocratic methods and structures, however, has produced a certain ambiguity in the end-of-ideologists' picture of the proper relation between pluralist and technocratic modes of decision making. In their early work on the new society they stress the conflict between these modes of decision making, implying the ultimate working out of a new synthesis involving a balance of these approaches; in their more recent work, on the other hand, they place the greatest emphasis on a technocratic image of the society, and tend to treat the earlier conflict as marginal or even already resolved. In retrospect, it becomes clear that these theorists have increasingly tended to assume that the recent spread of technical-managerial methods in government carries with it a "socially rational" mentality which favors the allocation of economic resources for social planning as well as the related political reforms this may require. In effect, the process of technocratic rationalization in and of itself, has come to be viewed by the end-of-ideologists as a major revolution aimed at furthering social progress and reform, in which social and physical scientists and technologists are destined to play a central role. As their work has matured, their early cautions and concerns regarding the technocratic impact on democratic pluralist structures have been progressively set aside as if no longer a matter of real consequence. In our view this is highly questionable, and we seek to examine in detail both the ideological orientation of the theory which supports it, and the political consequences which it may actually entail.

For the purposes of this examination, we will here provisionally define ideology as a set of socially shared assumptions regarding the world which integrate empirical ideas (facts, theories) about its nature and its relation to past and future with evaluative ideas (values, ethics) which provide an image of how the world ought to be (a desirable, "good" society), and which thereby motivate and justify the actions of those who share them.[58] A fully developed ideology may be viewed as an interrelated complex of ideas which constitutes both a theory of man and society, and a social ethic; a developed ideological *program* will combine an ideology with a strategy of action whereby the existing society may be changed to, or maintained as, a "good society." At the most general level, we will view ideology as a set of beliefs which serves to relate social theory to social action, not merely in terms of explaining action, but also by way of strategically affecting its course. The end-of-ideologists' theory of the "postindustrial" society will be examined not only in terms of the ideas and facts it marshalls about the present society and its likely development, but also in terms of its evaluative assumptions about what this course of development ought to be and who should properly guide it.

CHAPTER II

The Emergence of the "End of Ideology" as a Theory of Advanced Development

In this chapter we trace in a number of stages the development of the end-of-ideology thesis to its recent emergence as a theory of postindustrial development. In its earliest stages, the theory takes a crucial step beyond both the liberal analysts and the radical critics of postwar American society by positively embracing the society's new institutional forms as necessary to its integrated functioning as a social system. At this point the theory puts forward a picture of a restructured pluralist society in which new elements of conscious central management by "positive government" supplement traditional political pluralism, and lend it strength. The chapter goes on to discuss the theory's handling of these developments in their implications for the concentration of power in the society, and in relation to the rise of technocratic modes of policy making in government.

Pluralist Theory and Its Problems

As a theory of the overall development of contemporary American society, the end of ideology can be analyzed as one step in a series of postwar revisions of the traditional liberal-pluralist theory of "industrial-democratic" society. It represents an important intermediate phase of these revisions, which culminate finally in the theory of "postindustrial" society. This being the case, it is useful to state the major assumptions of the pluralist theory as of the 1960s and then to indicate how the end-of-ideologists have broken with these assumptions or introduced significant new ones which go beyond the original pluralist context.

As a political theory, pluralism has generally been concerned with the questions of the development and functioning of restraints on political power in modern democratic society. In its traditional version the major assumptions of the pluralist theory run along the following lines. In the first place, the overall structure of the society is viewed by the pluralists as a network of organized groups or "associations," insofar as a wide variety of private organizations is likely to emerge in a complex society, reflecting the diversity of social identities and economic interests present. Each organization concentrates the powers and resources of its members for the purpose of achieving their particular social and political ends. However, no single organization or small number of organizations can dominate, since a modern society produces many different specialized groupings with different interests and bases of political influence ranging from the possession of wealth or status to vital organizational roles or technical skills, to the exercise of the power of the vote. No one segment of the society has exclusive control over all these resources, so that the simultaneous pursuit of separate group interests from various power bases leads, to a large degree, to a counterbalancing of the political influence and power of any single group. If in some cases a group remains predominant its dominance is limited to its special field.[1]

In the course of history, this multi-influence pattern provides the context for institutionalization of a political system of checks and balances between group interests both outside government and between the institutions of government themselves. Over time, a system of political balance, supported by legal and constitutional sanctions, becomes the characteristic pattern for the procedural norms and institutions which allow expression of political interests in the society; through these institutions political conflicts are registered, negotiations facilitated, compromises arrived at. In American society, the resulting institutional pattern has taken the form of the familiar division of powers between the organs of government, and outside these formal governmental patterns there are the electoral system, interest bargaining, lobbying, opinion polling, etc., through which the formal system of government is interlinked with the complex network of competing political interests and attitudes of civil society. Historically, American electoral institutions encouraged the development of a two-party system, and the two parties, in direct competition for the broadest possible electoral support, have found it necessary to address themselves to a wide spectrum of social and sectional groupings rather than appealing to the support of a particular class or sectional base. According to pluralist theory, this has tended to make the parties responsive to a broad range of group influences in shaping their political programs, both while contending for governmental office and while occupying it.[2]

Thus, the main theme which runs through traditional pluralist theory is the dispersion and division of powers among diverse groupings and associations in civil society, outside of government, paralleled by the division of powers between the organs of government itself. No single organization or institution dominates; the powers of any single unit or coalition of units are generally counterbalanced by the powers of other units. The "animating forces" in the political system are group interests, so that the process whereby government policy is finally arrived at is conceived essentially in terms of shifting coalitions and conflicts between various group interests. These interests find political expression mainly through the functioning of various pressure groups and the political parties, whose working compromises are reflected in the statutes established by the legislature and implemented by administrative agencies.

In the early pluralist conception, the "state" itself (the institutions of government considered in totality) is viewed as an organization originally created by a voluntary "social contract" or agreement among the members of the society, based on mutual consensus regarding certain fundamental individual rights and minimal standards of public order which the state is entrusted to protect. In functioning to combine the power of various individuals, the state is not essentially different from nonstate associations; all associations in society are aggregates of social-political power. Unlike any particular private association, however, the state represents the basic social-political consensus. Thus it is vested with special powers to establish and enforce norms of relationship between individuals and between groups throughout the society, to the extent that these are deemed to have a public bearing. The state is, in effect, the official "custodian" of the underlying political consensus, with special authority to uphold the body of consitutional norms and legal statutes which express this consensus.

In addition, a major assumption of traditional pluralism has been that the political rules, laws, and policies entrusted to the state reflect "the equilibrium reached in the group struggle at any given moment," and represent at any given time "a balance which the contending factions of groups constantly strive to weight in their favor."[3] Since this equilibrium between social groups is not static, but constantly shifting, adjustments must be made from time to time in the body of rules. Thus the second function of government, besides the upholding of fundamental constitutional norms, is the provision of a socially recognized context for expressing political conflict and reaching political compromise between contending group interests within the larger constitutional consensus. Hence the pluralist image of the "broker" state in which political actors play the roles of mediators between competing interest groups.[4] In both these major aspects — that of constitutional "custodian" and that of political "broker" mediating between competing groups — the role of the state is conceived as essentially *reflexive*, in that its fundamental laws and its changing policies are viewed as reflecting the resolution of political conflict among private individuals and organizations in the society, whose consensus is prerequisite to its own political action. The legislature, for example, is seen as a "referee," ratifying the victories of the "successful coalitions" of interests, and recording the terms of group victory or compromise "in the form of statutes." In turn, administrative agencies "carry out the terms of the treaties" ratified by the legislators, and the judiciary is seen as an instrument for working out a coherent pattern from the various strands of legal statutes and administrative decisions.[5]. Though not merely passive, the pluralist state does not *initiate* political action, but either follows it or at most facilitates it; and then implements the political decisions which come out of the interaction of interest groups. From another angle, the traditional pluralist state does not act *independently* according to criteria which are separable from the ongoing play of political interests. In short, the traditional pluralist state, while not simply "passive," is not an independently "active" state either. We will elaborate on the significance of this point later in this chapter.

Such, then, are some of the major assumptions of the pluralist theory of politics; or at least the pluralist theory in its *simple* "interest-group" form. Later criticisms have objected, however, to the simplification of pluralist theory when viewed in this way as a "pure" theory of interest-group politics. Thus critics have attacked the simplistic version of pluralist theory as suggesting that public policy is merely the political "resultant of a parallelogram of organized pressure group forces."[6] Obviously "pure" interest-group theory fails to explain the actual complexities of the governmental process of policy formation. The modern state is far more than a mirror held up to the various forces in civil society, passively reflecting and recording their interaction. Today "the advanced capitalist countries . . . have an often substantial 'public sector' . . . through which the state owns and administers a wide range of industries and services. . . ."[7] In contemporary capitalist economies the state plays "an ever-greater economic role by way of regulation, control, coordination, 'planning,' and so forth." In addition, "the state is by far the largest customer of the 'private sector'; and some major industries could not survive in the private sector without the state's custom and without the credits, subsidies and benefactions which it dispenses."[8] Clearly the early pluralistic picture of the more or less passive state and its political figures neutrally reflecting or merely facilitating the play of social and political interests fails to convey the quality of these contemporary developments in the role of central state power.

Actually there are at least several serious weaknesses in the "pure" pluralist theory as applied to complex modern society. As we have already indicated, one such area relates to the role of the state and its agencies. Another concerns the problem of the more privileged classes of the society, possessing disproportionate resources with which to influence the political process. As some critics of the traditional pluralist approach indicate, the power of a group in the political process will vary "according to factors such as the social class, income, or education of the members. . . ."[9] This leaves open the possibility at least that some interest groups or classes exercise preponderant power in the struggle to influence policy. Focussing on this, the political sociology of Marxist theorists, for example, has long revolved around the theme that in modern Western society the state functions essentially at the bidding of the capitalist class, as the society's most powerful class, operating in effect, as an "executive committee" through which this class actually exercises political rule. In response, the modern pluralist position, particularly as formulated since the 1950s, asserts that in democratic society many organized interests, not only business interests, have an important impact on public policy outcomes; that "none of these aggregates is homogeneous for all purposes; that each of them is highly influential over some [policy] scopes but weak over many others; and that the power to reject undesired alternatives is more common than the power to dominate over outcomes directly."[10] Put another way, many interest groups, besides business, have the power to *veto* those policies which adversely affect their interests on particular issues of relevance to them (hence David Riesman's characterization of the active interest groups in American politics as "veto groups").[11] At the same time, it is unlikely that any single group can directly *dictate* policy favorable to its own interests, and even then only within a narrow scope of policy on a limited range of issues. Proceeding from this, modern pluralist theorists have tended to conclude that since the state in a democracy is "subjected to a multitude of conflicting pressures from organized groups and interests," it "cannot show any marked bias towards some and against others; its special role . . . is to accommodate and reconcile them all."[12] Just how accurate is this claim, and how valid is its representation of the resulting system as a balanced distribution of political power are questions which remain open to debate.

Another question on which the traditional pluralist position tended to be relatively silent is that of the internal relations between members within interest organizations. In its traditional form, pluralist theory assumed that "representatives" of group interests would emerge as spokesmen for these respective interests. In fact, there is much evidence that the role of representative has long since become subordinated to that of group leader, particularly in the sense of one who shapes the position and program of the interest organization, even in the face of considerable internal organizational dissent. This has been possible because of the increasing bureaucratization of the structure of voluntary organizations and the relative removal of their leaders from contact with members, and thus from the pressure to be responsive to membership sentiment. The modern pluralist response to these developments has been to embrace the new leadership role as a realistic adjustment to the growth in organizational scale and to the overall bureaucratization of society. Thus the contemporary pluralist position accepts the fact that relatively small leadership elites consisting of men at the top of their special fields of endeavor, whether economic, social, cultural, or political, serve to "represent" others whose institutional or social positions fall below them in rank in these fields.[13] In this way the modern pluralist recognizes that in a bureaucratically organized social environment the representation of interests in political bargaining is conducted through leaders who in their own spheres of action act as men at the top of institutional hierarchies. Though the result is a peculiar kind of "elitist pluralism," it nonetheless is viewed by the modern pluralist as "a prime guarantee that power in society will be diffused and not concentrated,"[14] mainly because it entails a fairly regular competition between different elites.

In addition to questions of the role of the state, its relation to the more privileged or powerful social interests, and the rise of elite-leadership in interest organizations, there is yet another matter which has taken on increasing importance as the society and its political system have grown in scale, and as the political system has formally opened its doors to some level of participation by the mass of the population, legally lowering earlier barriers of class, race, or sex. It amounts to this: despite the formal extension of the suffrage, the nominal opening of the parties to public participation over the past century, and the resulting claims that America is a "mass democracy," it is a well-known fact, documented by many students of poltics including the end-of-ideologists themselves, that participation in voting and in party activities is a characteristic mainly of the broad middle and upper-middle classes in America, in contrast to the relatively low participation patterns of the working and lower classes.[15]

During the 1950s this problem was responded to by pluralist theorists in various ways, mostly by seeking to minimize the significance of po-

litical participation to the individual, or by showing that too much participation could actually threaten the functioning of the political system.
David Riesman and Nathan Glazer took the tack that political activities,
like voting or maintaining interest and opinions regarding political issues,
actually may represent "apolitical" behavior, due to the growing possibility that they merely reflect conformity to the group norms on the part
of predominantly middle-class voters.[16] A high level of electoral participation was taken to mean *not* the concern of large numbers of citizens
for serious issues of government, but only group conformity or, at most,
an isolated political action for the sake of immediate self-interest. Viewed
in these terms, high-volume voting took on the connotation of "low
quality" political participation. The proponents of this position tended
to conclude that wide popular participation in voting should not necessarily be a political objective, or even a criterion by which to judge the
efficacy of a democratic political system. In fact, sudden high levels of
electoral participation have at various times been taken by pluralist
theorists to mean that "the tensions of political struggle are stretching to
the breaking point the will toward the constitutional,"[17] and are sympto-
matic of dangerous populistic, even revolutionary trends, or at least of
serious decline of political consensus in the society.[18] From this viewpoint, the long-term low levels (approximately fifty to sixty percent) of
voting participation which have been characteristic of American (national) elections for over half a century are indications of the electorate's
basic satisfaction with the conduct of government. The downgrading
of mass political participation which flows from this "antipopulistic"
pluralism is well expressed in David Riesman's remark that "bringing
sleepwalkers to the polls simply to increase turnout is no service to
democracy."[19]

As we noted in chapter 1, during the 1950s there emerged a strong
commitment among the major active political groupings in the society,
including business, labor, and politically involved intellectuals, to
the basic institutional forms of postwar American society. During that
decade, interest-group pluralism remained the dominant, received theory
of the society, partly out of "cultural lag" and partly because it expressed
intergroup political arrangements which had been arrived at and institutionalized by the New Deal, and which continued to function for the
groups involved. Nevertheless, a significant attack on the assumptions of
interest-group pluralism, particularly in its modern elitist, antipopulist
form was made by C. Wright Mills during the mid-1950s, opening the
way for mounting criticism of these assumptions by dissatisfied intellectuals and by newly activated interest groups such as blacks, students,
and others during the Sixties.[20] Mills' attack was some years ahead of its
time in that it had no mass base of support, but consisted of the critical

observations of a sociological theoretician regarding a viewpoint which seemed to pervade the social sciences to a point where its assumptions were taken as established fact; in the realm of the political culture the pluralist viewpoint had apparently penetrated so deeply as to become the main thread of the culture, inseparable from the taken-for-granted frame of reference for political action and generally accepted as the prevailing "public philosophy."[21]

In this context, Mills directed his theory of the "power elite" at several of the weaknesses in the pluralistic theory which we have described, particularly at the influence of the modern central state on the pluralist system, and the specially close relationship of the state and its agencies to the interests of the business elite. In the process, he produced a rather different picture of the society than that provided by the prevailing pluralist theory. In Mill's image, truly significant political decisions profoundly affecting the social structure of the society were now being made at a political level to which the public no longer was provided access by its various interest organizations. Instead of effectively linking the primary, local level of family and community to the national level of the state and other institutions of national scope, voluntary organizations like the unions and the political parties no longer had any significant effect on the major decisions of the time. Though the leaders of voluntary organizations still participated in the process of interest bargaining, which had become associated in the public's mind with the democratic process itself, the stakes for which they bargained were minor compared to those involved in the really important, war-or-peace decisions which were national in scope, and which were being made by a much more restricted group of leaders at a level above that of the voluntary organizations. A small and restricted institutional leadership elite now made nationally significant policy decisions beyond the control of the increasingly politically uninvolved and powerless mass of the society.

Though Mills conceded that interest pluralism as a politically representative system did indeed persist in American society, he claimed that the overall social structure had so developed that traditional pluralism was functionally limited to the level of local, intermediate structures, hence no longer relevant to the distinctive new processes of decision at the level of nationally significant structures such as the federal government and large-scale corporate enterprise. Indeed Mills viewed the local level of political and interest-group organizations as a kind of foil whose very accessibility tended to conceal the concentration of power in the hands of a functional coalition of major institutional leaders. Thus the problem for Mills was, in the final analysis, the legitimacy of the new elite coalition, hidden behind the facade of familiar local structures for political participation which (even while they reassured the interested public of the democratic nature of the system) had little relevance either to its operation or to the shaping of its further development.

One of Mills' main theoretical points was that the centralization of the economy, already evident prior to the Second World War, was now being followed up by the growth of an unprecedentedly powerful central state containing a massive executive bureaucracy whose most powerful and fastest rising agencies were those of the military. As a result, Mills looked beyond the intermediate level of power, as represented by the Congress and most of the organized interests and pressure groups, to the top level of the structure of power; he looked beyond the bargaining and logrolling of the wide variety of interests at the intermediate level of political power to the somewhat different relations of "executive co-ordination" between the managerial elite of the business corporations and the elites of the political executive and the military agencies. Mills believed that, under these circumstances, the influence of big business on government policy, and particularly military policy, could no longer be assumed to be effectively circumscribed by that of other interest groups in the polity. The growth of a militarily active central state during the Second World War and the Korean War, and the close coordination between military leaders, political leaders, and business executives during that period, had created a new mode of decision making, affecting the allocation of major social resources, yet involving only a very limited circle of institutional elites. Because of the size of the military sector, and its manifold connections with the economy, business was now able to influence not merely foreign military policy, but the subsidization of a significant segment of its own domestic development, *via* the medium of a powerful militarily mobilized central state.[22]

"Countervailing Power" and The New Pluralism

Interestingly, it was by way of the response to Mills's theory of the power elite and his related image of America as a "mass society" that the ground was first prepared for the theory of the end of ideology. The tack which sophisticated pluralists like Bell and Lipset took in their rejoinder to Mills in particular, as well as other representatives of the mass-society perspective, was to provide a revised image of the established pluralist model of the society. Daniel Bell, in an essay attacking Mills's analysis of American society, developed a new picture of the role of the state and emphasized its beneficent relation to unrepresented or underprivileged groups in American society.[23] Basic to this position, Bell noted the political or economic emergence since the New Deal of previously unorganized interests such as the unions and the buying chains which could now stand up to the economic power of the corporate sector. What he rightly emphasized was that much of this development of "countervailing power"[24] *vis à vis* big business had come about only with the aid and encouragement of the government, rather than as an automatic group response to unfavorable market conditions. By pointing out the crucial role of the state in this process, Bell took the notion of countervailing power somewhat further than the traditional pluralists who viewed it simply as an expression of "natural" tendencies toward intergroup restraint in a pluralistic society.

In point of fact, this was not the first time American government had taken steps to intervene on behalf of interest groups other than influential business interests; at least since the late nineteenth century government had become increasingly involved in regulating such areas of enterprise as banking, interstate commerce, and railroads, as well as the payment of subsidies to farmers, and, more recently, in the supervision of the public's drinking habits during Prohibition. Prior to the New Deal, however, much of this activity represented *ad hoc* concessions to the protection of rural and small town political interests, seeking to defend themselves culturally as well as economically against the encroachments of an expanding industrial society. What the end-of-ideologists emphasize however, is the contribution of the New Deal toward raising this kind of *ad hoc* governmental activity to the level of a general principle; i.e., the New Deal gave official legitimation to the idea that disadvantaged group interests such as industrial workers, the aged, veterans, minorities, etc., had the right as such for government support with respect to privileged interests, in matters ranging from the distribution of income to the protection of civil rights.[25] Bell's point is that in this way the state stepped in decisively during the New Deal to help the processes of countervailing power correct the inequalities of the marketplace as the regulator of economic power.

Bell's conception of the revamped, but still pluralist, structure of the American political economy combines the earlier pluralist image of a political "broker state" with the notion of decisive governmental intervention in the economy, to which he refers at several points either as a "political economy" or a "managed economy." In this politically managed economy, government increasingly becomes an active instrument for translating into economic programs political decisions arrived at through the process of interest-group politics. At the same time, since "welfare-state" government declares its support for the group rights of less advantaged interests, it will also intervene in the political arena itself, for the sake of correcting political disadvantage by establishing a reasonable balance among interest groups. It is this image of a beneficent, "positive government" which Bell employs in his response to Mills's theory of the power elite; a government which actively supports the development of countervailing power for the sake of political-economic balance. Now and then Bell qualifies this image in recognition of the continuing dominance of big business interests,[26] yet the point is not lost. Pluralism, even if somewhat lopsided, is still alive; no longer the simple pluralism of the past, contemporary pluralism consists of well-organized interests competing for the support and favors of an increasingly powerful, increasingly active, central government.[27]

In this respect, Bell, more adequately than liberal theorists like David Riesman, reflects the shift since the New Deal from limited, minimal government to government actively intervening in response to politically expressed social needs. Riesman pictures government policy as the outcome of a shifting stalemate between "veto groups" which can block one another, and occasionally government itself, from going too far in any given direction.[28] Bell sees government as a positive force for allocating economic and social values to groups, on condition that they can organize themselves in a politically effective manner. Thus Bell produces an image which goes considerably beyond the earlier liberal conception of a "night-watchman" state simply providing external defense and internal order; Bell's "positive state" actively intervenes in the conflict of competing socioeconomic interests so that some semblance of balance is created among them.

Consistent with this picture of enduring pluralism in American political and economic life is Bell's sharp criticism of the concept of America as a "mass society." The link which runs through the essays in *The End of Ideology* touching on this theme is the celebration of the variety and richness of American cultural life, which supposedly is the "underlying reality" obscured by the mass theorists' images of widespread cultural alienation and apathy.[29] Paralleling his emphasis on the enduring, though restructured, pluralism of the political economy, Bell emphasizes the enduring pluralism of American cultural life. Ostensibly, alongside what remains of the earlier ethnic pluralism of the immigrant working class, there exists an expanding range of taste in the emerging new middle class which bespeaks not a homogeneous "mass culture," but a spectrum of cultural styles, from "lowbrow" to "highbrow," from "popular" to "classical," among which American can choose today.[30] In addition, Bell stresses the continuing importance of participation in voluntary organizational activities in American life, which presumably "affords hundreds of individuals concrete, emotionally shared activities."[31]

To this point we have analyzed the earliest phase of the postwar revision of pluralist theory in which the ground is prepared for the later revisions made in the context of the end-of-ideology theory itself. The major theme which emerges during this phase is that pluralism has taken on new forms in political and cultural life, involving a fuller integration of interest groups into the policy processes of "positive government," and greater differentiation of individual life styles and organizational participation within the culture. The underlying emphasis is that these restructurings of political and cultural life have maintained — indeed strengthened—the viability of a pluralist social system in the context of the world's most advanced mass industrial society.

Beyond Pluralism: Technical Decision Making and The "End of Ideology"

In the framework of the end-of-ideology theory itself, the received pluralist image of government operating to assure a political balance of interests steadily recedes in importance. The focus shifts to the increasing centralization of political power in the postwar period and the growing bureaucratization of political and economic institutions. Moreover, the theory has it that the resulting concentrations of power were not consciously willed by the leaders of these institutions, but arose spontaneously in piecemeal response to domestic and foreign threats to system maintenance. The implication is that institutional centralization and bureaucratization do not really threaten the pluralist basis of American democracy; in fact they have actually strengthened major American institutions and improved their competence.

In support of this perspective, the image of contemporary American society presented by the end-of-ideologists takes as its point of departure an "affluent," highly productive society, whose productivity is based ultimately on a combination of managerial expertise and government action. The argument is that as a consequence of postwar tendencies toward centralization, bureaucratic administrators, corporate managers, and technical experts have come to replace their traditional forbears, the political and economic "bosses" of an earlier day, particularly in organizations which are national in scale. Thus, the end-of-ideology theorists tend to picture the basis for political rule in the society as having shifted from economic power to functional capacity, from the private possession of wealth to the ability to play highly technical roles important to organizational efficiency. In their image of the new society, not merely ideology but issue-oriented politics itself, comes to be deemphasized. This society comprises, at the core, a system of interrelated large-scale political and economic organizations in which ever greater reliance is placed on a new, more rational mode of decision: what Bell calls "technical decision-making."[32] Essentially, such decision making consists of the implementation by technically sophisticated management of policy decided upon at the executive level in the state or corporation. While policy is ultimately made with reference to the special goals and purposes of organizations, their purposes are depicted as beneficial to the collective well-being of the society as a whole. In the corporation, policy makers are ostensibly guided by aims of efficient production rather than motives of profit; in government, the most important determinant of policy making is the national security, rather than the influence of class or sectional interests. In this image, the managers of the corporation consider themselves responsible for the nurture and growth of a great organization, important to the well-being of its employees, stockholders, and the general community in which it functions; the bureaucrats and administrators of government, in turn, are dedicated to the national interest rather than any special interests, and the policies they implement are viewed as the most rational means for the nation's survival in a conflict-ridden world. Ostensibly, in the large-scale organizations of the new society, the values which guide the making of policy have changed from concern with particularistic special interests to the collective public interest. The underlying theme is one of beneficent managerialism.

Apparently, with the emergence of this well-managed, productive society, the traditional tensions of stratification between upper and lower classes have been markedly reduced. Both absolute deprivation and the relative distance between social classes has been reduced, as total national income has increased. Implicit in this position is the notion that resolving the tensions between different classes requires no fundamental redistribution of the social product, only its continued growth. Growth of the national product is viewed as a good in itself, and there is no consideration given to any possible negative side effects. To the extent that individuals can satisfy their desires for a material improvement of living standards, they lose interest in ideology and even in politics itself, even while they come to have a heightened dependence on the state, its programs, subsidies, policies, etc. Among the "new masses" of the managerially guided society, there is a general "de-ideologization" and "de-politization"—a turning away from the political arena to the home, the friends, the job, personal hobbies, recreation, etc.[33] In particular, the absorption of the unionized working class into the system removes the most important basis of the traditional ideological politics of the earlier industrial era, a politics based on objective economic discontent. In this view the decline of ideological politics is an index of the social and economic advances achieved through the managerial revolution in government and business initiated by the liberals of the New Deal and the innovators of the "new capitalism."[34]

Supposedly, the decline in class tensions which can be traced to the high productivity of the postwar economy, produces the "end of ideolology." Yet in the last analysis what the end-of-ideologists cite as the hallmark of the "new society" is not its unprecedented enonomic achieve-ment; it is instead the rise to decisive importance of administrative-technical modes of decision, owing to the change in the relative importance of the respective sectors of the American political system since the New Deal. That era, like no other before it, set in motion the rising importance of the federal executive as against the Congress and the states — a tendency which has continued ever since. The central executive of the New Deal in turn, through the large-scale administrative and planning activities involved in a variety of social and economic programs such as TVA, AAA, PWA and Social Security, made a signifi-cant contribution to the development of technocratic decision making. But, in the view of the end-of-ideologists, even more important to the rise of technocracy than the growing role of the federal government in the domestic economy has been the shift in the focus of politics from the domestic to the foreign scene, so that policy is today shaped essentially by international events, rather than being a reflex of domestic class or interest-group struggles. According to the "end of ideology" the major impetus to the new centralization of power and the rise of technocratic policy making can be viewed as deriving from this shift in the focus of policy concern.

Upon reflection then, we see that the theory of the "end of ideology" has its roots in a theory of political development in advanced society in which the loci of power and policy in the contemporary political system shift from the legislative to the executive branch, and from domestic to foreign politics. Moreover, this shift in policy focus is accompanied by a basic change in the way policy is made. The "simple" pluralist mode of policy making as the outcome of bargaining among the various inter-ests represented in the domestic political system gradually gives way to a technically dictated kind of administrative policy making increasingly preoccupied with foreign affairs. Though the New Deal may be viewed as an important early impetus to the growth of technocratic institutions in the executive bureaucracy, of considerably more significance has been our policy of military response to foreign affairs in recent decades. The military's expansion during and since World War II has been more re-sponsible than any other single factor for the rise of the technocrats and the emergence of a "postindustrial society."

This is the major theme which serves to introduce Bell's recent analysis of the technocratic basis of development in the new society.[35] The im-portance of the military technocracy in the shaping of postindustrial society is summed up in Herman Kahn's observation, cited by Bell, that military technology has supplanted the mode of production as "a major determinant of the social structure."[36] This is a theme which has grown in Bell's work ever since his own observation that the postwar military buildup had "reworked the map of American society" through the creation of a "dual economy" with new relationships between government and the defense sector, and a new role for scientists and planners in the political system and the economy.[37] As American society has taken on the features of a "mobilized society," basic resources, including scientifically trained manpower, have become geared to planned economic change. The adoption of a mobilized posture, entailing the rapid growth of the military and its technologies, has been the single most important stimulus to the expansion of technical decision making.

Essentially, Bell's argument is that "given" the post-World War II foreign policy framework of containment-of-Communism — formulated by publicly elected officials and their governmental advisers, rather than by any covert power elite — certain consequences followed, with profound impact for the very structure of society. He stresses that these developments are only the outcome of technical decisions made to implement policies which were themselves formulated by top government officials with only the overall interests of the nation in mind. Any resultant changes in the social structure, and particularly in the structure of power in the society, are to be viewed as merely the incidental by-products of decisions which were themselves "functionally rational" from the perspective of overall system requirements.

Unfortunately, this interpretation tends to obscure the very question which Bell posed in his sharp critique of Mills's power-elite theory; namely, just what is the character of the decisions made by those who have power?[38] By depicting the process whereby executive policy was translated into military programs and projects simply as "technocratic" decision making, and identifying this kind of decision making with "functional rationality," Bell tends to close off examination of the steps by which such decisions have fed the interests of certain powerful constituencies in postindustrial America. In particular, this explanation of the continuing expansion of the military sector tends to exclude consideration of the influence on the policy process of the considerable benefits which flow to corporate industry, to sectional and favored-state interests, to the federal agencies which administer the operations of the military, etc. If we look back into the policy process, to the initial executive policy decision itself, we see that by taking this decision as self-evident, as a "given," Bell is able to ignore the values that lie behind the choice of an essentially military response to postwar international developments, particularly in the "third world"; values which have been, moreover, consistent with the prevailing constellation of power in America which seeks to control development at home and abroad in accord with the common interests of its component members.[39] By ignoring the question of the values and interests that underlie basic policy decisions, Bell can proceed to explain the consequences purely in terms of the "fact" of military mobilization in its mutually supportive relationship with technocratic modes of decision. As a result, the emergence of a military-technocratic sector in American society is treated as a matter of facts, of means, of implementation, rather than as a question of goals, aims, or interests, in the "value-free" context of the end-of-ideology theory. In this way, the end-of-ideology theory produces a curious new separation in the relationship of policy to political power. On one hand, policy is no longer viewed as the response of government to the interests and demands of those who can exert effective political influence but as a decision made in the general interest by official representatives standing above these influences and guided by superior technical information and advice. On the other hand, changes in the structure of power are not the conscious intention of policy, but only incidental, technically dictated consequences. Treated in this way, the concept of technocratic decision making becomes a screen between power (the structure of interests with influence on the decision process) and policy (the outcome of the decision process). Allegedly, if powerful interests benefit from policy decisions, this occurs not because they have used their power to influence these decisions to their own benefits, but only as an unforeseen consequence of the technocratic implementation of policy.

As we have already noted, from its early stages the end-of-ideology theory accepts the restructuring and integration of the American political and economic systems as beneficial to the larger society. The resulting concentration of power in government and the corporate economy is explained in the intermediate phase of the theory as an unintended consequence of these developments. In this perspective, the new managerial elites are viewed as the agents of progressive social development, oriented toward the collective benefit, rather than toward private interest. In its later stages, the theory combines these developments in a theory of decision making which has its roots in the technical-military exigencies of the war and cold-war period. In the process, the theory produces an interesting separation between policy making and the wielding of political power in the society. The nonrational, special-interest side of power is minimized, and power is viewed simply in terms of the contribution it can make to the protection and rational operation of the overall society.

We question whether power actually functions in this manner in American society today. The theory of "technocratic" or technical-administrative decision making, which is first broached in the end-of-ideology theory and then in ensuing work on the postindustrial society, is an elegant and powerful summing up of a tendency of the first importance in advanced industrial society; but it frequently overlooks the fact that the underlying shift in the focus of decision making from the arena of interest-group politics to the executive agencies of the state, is still only an important tendency rather than a completed process. Interest-group politics is far from dead at any level of American society today, though we do tend to agree with Mills' picture of a narrowing of *significant* political access to a small circle of institutional leaders the closer we approach the top level of decision making of national scope. Thus the notion of "elitist" pluralism seems a good approximation to the *overall* political situation in a society characterized by bureaucratic organization, hierarchic leadership, and a diversity of competing specialized elites.[40] Rather than the end of interest-group politics at the national level, there seems to have occurred an integration of such politics with the functions of the relevant administrative agencies. Decision making by technical experts and administrators in government agencies and private bureaucracies is not simply a cool, detached, scientific-rational process insulated from the influences of political pressure and conflict. To the contrary, we will argue that the technical experts have been absorbed into the various institutions in which they are based, effectively placing their knowledge and expertise at the service of the elites which control those institutions.. In sum, we submit that the technical mode of decision making has itself been institutionally "pluralized," with technocratic experts distributed mainly among those organizations which can pay for their services and supply the necessary "intellectual technologies" for their work.

It is our thesis that what the end-of-ideologists, as theorists of technocratic decision making, have done is to put forward a "premature" theory — one which prematurely proclaims the dominance of newly emergent social structures, and which tends to overlook the fact that even the most profound, revolutionary social changes typically carry over with them important elements of the preceding historical period. These residual elements become features of the new society, which during the process of absorption themselves tend to modify the characteristic institutions of the new society.[41] As a "premature" theory the thesis of technocratic decision making serves also as an ideology, representing the perspective of social scientists who seek the functional rationalization of the political system and its better integration with the economy. That is, they express through this theory their preference for overriding the interest-group system, when and where possible, by way of administrative state controls. (This preference comes through clearly enough through repeated usages which connect the pluralist arena with irrational modes of decision, as against the superior rationality of the technical-administrative decision mode.)[42] As such, they function not only as theorists of technocratic development in advanced industrial society, but also as prophets and ideologists of such development. At the same time, however, their position is finally ambiguous, since they are unable to outline what they consider as the proper relationship of business, currently still the most powerful set of interests in the pluralist arena, to government. At times, they see government as making its most important decisions for the welfare of business,[43] and at other times, they suggest that government and the emerging university and research agencies (Galbraith's academic-scientific estate) are institutions in the service of disinterested rationality rather than private profit, and oriented toward the satisfaction of social needs rather than the wants of private consumers. In this, these social scientists tend to overlook the possibility that government programs and the work of the educational-scientific estate may serve the interests of business, particularly large corporate business, at least as much as they do the rest of the society, and certainly as much as they do the "public sector."

Rather than alerting us to these possibilities in the emerging postindustrial conjunction of central government and centralized corporate business, their theory and the major terms and symbols through which it speaks (such as the notions of "postindustrialism" and the related concept of value-neutral "technocratic planning")[44] serve to obscure these possibilities and their problematic aspects by suggesting that the new political economy is well on the way to transcending private industrial and business interests, and planning for the "communal" welfare. The intention of the present work is to critically investigate these broad and generally optimistic images of the theorists of postindustrial society, by examining their validity as representations of the emerging political economy and its structural arrangements, and by identifying the ideological bias which they express.

CHAPTER III

Postindustrial Society
and the
Role of Technocracy

To this point we have traced the underlying assumptions of the end-of-ideology theory through its development as a theory of ideological decline, on to its transformation to a theory of technocratic development. In its most recent stages, the end of ideology has become explicitly a theory of society as it moves into a "postindustrial" phase; though this is a general trend of Western societies today, the theory points to the American case as the most fully developed example of the mechanisms and consequences of this trend.[1] Accordingly, in this chapter we review the theory's treatment of postindustrial development in relation to the development of technocratic structures in American society. In addition, we discuss the implications of this process for pluralist political institutions inherited from the industrial era, and its connection with the emergence of a new "technocratic class."

Postindustrial Society and "Technocratic Rationality"

The "postindustrial" society, according to the end-of-ideologists, is already upon us. This is a society in which manufacturing, the productive core of the preceding industrial society, is in process of being displaced by a growing "service sector," including personal, professional, and repair services; general governmental services; and such private activities as trade, finance, insurance, and real estate. (Essentially, "services" are activities which do not produce tangible goods such as food, clothing, housing, etc.) This shift in economic activity is reflected in a changing occupational structure, particularly in the rising proportion of white-collar workers to a point where they now outnumber blue-collar workers by "more than five to four." Of particular relevance to the thesis of an emerging "technocratic class" is the rapid expansion in upper white-collar positions (managerial, professional, and technical) on which is based the "heart of the upper-middle class in the United States."[2] We will detail some of these trends below.

In the first place, there has been tremendous growth in national product since WW II, sufficient to give the American population 50 percent more income per capita in 1970 than in 1946, even though population has at the same time grown by about 40 percent. Contrary to early predictions of postwar depression, 20 million more jobs have been created in the economy, and about 30 million homes and apartments have been built in the past 20-odd years. These phenomena have been the bases for declarations of an "affluent society." Moreover there has been a diversification of consumer patterns, with increasing proportions of added consumer income being devoted to spending on education and a variety of services, as against durable goods.[3]

The rise in spending for services by individual consumers has been accompanied by expanded expenditures by government for services such as health, education, and technical research, and by industry for various business and banking services, as well as for research. The rising investment in the services sector and in general government has produced a significant rise in services-government employment. In fact most growth in employment since the end of World War II has occurred in the services-government sector, so that today over 60 percent of total employment is in this sector, and this is expected to continue rising. In this respect, there is justification to speak of a "postindustrial" society, for while employment in traditional goods-producing industries such as manufacturing, construction, and mining has grown in absolute terms since World War II, their relative share of total employment has declined due to the much more rapid growth of employment in services-government.[4]

Interestingly, the developments of the New Deal, world war, and postwar periods have produced such an expansion in government and other services that the proportions of employment since 1920 have been reversed, with goods-producing industries, including farming (i.e., the "primary" and "secondary" sectors), employing 61 percent of the labor force in 1920, and only 39 percent in 1970, while services-government (the "tertiary" sectors) have increased their share of employment from 39 percent to 61 percent over that period.[5] In this sense a "silent revolution" has taken place, at least with regard to the structure of employment, and increasingly the "white collar" of the technical, professional, and clerical worker in the services-government sector has replaced the "blue collar" of the factory worker, and the work uniform of the farmer. While most of the growth in white-collar employment has been accounted for by the expansion in the female clerical and sales forces, nonetheless 41 percent of the male labor force, or almost 20 million men, held white-collar jobs as of 1970, as against 25 percent in 1940 and 15 percent in 1900. Out of these 20 million white-collar male workers, about 70 percent, or 14 million, hold managerial, technical, or professional jobs, and this group is the source of the "technocratic class" which the end-of-ideologists expect to play such an important role in the postindustrial society.[6]

Clearly, the expectation of the end-of-ideologists is that this class will provide serious competition to the established leadership elites of the society. According to them, the growth of this class, particularly its professional and technical components, reflects the displacement of a society in which property and political position have been the bases of power, by one in which systematic theoretical knowledge becomes the new power base. Moreover, the kind of knowledge which will be central to the government and development of the new society involves the capacity to manipulate the natural and social environment through highly sophisticated scientific techniques. So, for example, the role of computer technology seems destined to grow, since its techniques enable theoretical simulation of complex social-economic systems and experimentation with reference to simulated social environments. Inevitably then, the making of social decisions will have an increasingly technical character, requiring special skills which the members of the technocratic class are uniquely qualified to provide. Though it is, for example, Daniel Bell's belief that this class will challenge the established leadership of the society, and possibly in time displace it, his position with regard to this challenge is not entirely clear, since he refers to the dominant institutions of the industrial era as those of the business elite, while the leading institutions of the postindustrial era will increasingly be those of the "knowledge elite."[7] This would imply a basic conflict between the business elite and the technocratic elite (the leading policy-concerned members of the larger technocratic class); yet the conflict about which Bell expresses concern is the potential struggle between the technocrats and the established political elite. This position can be contrasted with that of Robert Heilbroner, writing on the emergence of new institutional elites and their impact on the corporate capitalist system.[8] Unlike Bell, Heilbroner's emphasis is on the likelihood of conflict between the established business elite and the emerging "nonbusiness elites," among whom he includes the professional academic experts, the technocratic government administrators, and the new military administrators; taken together, roughly the equivalent of Bell's technocrats. Actually at one point Bell lays down the basis for a similar argument, but never pursues it. He notes that "in the most general ways . . . the major decisions . . . have been made by business, and latterly by government, which gives major priority to the welfare of business."[9] This would suggest that the struggle to replace the particular-interest perspective in the policy process by a public-interest perspective will involve conflict not merely with the politicians, particularly the traditionally interest-oriented establishment in Congress, but also with the business elite.

Perhaps most important for future development is the possibility that government in postindustrial society will become increasingly active with regard to planning for the needs of the public sector. For this is a society which is coming to be more conscious of its developmental needs as a social system, owing to the increasingly public, collective nature of needs in a wide range of areas such as urban development, education, public transit, and the like. As Bell puts it, the society is getting increasingly "communal" and "future-oriented" at the same time; that is, aware of the desirability of planning ahead to meet its growing public needs. In this context, the demonstrated effectiveness of techniques already employed in the military sector, such as centralized systems analysis and program-budgeting techniques, as well as the application of sophisticated methods of fiscal control over the private economy, all suggest the benefits to be derived from the exercise of some combination of centralized, technocratic controls over the development of the public sector. Significantly, Bell tends to assume that the technocratic mode will not remain confined to the military sector, but will somehow spill over into the civilian economy in transition from an industrial economy producing goods for private consumers to a postindustrial economy providing a variety of services, both private and public. As public needs for services such as education, medical care, and urban planning become ever more urgent, government decisions will probably continue to replace the market in the making of various developmental choices in the economy.[10]

In sum, as society becomes increasingly "communal" and "future-oriented," government will probably engage in more planning, continually replacing the market in deciding the lines along which social and economic development will proceed. Already, notes Bell, there exists a political commitment to domestic economic growth and to the need for assessing the consequences of growth in an increasingly complex society. All of this has led to what amounts to, against the background of prior attempts during the New Deal, a revived interest in planning based on a heightened awareness of the need to define national goals and long-range objectives. With the further development of sophisticated simulation techniques, long-range objectives could possibly be portrayed in the form of computer profiles of "alternate futures" implementing different sets of national goals; the drafting of such profiles would be another important responsibility allocated to technocratic planners, in the projection and management of social development.[11]

Much of this outline of the postindustrial future is left to the rise and growth in influence of the "technocratic class," which is defined rather broadly as all those who deal with "theoretical knowledge," thereby encompassing "scientists, engineers, technicians, or intellectuals" in one loose category.[12] This new class can be expected to affect the political system in a number of ways. First, as scientific, economic, or administrative experts, its members should play important roles as government administrators and planners, and as technical advisors to politicians and bureaucrats in government. Second, they should act as a new political constituency in their positions in universities and research laboratories seeking government support, particularly for research activities. In this respect their political participation as claimants for government support will be carried on mainly through the channels of the administrative bureaucracy, rather than through the electoral system. Third, as people of education and some taste, they will probably tend to introduce into the political process, including party politics, demands for a general improvement of the quality of public life. Such demands would be directed toward the improvement and updating of the educational system, the provision of more cultural amenities, better urban planning, etc; all of which taken together bears an interesting resemblance to the current liberal political agenda for "qualitative reform."[13] We have here a long chain of conjecture which seems to take for granted both the growth in influence of the technocratic class, and a high degree of political unity among its members in favor of the necessary public service programs to carry out these reforms.

However, technocratic planning has so far been widely instituted only in the process of military policy making, an area in which policy seems to proceed from certain broadly accepted "givens" on which there is considerable agreement in the political system. Moreover, Bell's discussion suggests that where military policy is concerned, the usual "political criteria" of the pluralist system are suspended, and a more technical kind of rationality takes over.[14] This raises an important question which deserves further exploration. If "technical rationality" is to prevail in the public sector as well, how long can policy making for this sector continue to be characterized by the process of pluralist bargaining among private interests? For many of these interests still seem to view the satisfaction of public sector needs as the proper domain of private enterprise and are only grudgingly willing to empower government to do an adequate job of providing these services to the public. Yet Bell tends to assume the spillover into the public sector of technocratic methods and the implications they carry of long-term planning. On what does he base this assumption?

Apparently this expectation can be traced to the rapid growth of the role of the executive in the policy process in the past generation, and the assumption that this role will continue to grow. Moreover, the same political developments which have given the Executive the initiative in government policy making have led to the institutionalization of a variety of technocratic agencies as its functioning arms:

> In the United States we have seen, in the past twenty-five years, the enormous transformation of the Presidency into the Executive Office of the President with the addition of new staff functions — such as the Bureau of the Budget, the Council of Economic Advisors, and the Office of the Science Advisor — directly within that office.[15]

In this way, an executive technocracy has grown up engaged in technical decision making within the framework of established imperatives of national interest.

The situation which has developed as a result of this sudden and unanticipated growth of the executive branch is one of considerable potential and actual tension between that branch and the other elements of government. It now becomes more clear what is involved in Bell's depiction of the relation between technocrats and politicians as a "conflict between technocratic rationality and political bargaining."[16] Apparently his reference is to the relations of the executive technocracy, which articulates and administers the general policies of the political executive *vis à vis* the pluralistic polity, i.e., the Congress, the states, and the various private interests in the political system. What is actually at stake here, then, is the relationship of executive government, with its growing technocratic appendages (nourished from the "inside" by the advisory "brain-trusts," the regular White House Staff, and the departmental and agency staffs, and from the "outside" by university and research-based consultants), to the inherited institutions of the pluralist polity, particularly the Congress, still acting as broker among the various special interests which may frequently be indifferent to the contemporary imperatives of national policy.

Lying behind Bell's abstract formula of technocratic rationality *versus* political bargaining is really the clash of two ideal types of government, and the institutional structures which embody them: executive-administrative government, standing above the particularistic struggles of the pluralist policy, authoritatively deciding the policies required to protect the "national interest"; and parliamentary-legislative government, representing the earlier established system of "interest bargaining." In Bell's discussion, it is the executive-technocratic state of "postmodern" vintage which stands in an increasingly stronger position with respect to the pluralistic legislature, and if "technocratic rationality" is to be extended to the public sector it will most likely be primarily through executive initiative.

Though this position seems plausible, it involves some drastic simplifications which must be carefully examined to understand the obstacles which remain in the way of planning for public civilian-sector development, even while technocratic planning takes on a larger role in the military sector. We will close this section by looking somewhat more closely at the process of governmental policy making.

Technical Decision Making: Some Obstacles in Government

The process of public policy determination in America today can be analyzed provisionally as a three-cornered affair, involving the executive, its technocratic bureacracy, and the pluralist polity. As a consequence, policy making in the public service sector will tend to be considerably more complex than in the military sector, since, structurally speaking, it involves the pluralistic polity far more actively than does military planning while, ideologically, it entails a good deal more conflict of values and interests.

Indeed, Bell's picture of technical decision making in the military sector is itself considerably simplified; from his account, it would seem that this is little more than a working-out by technical experts in federal agencies such as Defense, of policies handed down by the Executive. But Bell pays too little attention to the persisting involvement of particular interest groups and occasionally the Congress in the implementation of defense policies; the case of the TFX plane is a classic example, and can hardly be said to have been free of sharp conflict between differing preferences as to how military appropriations should be translated into a specific defense program.[17] It is, in fact, only by comparison with the even *greater* complexity of the policy process in the public service sector that the situation in regard to defense policy seems simple. Yet, even in the defense sector, policy making is hardly the clearcut rationalist process which the term "technical decision making" tends to convey. As Huntington has pointed out, it is only in issues of *strategic* policy, such as the determination of requirements for military forces and weapon systems and programs for their deployment, as opposed to *structural* policy (structural organization and conditions of military service), that effective decision power rests with the executive. Thus, in the case of strategic policies and programs, the basic decisions have tended to be confined to executive agencies and committees such as the Bureau of the Budget, the Joint Chiefs of Staff (JCS), the National Security Council (NSC), and the Department of Defense (DOD). Insofar as technical decision making tends to be located in central executive institutions rather than the public or its representative institutions, and to have available to it sophisticated intellectual technology for specifying programs and resources required to carry out policy, the strategic military policy process has resembled "technical decision making," over the postwar period. Yet even here the features of bargaining, disagreement, identification with alternative positions, etc., which are so typical of the broad pluralist polity, particularly the Congress and its interest clients, have been characteristic of the relations among the various executive agencies and the central executive. This suggests that while the *locus* of decision has largely shifted to the executive branch, the *mode* of decision has in many ways remained that of pluralist interest bargaining. Indeed, the reason for the shift in locus is primarily that the major interested groups are located or represented in the executive agencies rather than in the Congress. As Huntington explains, no congressional committee can of itself balance competing military programs against each other and against the needs of domestic and nonmilitary foreign policy programs; not because the committees of Congress lack technical competence (many of the chairmen and senior members have accumulated considerable technical knowledge and expertise over the years), but because they lack the legal authority and political capability to bring together all the conflicting interests required to hammer out a compromise and arrive at a final decision.[18]

In light of the importance of pluralist bargaining even within the supposedly "technocratic" military agencies in the executive branch, how shall we characterize the situation with regard to policy making in the civilian public sector in which the Congress, as the major pluralist institution, still plays such an active role? Can this by any stretch of the imagination presently be portrayed as an instance of "technical decision making," or even as unambiguously tending toward such a decision mode? In the first place, compared to the general agreement on the importance of defense expenditures which has prevailed over the past two decades of recurring war and Cold War,[19] the pluralist polity and its representatives in various interest groups and the Congress often seem to have been seriously split on the value of social programs *per se*, much less programs of a magnitude comparable to defense programs. (Consider the difference in response to a rat control bill, with marginal implications of aid to the ghetto, and the response to provisions for strengthening police and national guard forces, in the eventuality of future ghetto riots.) Even assuming that a strong executive branch places its full support behind a given social program, Congress is capable of blocking it at the level of decisions regarding the amount of appropriations, when they are to begin, for what duration, etc.; all important indicators of the priority the program deserves. And even if Congress is generally agreed on the broad concept of a given program, it may be seriously revised or distorted at the level of legislative decisions on the nature of administrative controls; over how much control should be given the states or localities over the distribution of funds, the composition of administering agencies, etc.[20] Thus we see Congress and the localities operating in the area of social service programs much in the manner of political and administrative "veto groups." By contrast, the much higher degree of consensus on the priority of defense programs has tended to limit pluralist disagreements and negotiations to the matter of which particular interests should benefit by what programs — specifically, which states, companies, projects, etc., should be favored in any given instance — rather than the more fundamental questions that have often faced social service programs, including their very right to exist.[21]

The "Technocratic Class" in Postindustrial Society

If, as Bell suggests, the "technocratic class" has a critical role to play in providing politically effective support for government programs addressed to public, nonmilitary needs, then the task which it faces today is great indeed. In order to better understand the nature of this class and Bell's expectations for it, it is useful to compare the recent work of John Galbraith on the nature of advanced industrialism in the United States.[22] In Galbraith's "new industrial state" the notion of technocrat refers not only to the experts who work in the governmental bureaucracies, or to the specialist members of the academic and research world who come to government as consultants or advisors, but also to those technical specialists who work in the private corporate economy. At the least, a three-part classification of the technocracy seems called for: (a) the government agency specialists, (b) the academic experts, and (c) what Galbraith calls the corporate "techno-structure." This last is the organization of technical specialists which has arisen in the contemporary "mature corporation" in response to the demands of the advanced technology now employed by such firms. Viewing the corporation as a series of concentric circles, the technostructure can be located at the circle immediately adjacent to the corporate center, composed of executives and management; the other circles are composed, successively, of the routine supervisory and white-collar personnel, the production workers, and the stockholders.[23] The technostructure is made up of all those in the corporation who bring specialized knowledge or skills to "group decision making" (e.g., technicians, engineers, sales executives, scientists, designers, and other specialists); its key function is to plan the development and employment of the corporation's advanced technology. Hence, according to Galbraith, it is the technostructure which is the working intelligence, the "brain" of the contemporary corporation[24] (though ultimately we would regard this technical "brain" as subordinate to the corporation's executive managerial core — the corporate "soul," as it were — and available to it for technical research and advice).[25]

The "Technostructure" and Government

The analysis of the "technocratic class" into several distinct institutional components suggests a number of interesting new interrelationships, each with its own special problems. For example, what does the technostructure's role of corporate "brain" imply for corporate relations with the technocratic agencies of the state? We can begin to answer this question by considering that, with most important activities of the corporation today centered on the development and employment of highly complex technology, the preoccupation of corporate decision makers is with a new kind of planning. Corporate planning is no longer merely a matter of foresight with regard to acquiring and combining the factors of production. To be successful, corporate planning must go further than seeing that the firm responds intelligently to the demands of the market. It must incorporate that market, not merely theoretically, through market estimates, but functionally, through exercising control over the markets which supply it with the elements of production, and over those which absorb its finished products. In other words, the corporate structure must see to it that the markets which supply it with labor, materials, and equipment, and the markets which receive its subsequent outputs, are reliably integrated with its operations; to a large extent, "it must replace the market with planning."[26] The firm must exert this kind of market control because of the uncertainties of a free market in supplying the scarce, expensive factors of production required by advanced technology (e.g., technical components, special materials, and skilled labor) at economic cost. Equally important, the firm needs market control to assure a demand for its highly specialized output when the heavy investment involved finally comes to fruition in the form of a marketable product. These uncertainties can be eliminated only through "planning" which *includes* market control. While this leaves the structure of the market formally intact, it eliminates or drastically reduces dependence on the action of buyers or sellers by the "mature corporation" which is powerful enough to exert the necessary market controls. Accordingly, its "planning," by assuring favorable market conditions, also assures adequate income for the purpose of reinvestment, and tends to eliminate dependence on external financing. Thus the key to modern industrial policy is a potent kind of planning which is more than just a set of intellectual operations, and through which the "strategic cost factors" of capital and labor both become subject to internal decision by the corporate technostructure.[27]

Yet, even though the corporation has at its disposal a number of kinds of market control (vertical integration, administrative pricing, etc.) these controls are partial, effective only within the firm's immediate markets, and thus incapable of insuring the requisite demand over the entire economic system to absorb the products of industry as a whole. In addition, under conditions of full employment, the system is subject to dangerous inflationary tendencies, and becomes incapable of holding prices and wages stable, a key condition of profitable production. Also, the industrial system requires trained manpower at various levels, not least of all at the level of the "technostructure" itself. It is at such points, where the "planning" of the technostructure is unable to provide for the functioning of the industrial system as a whole, that the state has increasingly tended to step in over the past generation.[28]

In the postwar period the state has come to underwrite the functioning of the industrial system in a number of ways, particularly through the provision of capital outlays for the highly expensive technologies now characteristic of the most advanced sectors of corporate industry. Today the state provides substantial stimulus to advanced technological development in industry, mainly through its contracts for sophisticated weapons systems and related "hardware." In the process, the corporation and the federal agencies which oversee this kind of development have become functionally integrated in a number of ways. In the first place, they have come to share one another's goals, since both are today committed to stable economic growth; to the scientific innovation which nourishes this growth; and to the expansion of scientific and technical education which is the reservoir of innovation. Second, they regularly share one another's manpower, with retired military men coming to sit on the boards and in the management of various corporations related to defense procurement, and corporate consultants on loan to government agencies involved in procurement.[29] Finally, they divide the process of decision concerning the direction of advanced technological development. In conjunction with the armed services and related federal agencies (Defense, AEC, NASA), the industrial system as a whole is a major source of estimates of the requirements of the military sector. These estimates, which tend to dovetail with industry's own productive capacities and interests, become in turn a significant part of the working materials of policy makers in the area of armament and disarmament. The private firm which is given the responsibility for developing a new generation of weapons is in a prime position to introduce its own productive capacities and market needs into weapons design specifications. But ever since the 1950s the practice of the government's military agencies has been to foster the growth of just such companies. Moreover, these firms have been delegated the responsibility of making major decisions about how governmental appropriations should be spent, through their assigned role in the selection of subcontractors. Sharing the same basic biases in favor of the continuing expansion of military development, both the agencies and the corporations have supported the direction of public expenditures toward military programs, as against the public services which government is increasingly being called upon to provide.[30] Thus, contrary to Bell's image of a technocratic class more or less unified in favor of public sector improvements, many technocrats, particularly those located in corporations with defense contracts or related government bureaus, may well represent an influence for development in a rather different direction.

Perhaps the major theme in Galbraith's description of the "new industrial state" is the essential unity which now links the corporation and the state; in one respect, a unity of outlook, in another, a unity of function. No sharp line can any longer be drawn between the state and the mature corporation: each shares the same broad goals, each adapts these goals to its own particular needs and objectives. The earlier image of a competitive power relationship between state and corporation, in which each seeks to dominate the other, emerged during the day of the entrepreneurial corporation, and must be viewed within its historical context. The political influence of the "corporate octopus" was considerable, in its heyday, with state legislatures and large segments of Congress "owned" by the trusts. Nonetheless, the tactics of bribery and corruption, though productive of political influence in an earlier period of industrialization, were symptoms of the separation of politics from the economy, and the need to establish a relationship through extrinsic means, through "buying one's way in." Today the "mature corporation" does not *need* the influence over the legislature which the corporate entrepreneur so ardently sought. The corporation no longer has to "buy its way in"; it is already there, linked to the governmental bureaucracy as a functioning "arm of the state," as Galbraith aptly puts it.[31]

Clearly Galbraith's description of the "mature corporation" is a metaphor which best fits the large defense industry corporations, such as General Dynamics, or Lockheed, working mainly on government contract today, rather than the large corporation *per se*. Most of the major corporations still have the greatest part of their markets in the private economy rather than government, and cannot be considered as simply "arms of the state," since the bulk of their production is neither intended for, nor demanded by the government. Still, the "mature corporation" as an "arm of the state" is a useful image, since it gives a sense not only of the relation of the fully defense-oriented corporations to the government, but also of some important postwar tendencies in the relations of the large nondefense-production corporations to the government especially as they have become engaged in doing work on government contract. Perhaps the most significant aspect of these relations is that they are reciprocal; if the corporation is in effect used by the state to satisfy requirements for defense, or space exploration, or nuclear development which are deemed in the "national interest," the state is in turn an instrument of the corporate system.[32] While governmental activities, such as the maintenance of a large public sector supported by corporate and individual taxes, were once viewed as damaging by the entrepreneurial corporation, they are today regarded as beneficial by the mature corporation, since they subsidize its research-and-development (R & D) activities, and assure a market for the products which R & D yields. At the same time, the state is assured of the growth of the economy, under conditions of relative stability. In short, the influence of the mature corporation on public policy goes much deeper than that of the entrepreneurial corporation of an earlier day which was based mainly on pecuniary relations.

Today, observes Galbraith, corporate influence is based on the coincidence of the corporation's functional requirements with those of the state, ideologically expressed in a coincidence of "goals" and structurally expressed in the linkage provided between the Office of the Executive and the policy makers of the technologically advanced corporations, by an array of governmental agencies ranging from the Defense Department to NASA and the AEC. In the federal agencies committees of technical specialists and agency administrators, working in conjunction with corporate representatives and consultants, make "framework" decisions about the requirements for a given weapons system or space vehicle, with the result that Congress tends to have an increasingly limited voice in basic military decisions. In this way, the governmental bureaucracy performs the vital role of direct liaison between the corporate technostructure and the political executive at the core of the government. What this means in the larger political system can be glimpsed by applying Galbraith's imagery of circles of authority and influence to the political sphere. Here we would place the government agency technocrats in a circle immediately adjacent to the political executive, followed by concentric circles representing the Congress, the lobbies and pressure groups, and the general public, in that order. Taking the corporate executive (including top management) as the fundamental policy-making center of the corporation,[33] we see that the technocrats of business and government act as a major channel through which are linked the executives at the core of their respective institutions. Through arrangements like this, the pluralist polity (Congress and the electorate) is quietly bypassed as an arena of political decision, and the "free market" is regulated as a secure framework for corporate economic activity, in a society whose public ideology is still that of "free enterprise" and "democratic control."

The "Technostructure" and Academia

As we have indicated, the "mature corporation" has vital relations with the agencies of the state which are the ultimate guarantors of its "planning." At the same time, it also has important relations with the "educational and scientific estate,"[34] or as we shall call it simply, the academic community. From the standpoint of the corporation, the academic community bears it the same relation as that of the banking and financial community *vis à vis* the entrepreneurial corporation in an earlier period of industrialism. In that period, the decisive factor of production was capital, since it was the scarce resource without which production could neither be continued nor expanded; and an intricate network of banks, brokerage houses, and insurance companies came to play the role of suppliers of this crucial resource. Today, the corpoation no longer needs to rely on such sources for its capital requirements; its secured earnings, acquired through the complex technocratic "planning" described earlier, assure it the capital it requires for reinvestment, after payment of dividends, bonuses, etc. Today the scarce resource in the economy is no longer capital, but specialized, highly skilled manpower, whose major source is the complex of educational institutions and research organizations which have grown so rapidly since WWII, the "educational and scientific estate," as Galbraith so grandly puts it. However, unlike the financial community, academia today does not enjoy exclusive control over the supply of skilled manpower in the way the banks once controlled the supply of capital. The new element in the picture is, once again, government. For, at the same time that government subsidizes the R & D activities of the corporation, it subsidizes the training of manpower to do this work through its support to colleges and universities, and to their research activities. This insures at least the functional compatibility of the academic community with the corporation. Further, the ostensible identification of the technostructure with nonpecuniary motivations ("social goals") tends to remove the conflict which existed between the more narrowly profit-minded corporate leadership and the socially concerned academia of only a generation ago. The acceptance of the intervention of government in the economy for a range of public purposes brings the contemporary corporate leadership in agreement with governmental policies which an earlier corporate leadership had vehemently decried — policies which have been associated, whether rightly or not, with the academic community.[35] But whether Keynesian practices were introduced on account of academic persuasion or of economic practicality, the fact is that these innovations have by now been fully embraced and absorbed by the corporation in the course of its recent evolution, and with this an ideological source of tension between the corporation and the academy has been removed.

Notwithstanding these unforeseen changes in corporate attitude, the removal of these old sources of difference does not spell widespread or lasting agreement between academia and corporate enterprise. With some equivocation, Galbraith points out that there are a number of areas of potential conflict which may flare up in the future. In particular, while technostructure and academia today both see themselves as motivated by "social goals," it is an open question just how much these goals actually coincide. On its side, the technostructure's major goals are related to assuring continuing growth through the exercise of significant control over its economic environment. Such control is achieved partly through the integration of suppliers and mass advertising, and partly through government defense contracts, which tend to assure a market for the product of the "mature" corporation's R & D. Moreover, by doing defense work the corporation can claim to be serving the broader "social goal" of contributing to the nation's security.

In view of the rather close fit of defense production to the interests of the contemporary corporation, it might be expected that such claims would be viewed with a certain amount of skepticism, certainly in academia, if anywhere. Yet surprisingly Galbraith gives the impression that there has been very little questioning of corporate activities in academia. To the extent that he discusses the response of academia to the technostructure, he does so in the framework of an emplicit theory of the cooptation of academic interests. He draws a sharp contrast between those faculties such as mathematics and the physical sciences, which have an

interest in research or employment that is supported by the modern corporation, and those which lack such an interest: "the classics, humanities,
some of the social sciences (*sic!*)." This provides the ground for a simple
theory of co-optation, on the grounds of occupational interest. While the
scientists will probably be co-opted to the purposes of technostructure
or state, the humanists will continue to represent the "older goals of the
academy":

> They will criticize their scientific colleagues for doing excessively
> purposive research . . . and implicitly, for abandoning the vow of aca-
> demic poverty. The scientists will reply with hurt protestations of the
> immunity of their virtue to pecuniary corruption and the need for some-
> one to pay their bills. . . .[36]

This statement reproduces the simplistic "two-cultures" image of a clear-
cut cleavage between the political and cultural orientations of humanists
and scientists, ignoring the considerable involvement of scientists, for
example, in various political activities directed against government
policies in the areas of national security, military spending, etc. But what
is most arresting, and at the same time most disturbing, about Galbraith's
position is that it pictures the academic community of the mid-1960s as
being essentially passive with regard to questions of social value orientation. On its side, the technostructure apparently has clear-cut, definite
goals ("planning"), to which it assimilates the goals of the state ("national security") so that the two become indistinguishable; with this, the
corporation's goals can then be projected as the goals of the society as a
whole. By contrast, the academic community can only accept or reject
the goals of the technostructure, but of itself lacks the power to authoritatively put forward its own goals for the larger society. Much of Galbraith's book is in fact written on the assumption that academia is in
need of a broad, unifying social consciousness, and that his ideological
prescriptions can fill this need. The adequacy of these prescriptions will
be a subject for later discussion. For now we will only note that those
goals which Galbraith recommends seem to be so couched as to stimulate
the least possible conflict with the aims of the "technostructure." In his
view, the goals of authoritative planning and continuous growth are un-
objectionable because "inevitable" from the viewpoint of being absolutely necessary to economic order and satisfaction in the "new industrial
society."[37] In consequence, his critique of the technostructure is often
more stylistic than fundamental, being directed against the forms in
which the new technoindustrial system's purposes are expressed, rather
than the purposes themselves and the socioeconomic structure in which
they are grounded.

With this in mind, we can understand why Galbraith's discussion gives so much attention to the question of corporate marketing methods as a source of conflict between academia and the technostructure; in particular, the matter of the techniques of persuasion and manipulation employed by the technostructure in advertising its products. The academics look with disgust on the meretricious means by which products are introduced to the general public, considering themselves superior to the banality and raucousness of the advertising media. In response, the technostructure protests that these operations are absolutely necessary to the welfare of the economy. Of course, the paradox is that the same economy which requires "organized public bamboozlement" also nurtures an academic-intellectual subculture which deplores it as intellectually corrupt. Yet, in terms of Galbraith's extremely broad definition of planning, the technostructure's management of consumer demand is itself quite justifiable. In the complex industrial economy in which such planning plays an essential role, "the needs of the producing mechanism take precedent over the freely expressed will of the individual." Hence the inevitability of conflict between individualistic intellectuals and the corporate industrial system. However, insofar as the intellectuals' protest is directed against the manipulation of consumer behavior it is essentially futile, since it ignores the basic requirements of the system for such manipulation.[38] While Galbraith's discussion of corporate advertising techniques suggests that he sympathizes with the intellectual critique of prevailing methods of consumer persuasion, his acceptance of the contemporary requirements of large-scale corporate enterprise produces a critique that is generally more concerned with the style in which corporate economic goals are currently pursued than with the substantive questions of the social control of economic power which are entailed.

Insofar as Galbraith is critical of the corporate sector of the new industrial society, it is not with regard to the technocratic structuring of that sector, but with regard to the particular policies which its members have pursued. If these policies could be redirected, the heart of Galbraith's critique would be satisfied, yet little would change in the day-to-day functioning of the contemporary corporation. Galbraith views the essential conflict of the academics with the corporation as one involving a modification of the policies of the corporation, without necessarily involving an attack on the hierarchic structuring of its policy-making process. To this point of our analysis, then, the major value of Galbraith's work lies in clearly differentiating the several segments of the "technocratic class" — industrial, governmental, and academic — which Bell casually lumps together, and analyzing them in terms of their respective functional roles in the new industrial system, thereby alerting us to the possibilities of political conflict between them.

The Technocrats in the
Postindustrial Polity

In describing the rise of the technocratic class and in projecting political roles for it *vis à vis* government and other major contemporary institutions, Bell and Galbraith attempt to delineate some of the emerging dimensions of the political system as we enter the postindustrial era.

A close comparison of their work indicates that they actually provide us with images of two different political systems, entailing different confrontations of ideas and values, through their differing emphasis on political participants. In particular, Bell reflects the widely acceptable image of scientists and technologists as a technocratic elite possessed of special expertise and knowledge which has catapulted them virtually overnight into positions of great influence in the making of government policy.[39] Over against the "politicians," the chief policy elite of the late-modern era, he sets the supposedly nonpolitical "technocrats" as the major contenders for this position in the postmodern era. According to Bell, what brings the "nonpolitical" technocrats into the political arena are their roles as active representatives of a new scientific rationality in the policy process itself. In this they stand in contrast with the politicians, who represent a mode of policy formulation based on the complicated and often nonrational balancing of constituent interests. Representing multiple constituencies, the politician becomes the symbol of the pluralist aspect of an advanced industrial society composed of many groups pursuing different interests, while the technocrat moves to center stage as representative of the technically rational and beneficent central administrative state which has lately emerged over and above the fractionated pluralist society.[40] At the same time, though Bell recognizes in his early work that industrial society has been essentially a "business society" in the sense that business interests and business values have dominated its community life and politics throughout the modern period, he virtually drops any explicit mention of these interests in his later analysis of the postindustrial society. The effect is to imply that business interests need no longer be given special attention as the society's dominant political interest configuration, but that they have taken their place alongside other social and organizational interests numbered among the society's various political constituencies.

In contrast to this simple image, Galbraith gives us a somewhat more complicated and comprehensive picture of the participants and interests in the political system. At the core of the system, there are the technicians of corporate power (the "technostructure") dealing closely through administrative channels with the technicians of governmental power (agency bureaucrats and administrators). Owing to their common interests and goals, and a frequent interchange of personnel and information, these technocratic figures at the functional center of the new industrial system are largely able to dispense with the pluralist legislature as a means of mutual communication and influence; corporate business has become closely linked to executive government today through the administrative bureaucracy, and this tends to supersede earlier ties involving the Congress. This makes it possible for crucial national policies, particularly those involving defense, to be made in a closed circuit of communication between corporate and government technocrats, with the pluralistic polity shunted aside. At the periphery of this emerging system stands the broad public, its elected representatives, and nontechnocratic intellectuals and academics. Galbraith views the latter as potential spokesmen and leaders of public opposition to the militarist and materialist expansionism of the new technocratic industrial state. It is to them that he looks for leadership in the reorientation of state policies, through the medium of a pluralist polity revitalized through their participation and directed toward larger issues than traditional local pluralist concerns.

Despite some misgivings about their lack of a clear-cut ideology incorporating definite programmatic goals, Galbraith is encouraged by the growing skepticism of nontechnocratic academics and intellectuals regarding government policies toward the Cold War and the military-industrial complex. Accordingly, he views the alienation of students, intellectuals, and some academics from the life concerns engendered by the "new industrial system" as a symptom of an emerging tendency to question, not merely the politics and economics of this society, but its character as a culture as well. In this, his attention is focussed on what he calls the "world of aesthetic experience": the ecology of city and countryside, and the quality of public cultural life as transmitted by the mass media. Here is a world beyond that of economic goods and services, a dimension of experience which must be protected and encouraged against the ugliness perpetrated by the industrial system. This will call for the active participation of men of cultural taste and perspective as a new opposition in the political system, particularly in view of the political and ideological absorption of the working class into that system contrary to historical expectations. The humanist intellectuals' participation can serve as a necessary corrective to the increasingly monolithic nature of the political-ideological system; through them Galbraith hopes the current monopoly of the industrial system over the establishment of social purpose and the quality of the life environment may yet be broken.[41]

By contrast with this, the end-of-ideology theorists tend to play down the political role of those intellectuals who have reacted against technocratic tendencies in the society. (Of course, this reaction has not been

limited to those in the humanistic disciplines; many in the sciences have
expressed concern over the technical-administrative "mobilization" of
science and of the larger society for military purposes, and over technological exploitation of the environment which results in pollution and
disturbance of ecological balance.) To the extent that Bell gives these
intellectuals any attention, it is to picture them as today standing outside
of society, either as irresponsibly romantic cultural nihilists or as extremist revolutionaries. As nihilist critics of the postindustrial society they
have abandoned the traditional humanist concern for the shaping of social
values; they have stepped outside the circle of society and culture
altogether, and oppose the very notion of social or cultural order as
absurd. As apocalyptic revolutionaries, they seek the overthrow of
present structures and the culture which they support, through extra-
parliamentary, violent means if necessary. In either case, they have abandoned any role or influence they formerly may have had with regard
to the established political process.[42]

Despite the fact that both claim to support liberal pluralist values,
there is an important difference between the political role which Galbraith
ascribes to the liberal intellectuals, and the absence of any such role in
their depiction by Bell. For Galbraith, the liberal humanist intellectual
has the extremely important function of sustaining political and cultural
pluralism by challenging the industrial state's tendency to monopolize the
determination of social purpose. Bell, on the other hand, regards those
intellectuals who separate themselves from the dominant goals or institutions of the postindustrial society as radical extremists standing outside
the role structure of the society. His analysis actually tends to absorb
the liberal intellectual into the broad "technocratic class" which serves the
purpose of the new industrial state, and he suggests that "technocratic
rationality" is the best instrument for the realization of the liberal's desire
to enhance the quality of public life. By contrast, Galbraith does not take
the new technical rationality for granted as an instrument of humanist
aims; he views it as primarily serving the industrial system's goals of
continuous economic expansion; even if these are necessary to maintaining the high living standards of an advanced industrial culture, they
are by themselves too narrow to be sufficient to a satisfying cultural life.
Accordingly, he makes a clear separation between the liberal humanist
intellectuals and the technocrats; the liberal intellectuals stand outside
the "industrial state," while the technocrats serve as its executive and
managerial saff. Where Bell pits the technocrats, as representatives of
rationality, good taste, and consciousness of the public interest, against
the politicians, Galbraith opposes the liberally oriented intellectuals to
the interlocking technocracies of big government and big business.

As models of social reality, both of these tend to overdraw the actual relations involved between "politicians," "technocrats," "intellectuals," pitting them against one another in the political arena. Though Galbraith's model has the advantage of being somewhat better articulated than Bell's (particularly with respect to the divisions within the intellectual-academic-scientific "class" today), not all intellectuals or academics in the humanistic disciplines have reacted in disfavor to the technocratic organization of society (witness Marshall McLuhan and others as advocates of the electronic integration of the culture). Nor by any means have all scientists lined up in support of official policies of technological mobilization, as in the case of scientific opposition to H-bomb development or nuclear testing. Galbraith's model of liberal humanists pitted against science technocrats does not help us understand how it has come about that the scientists, for example, have taken such widely divergent positions in the recent history of science-technology politics in America.[43] In this respect, it is best to keep in mind the looseness of the concept of a "technocratic class"; that while there are "technocrats," it is quite another matter to portray them as sharing a common "class consciousness," or necessarily cooperating for the achievement of common political goals. Both Bell's positive image and Galbraith's critical image of the technocracy require modification, since both assume more power in the hands of the technocrats than is presently warranted. Though an important functional group in the postindustrial society, the chief role of the technocrats has been to serve those who hold power, whether in government or industry.

Under these circumstances, we should neither expect the technocratic functionaries to constitute a unified movement for ameliorative social change nor should we charge them with ultimate responsibility for the ongoing centralization of politicoeconomic power or the decline of the pluralist legislature. As we view them, the technocrats are no more or less than a knowledge staff for the executive-managerial elites of the major institutions of the society, performing the technical functions of research and program planning which are required as sources for the ultimate framing of policy by top institutional executives. The technocrats are not a homogeneous class either in occupational composition or in status; the technocratic class is itself stratified by skill, training, experience, and responsibility. The few who rank highest in these attributes are most eligible for possible recruitment into the executive elite which their class as a whole serves.

The pattern which presents itself in sharpening outline since the mid-1950s is one in which scientific and technical personnel, scattered through the agencies of government and through the major institutions outside

it, have tended to adopt the perspective of their respective client institutions for whom they have so far performed essentially as advocates.
In fact, after a while, the powerful men at the helm of these institutions
have learned to speak the language of their technocratic functionaries and
to penetrate their technical jargon, in the process losing awe for the
technocrats' special expertise which they have gradually come to assimilate to their own purposes. As Daniel Greenberg puts it in a pene-
trating review of the postwar relation of the physical scientists to the
seat of political power:

> [S]cientists, rather than being the new men of power in American
> politics, comprise a very much misunderstood and politically fragile
> group whose proximity to power is easily confused with the real stuff
> of power.[44]

For good or ill, the possibility of scientific technocrats becoming a
coherent power elite seems rather remote. Unlike such established interest groups as business, labor, or the farmers, the technocrats have not
come to power centers such as Washington backed by a constituency
mobilized to enforce their demands by coercive action. As Greenberg
observes, though the scientist is a familiar figure in national affairs today, anyone who believes the political community is ready to give the
scientist "blank checks for money or policy" is being seriously misled by
a bogus stereotype. Though the scientists are to be found everywhere in
Washington, far from being a sign of their "take-over," this is testimony
to the politicians' recognition of the many ways in which scientific coun-
sel can be useful to the policy maker. Unlike the other interest groups
in Washington, it appears that social as well as physical scientists are a
kind of "kept" interest that has little to rely upon but the goodwill of
the political community when vital matters are at stake.[45] Probably the
images of the new commanding role and potential of the technocrats provided by both Galbraith and the end-of-ideologists will both have to be
basically revised.

CHAPTER IV

Postindustrial America
and the
"Contract State"

In this chapter we trace the basic development of a unique American politicoeconomic subsystem which was initiated during the Second World War and which has crystallized during the postwar period around the large-scale production of military hardware and technology, with profound effect on the overall society. This subsystem, often popularly described as the "military-industrial complex" (and here referred to as the "Contract State"), incorporates major productive units of the regular civilian economy as well as more narrowly specialized defense and research firms, linking them together with political-organizational allies in related government agencies and the broader polity. By way of illustrating the larger dynamics of growth of this state-within-a-state, we will briefly review the specific case of the Air Force in promoting the growth of a defense-industrial complex related to its military operations, and in using nominally civilian-controlled agencies such as the National Aeronautics and Space Agency to foster these aims. Finally, pursuing these developments, we can identify the "Contract State" as the essential matrix of military-industrial relations within which there has in recent years been established an explicitly centralized political-technical system of coordination, located in the Pentagon.

The Evolution of the Contract State

As a result of the postwar growth of defense-industrial contracting empires, there exists today an interlocking structure of federal agencies, their industrial constituents, and their joint political allies, which has come to constitute a significant political economy within the larger society. This internal political economy, a virtual state within the larger state, has come to be referred to as the "Contract State," owing to the central role played within it by the government contract as the binding element between the different interests included in it.[1] It is this structure which serves as the relevant context for the political-technical role of the scientists and technocrats connected with government-sponsored programs involving technical research and development.

From the launching of the first Russian "Sputnik" satellite in 1957 to the end of the Kennedy regime, the military services engaged in a free-wheeling competition in the newly developing aerospace field. Through the power to choose industrial contractors in states across the country, the military services came to develop their own widespread and powerful industrial and political constituencies, which returned the favor through political and technical support for further space and missile development. The system of delegating various management responsibilities to prime contractors in overseeing the work of a host of subcontractors in a pyramid-like contracting structure enabled favored corporations to become powerful industrial brokers in their own right in the R & D sector. By virtue of the authority vested in them by government contract, they could now disburse vast public funds through the award of subcontracts, thereby strengthening their economic position, and enhancing their own local political influence, through the building of subcontracting constituencies. Moreover, operating under a largely noncompetitive system of negotiated contracts, and in the absence of any objective economic yardstick, industrial contractors could safely inflate costs and charge contract overruns to the contracting agency, thereby permitting many levels of hidden profits.

Since the bulk of government contracting to date has been directed toward the purchase of military supplies, weapons, and related research, the background to the Contract State may be traced through a brief review of government policy in this area.

Following a series of contracting scandals involving profiteering during World War I, federal legislation established that government would henceforth seek to provide its own military supplies through public-owned facilities, whenever economically feasible. The aim was to maintain a system of "in-house" capability which would serve as a yardstick by which to measure the performance of industrial contractors, as well as to provide expert advice on weapon-systems development. (Much the same concept was involved in the later creation of the TVA as a yardstick for the performance of private power companies during the New Deal.) This led to the establishment of shipyards, arsenals, and research laboratories by the military services after World War I, continuing through World War II and the early Fifties.[2] The military emergency of World War II led the government once again to depend on private contractors for weapons development, as reflected in major changes in contracting procedures which became basic features of much of postwar military contracting. In order to encourage prompt industrial response to the government's vastly enlarged war needs, military agencies were freed from procurement practices based strictly on competitive bidding among contractors.[3] Instead the cost-plus-fixed-fee contract, with contractor's fee calculated on the basis of estimated costs, became the typical mode of military contracting until almost the mid-1960s. In this system, unrealistically low initial cost estimates frequently led to renegotiation of contracts to cover contractors' cost overruns, with an additional fee added. This in effect provided an inflatable "sliding fee" for contractors similar to that which led in the first place to establishment of in-house facilities.[4]

The initial intent of the in-house system to strengthen the hand of government in industrial contracting has further been weakened by the employment of private corporations as "systems managers" for weapons development. In the postwar period, the traditional practice of contracting specialized components to subcontractors was transformed into a means by which "prime contractors," subsidized by government funds, were given many powers formerly reserved to government agencies. Through this management approach, private firms designated as prime contractors took on the role of "systems engineers and technical directors for multibillion dollar R & D and production activities involving hundreds of other corporations."[5] In this role the primes have exercised many of the functions of government itself, in relation to subcontractors and supplies. According to a report of the House Committee on Governmental Operations:

> These companies establish procurement organizations and methods which proximate those of the government. Thus large prime contractors will invite design competition, establish source selection bids, send out industrial survey teams, make subcontract awards on a competitive or a negotiated basis, appoint small business administrators, designate plant resident representatives, develop reporting systems to spot bottlenecks, make cost analyses of subcontractor operations, and request monthly progress and cost reports from subcontractors.[6]

In consequence, the granting of prime contract status to a relative handful of large corporations has given them a position of enormous discretionary power and managerial leverage over their numerous subcontractors. Under the terms of its contract status, the prime contractor is granted power over the fortunes of dozens of subcontractors, investors, bankers, businessmen, and employees, often entailing the economic well-being of whole geographic areas. As an officially designated "systems manager" it has the power to contract out or do work itself, to acquire subcontractors' proprietary information, to exert pressures on subcontractors to sell out, and even to create dummy subcontractors which can be useful in concealing profits or proprietary information from the government. In general, the prime will use its subcontracting power to stabilize its operations by expanding or curtailing subcontracts in phase with swings in government business. In addition, the prime contractor, standing at the top of its "system-management" hierarchy, can buttress its own economic position among other large corporations by "mergers, acquisitions, and investments in the flock of companies dependent upon them for government largess."[7] In this light, the government contract can be viewed as a cushion which helps secure and enhance the economic position of the favored corporations whose productive capacities and political influence qualify them for prime status.

The trend toward the employment of private contractors for government work on a system-management basis first became pronounced during the Eisenhower administration.[8] Its most important stimulus was the expanding need of the rapidly growing Air Force for R & D capability. Unlike the Army, of which it was only a post-World War II offspring, the Air Force lacked the in-house facilities for research, engineering, or management which were integral to the Army's system. Thus the Air Force resorted to private contractors to perform what would normally have been in-house functions. In the intense interservice competition for jurisdiction over new weapons systems which marked the 1950s, the Air Force promoted the growth of private companies which ultimately took over a substantial segment of regular military operations, from routine aircraft maintenance to the technical management of a host of military-related subcontractors. The Air Force's lack of in-house capacity, far from hindering its competitive efforts, gave it a major advantage, allowing it to pare down personnel levels in keeping with administrative policies, and at the same time to put together a huge industrial and political constituency with a stake in the continued heavy funding of its weapons systems. So successful was this approach that other federal agencies, including the other services with heavy R & D requirements, soon began employing it, and this encouraged a new era of intimacy in government-corporate relations, embodied in the notion of the Contract State.

Profit and Power in the Contract State

One major result of these developments was that the government's capacity to independently evaluate private R & D performance was seriously reduced, while a procurement system highly vulnerable to abuse by private interests came into being. Though the firms which do the bulk of their business on government contract are organized as private enterprises, they have rather special and unprecedented relations with government, through which the mechanism of an open competitive market has been replaced by the complex and obscure processes of government agency contracting. Low performance standards have been facilitated by the permissive nature of much of government contracting, as embodied in such practices as the tolerance of overspending, failure to meet schedules, lack of adequate product specifications, faulty cost estimates, charging of private overhead to the contract, etc.[9] In addition, the complexities of multiple subcontracting constitute a "labyrinth" largely impervious to government inspection, so that the average contractor fee of about six percent does not indicate the various layers of overhead and concealed profit in hierarchic subcontracting by prime contractors, who can charge the total subcontracting costs, "including profit fee for the sub," to their own costs.[10]

Under the Eisenhower administration, the abandonment of government in-house facilities was openly encouraged as part of the move back to "free enterprise" in reaction to the excursions of government under the New Deal into the private domain. During this administration, many installations and factories built during World War II were sold to industry, usually at a fraction of cost; TVA itself came close to being dismembered and sold to private power companies in the Tennessee Valley area, under the Dixon-Yates scheme. Other installations were leased at nominal fees to contractors who then received government contracts to make their use profitable; in some cases new facilities were built and then leased by the government at low fees. Contractors were also allowed to use leased facilities for commercial production outside their contract obligations, at no cost to themselves. These publicly encouraged arrangements were consistent with practices already well under way during the Truman administration.

Over half of the fifteen hundred government-financed industrial plants built during World War II at a cost of almost $13 billion by 1949, were either sold to private industry at nominal cost or held by the military services under the National Security Act, reserved for their original use; the value of the plants involved is estimated at "over nine billion dollars." In this way the government was able to directly and indirectly subsidize "extensive capital expansion" sought by political leaders, while at the same time the military establishment was assured that war-built defense plants "would remain oriented to military production."[11] The Eisenhower administration merely stepped up the process of selling or leasing these facilities to private industry. Though the intention was ostensibly to cut military expenditures by substituting private contractors for government in-house work, the cost of military R & D quadrupled over the course of the Eisenhower administration.[12] The costs of R & D increased not merely because there was considerably more of it by the late 1950s than at the beginning of the decade; also contributing to this precipitous rise was the inflation of costs under negotiated contracts which often permitted overpricing, duplicate billings, technical errors, mismanagement, and overhead charges to the government for costs actually applicable to the contractors' private commercial work.[13] In large part this was the consequence of the great discretionary authority allowed by negotiated awards to federal agencies and their contract officers,[14] allowing them to commit large sums to contractors on the basis of often inadequate specifications, estimates, and reviews.[15] Yet, despite these drawbacks, with the emergence of the Contract State, negotiated contracting had come to comprise almost nine-tenths of the dollar volume of government contracts by the mid-1960s.[16]

The prevailing system of government contracting has to date contributed not only to inflationary trends, but also to the acceleration of corporate concentration in a variety of ways. In the whole economy, only 300 major corporations perform 97 percent of all federal R & D; at the same time they also account for 91 percent of all private R & D, much of which is a means of maintaining capability for government work, and is generally paid for by government in the form of overhead on other contracts. But even this does not give an adequate idea of the degree of concentration in the R & D sector. In the 1960s prime contracts accounting for more than half the total R & D and production business in the aerospace field were held by a few giant corporations, such as North American, Lockheed, General Dynamics, and Thompson-Ramo-Wooldridge, which specialize in aerospace work; together with a small number of old established commercial giants such as GE, GM, Westinghouse, Chrysler, Ford, Socony, Firestone, Philco, Goodyear, etc., which moved into the field. In this way, the private corporate sector and the government contract sector have become closely interconnected.[17] In fact some of the newer aerospace corporations seem to be merely legal fictions, facades for interlocking arrangements between established industrial corporations. Thus the House Judiciary Committee cited the five largest aerospace firms in 1965 as examples of corporate interlock. In one case an aerospace firm had interlocking directorships with 18 financial institutions and 28 industrial corporations; it was also found that companies in the field frequently hold stock in nominal competitors. According to the anti-trust subcommittee staff, interlocking directorships are today as wide-spread as when the Clayton Act of 1914 was passed prohibiting such interlocks; in about 75 major corporations it was found that approximately 1500 officers and directors held a total of about 4500 positions.[18]

Recently a number of observers have remarked that there are in effect two economies in America today: one dominated by the huge corporations which command advanced technology and are relatively independent of the traditional commercial market, and the old-fashioned market economy consisting of small and middle-sized entrepreneurs, characterized by an increasingly outmoded technology and depressed or marginal labor conditions.[19] Clearly it is the corporate economy which is now the dominant and determinant element in the overall economy, and its on-going development is closely linked to our movement into a "postindustrial" era. Moreover, the most dynamic element of the corporate economy is the R & D sector, funded by huge sums of government money each year, and increasingly interlocked with government through contractual relations. Thus, through the government contract, private corporations have become the agents of an essentially new economic subsystem which combines features of private enterprise such as private ownership and profits, with state-monopoly aspects of the "corporate state" which achieved fullest development under European systems of facism little more than a generation ago. A handful of corporate giants, acting as "systems managers," have been granted governmental authority to oversee R & D and production activities costing billions of dollars and involving hundreds of smaller firms. In dealing with these subcontractors, the prime contractors take on the role of government itself, from the making of subcontract awards to the supervision and cost analysis of subcontract operations. In the process, the corporate prime contractor has become a quasi-public organization, a veritable "arm of the state."

In this perspective, the government contract can be viewed as a significant instrument for linking up that complex of organizations and institutions (both defense and nondefense oriented) which are the structural core of the postindustrial society. Government and corporate industry are the focal institutions of this society, commanding its major economic and administrative resources, deciding its major public policies and their administration, employing most of the technocrats who are its most vital manpower and its scarcest resource. Alongside them, the universities play an extremely important ancillary role in doing much of the research and training most of the manpower required by this system. Today these three institutional areas are interconnected as never before through integrative relations which increasingly take the form of government contracts. Government agencies employ major corporations to engage in functions formerly reserved to in-house facilities: NASA employs GE to integrate and test its space equipment, and Bellcomm (an AT & T subsidiary) to manage its R & D and engineering operations; the Air Force employs a single corporation, Aerospace, to do both.[20] Major universities do the greatest part of their research for federal agencies under government contract; government labs are operated for government by industry or universities under government contract; "nonprofit" institutions such as Rand and the Hudson Institute conduct computer studies of policy matters for federal agencies, under government contract.[21]

In this way, the new, highly integrated political economy of the Contract State is embodied in large-scale organizations operated most frequently on a profit basis (but also, particularly in the academic world, on a nonprofit basis), which have officially been granted the power to dispose of enormous resources, often holding sway over a host of economic dependents. At the inner core of the postindustrial society in America, earlier distinctions between "public sector" and "private sector" have increasingly tended to lose their meaning while private economic interests have come to enjoy a highly intimate relationship with the agencies of government, largely without the knowledge or consent of the general public.

Interest Investment in the Contract State

The contemporary loss of distinction between the "public" and the "private" sector appears not only in terms of the interlocking functions of organizations once functionally quite distinct, but also in terms of the growth of structural interrelations between organizations. One important mode of interorganizational linkage is provided by those who have leadership roles in different organizations; Nieburg suggests that connecting the organizations that stand at the core of the Contract State is a group of probably no more than few thousand men, predominantly industrial managers and brokers, with closely related roles in the system. Moving between private corporations and government tours of duty, sitting on boards of directors, consulting with government agencies, serving on agency advisory committees, and acting as managers on behalf of government in the distribution and supervision of subcontractors, this managerial elite constitutes an essential element in the structure of the Contract State.[22]

Though Nieburg is certainly correct in naming industrial broker-managers as a crucial and powerful interest group in the system, his own discussion of the Contract State indicates that, in singling them out as the strategic elite, he is focussing on but one side of the contract relation. The point which needs to be made, it seems, is that the Contract State is built around a structure of relations between a number of strategic elites; that it is based, in fact, on an evolving reciprocity of elite interests which have by now come to formal expression in the government contract itself. In this respect, the core of the Contract State is both elitist and pluralist; rather than a monolithic ruling class at the center, we have a pluralism of powerful elites. Who are these elites? In the professional as well as the popular literature, there are a number of favorite candidates for this role, besides the industrial managers:[23] the agency heads and bureau chiefs in the government agencies; the leading figures in office and in the political parties; the chairmen and senior members of congressional committees responsible for agency oversight; and the scientific-technical advisors to government agencies and the executive office (though in light of our discussion in preceding chapters, we would tend to discount the latter as a group having significant power in the making of basic policy).[24]

In order to develop a model of the relations between these elites that reflects the manner in which their interests bear on the making and administration of policy in the Contract State, we begin with the formal structure of government to which we then relate the ongoing structure of elite interests. The structure of government can be looked upon as simultaneously an investment firm and an investment market. In the first instance it is by now something of a commonplace to note that the government is the largest firm in the nation. However, it is not basically a production firm; its productive output is relatively small compared to GNP and has been cut back since the 1950s with the closing of various in-house government facilities. It does in a sense engage in "productive" activities; these, however, are political rather than economic, though they do have ultimately significant economic impact: the "production" of policy for achieving and maintaining social standards in a wide range of public concerns, from public health to public order. Its major economic function is making socially sanctioned (politically legitimated) investments and purchases out of public revenues through a variety of programs, in accordance with the broad outlines of its policy. Those investments take on the form of subsidies, grants, contracts, etc., from which a "return" of some kind is expected, from agricultural price stability to the stimulation of scientific research, to the actual production of governmentally required goods or services, in the case of the government contract. The return, as in the cooling of "long hot summers" *via* poverty grants, is not always measurable primarily in economic terms, though there may be economic as well as social, political, or cultural benefits that flow from any given government investment, such as the assurance of a normal level of small business activity in riot-threatened slums.

Viewed as a market for investment, the formal structure of government represents a differential structure of opportunities for "interest investment." This type of investment has both an economic and a political component; e.g., the industrial contractors interested in obtaining defense contracts are extremely active employers of retired ex-military officers. This is surely the kind of economic investment which it is also "politic" to make, and which has real political consequences in the sense of the influence it brings to bear in the competition for contracts. We find that the level of "interest investments" of this kind does in fact correlate fairly closely with the granting of contracts by given agencies.[25] The contractor "invests" politically in such-and-such an agency or several agencies by way of lobbying, securing personal contacts with agency administrators because they offer contracts in areas related to his general productive capability. He may find himself, after having done business with a given agency, invested more heavily in it than in others and not inclined to invest in the others; on the other hand, if a given agency's appropriations are cut, or particular programs on which his contracts depend are cut back, he will have to redirect his political "investments" to other agencies relevant to his interest in government contracts. In either case, the executive branch, composed of these various agencies, appears to him as a structure of various investment opportunities of differing attractiveness and risk, somewhat like the conventional investment market. In this context, the formal meeting ground for the industrial contractor and the government agency is the negotiating table. The formal negotiating process is, however, typically preceded by numerous informal managerial contacts and explorations, and supplemented by formal contracts such as are provided by agency meetings with industry advisory committees on which favored contractor representatives sit. Such at any rate is a simplified version of the reciprocal entrepreneurial relations between contractor and agency — each facing an investment "field" or market, either in the spectrum of agencies, or in the array of contractors, which confront it at any given time, each choosing to make an investment in a given agency or market based on the maximization of its own particular interests.

In this way, the "military-industrial complex," whose major actors were the chief elements of the Contract State until almost the mid-1960s (prior to the development of central budgetary control elements in the Defense Department), constituted itself as a new kind of market, in which contemporary economic-entrepreneurial relationships with all their own complexity (involving "administered" prices and "integrated" markets), were embedded in a political context marked by its own peculiar intricacies. At least in part this owed to the fact that the executive branch of government, from which contracts are to be obtained, had itself become an enormously complex apparatus, standing at the center of

a number of political conflict relations — on one hand, the conflict between presidential and congressional authority; on the other, the conflict
of presidential and agency authority, which is closely related to conflict
between agencies. In each of these instances, the Presidency, as symbol
of the central political authority and of the public interest, is under challenge. But there is something else in common between these challenges
to presidential authority; typically, those who are the central actors in
offering the challenge are members of what has been called the "bureaucratic subsystem" of government.[26]

The bureaucratic subsystem is the structure of relations between the
leading members of the Congress — the chairmen and senior members
of the standing committees, as well as the party leaders in each house —
and the leading members of the executive bureaucracy, the agency chiefs,
and bureau heads. Moreover, as Charles Jacob points out, both sets of
actors in the policy process are "specialists, technicians with wide experience in a particular area of policy,"[27] both enjoy considerable continuity
of position, often outlasting the regime of one or more presidents, and
both have a good deal of autonomy in the formulation of policy relevant
to their special area of competence. It may come as no surprise to hear
the agency person referred to as a technician, but the conception of the
politician as a technical specialist is of particular interest in light of the
sharp distinction which Bell has drawn between the politician and the
technocrat, and makes that contrast appear rather overdrawn. In any
event, in the context of the growing technicality of government affairs,
these capacities qualify their possessors as leading actors in the administrative subsystem which functions as a kind of permanent administration
below the surface of a succession of changing presidential administrations. Thus, any given interest group, such as the corporation seeking
government contracts to secure its influence in the policy process, will
have to make interest investments in both sectors of this infrasystem.

Of course, it is to be expected that Congress will present itself as a
focus for interest investment; its formal role of representation invites its
various constituencies to vie for influence which may bear upon their
fortunes in the policy process. On the other hand, the only interest of
the executive agencies is, theoretically, the execution of policy in terms
of the "functional rationality" of which Bell speaks, i.e., the efficient
execution and administration of broad government policy. Even if Congress or the executive tend to favor particular constituents because of
the political value of their support, the agencies of the executive are no
more than operating arms, and should ostensibly themselves have no
particular favorites, no "constituents." The autonomy and expertise
which agency officials possess should insure their political neutrality and
their indifference to attempts at interest investment by groups seeking
influence or benefits with regard to agency programs.

In practice, however, it is the nature not only of the Congress but also of the executive agencies to invite a kind of "interest investment" by the various interests found in contemporary society. As a matter of course, a variety of interests, not merely economic, but also social, cultural, and ethnic are drawn to these agencies to insure that they will not be excluded from the beneficence of the state. The fact that government agencies are often in conflict themselves, tends to invite the involvement of various interests, and vests these interests with considerable influence in the making of agency policy in return for their support in the Congress and the broader polity.

Since World War I, and particularly since the New Deal, there has been a proliferation of agencies with overlapping functions whose roughly equal status has made for interagency conflict over their respective lines of authority. Theoretically, of course, the President has the constitutional power as the chief executive to impose his concept of policy on the executive departments; in reality, however, the President finds himself limited to formulating general principles of policy which he hopes will not suffer too much in the process of execution. The result is a system of policy formation in which the ostensible technical instruments of policy take on a policy role of their own; rather than merely executing public policy, the executive agencies become in practice independent centers of decision to which there have fallen important segments of the executive's authority to make public policy. As Hans Morgenthau observes:

> The executive agency, competing for the determination of policy with other agencies, more and more resembles a feudal fief that owes its existence to the delegation of powers by higher authority but becomes an active operation and autonomous center of power, defending itself against other centers of power and trying to increase its power at the expense of others. . . .[28]

In the process of acquiring autonomy, the executive agency takes on characteristics typical of elected centers of decision, including the development of constituencies within those groups in the society interested in its activities; these are its primary constituency. Moreover, due to the importance of these constituencies to the Congress, the agency takes on segments of the Congress itself as a secondary constituency.

Administrative Autonomy versus Centralization in the Contract State

It is within this framework that we can briefly examine the establishment of NASA and its administrative capture by the Air Force in the late 1950s. In the opening phase of these developments, prior to the Russian launching of "Sputnik," there was already an on-going relationship of reciprocal interest investment between the Air Force and its industrial contractors. At the same time, there existed another such relationship between strategic members of Congress and these same industrial constituents, who have generally represented prominent elements in the economies of those states which are locations of aircraft and missile production. Shortly after Sputnik, the administration bill for NASA, incorporating the recommendations of the President's Science Advisory Committee, came down for congressional action. Despite strong service opposition to a civilian space agency, the bill had too much public support (owing in some measure to the prestige of the President's science advisors) to be rejected outright by the Congress. Instead, the Department of the Air Force, together with its constituents in the missile industry and Congress, obtained important modifications of the bill so that a civilian NASA would not have jurisdiction over the space programs of the Defense Department. In the legislative process, the executive military agency, through its expert testimony to the Congress and through propaganda aimed at public support and claiming special military-technical knowledge of the requirements and opportunities of international space competition, acted as a technocratic voice for the economic and political space interests which were at the same time its own constituents. But this is not where Air Force action ended. Next, apparently through its industrial constituent Thompson-Ramo-Wooldridge Corporation and its congressional allies, the Air Force affected the choice of the NASA administrator thus facilitating the use of the agency as a magnet to draw away the programs and facilities of its service competitors. Finally, having prevented NASA from becoming a possible lever for reducing its influence over space programs, the Air Force, partly through its enhanced influence at NASA, bypassed the Defense Department's Advanced Research Projects Agency and stripped it of working authority over military space programs, thus neutralizing the very instrument of centralization by which its own autonomy might have been curbed.[29]

The possibility of even beginning to correct such a situation did not really present itself until the Kennedy administration, with the advent of Defense Secretary McNamara, committed itself to the establishment of effective centralized controls over the military agencies, particularly in the matter of imposing a central managerial perspective and appropriate operating controls on the process of military planning and budgeting.

Coming from the presidency of a major industrial corporation with a reputation for modernizing efficiency, McNamara represented the administrative technocrat par excellence, and he lived up to his reputation on many counts. Ultimately, he forced the services to define and justify their military strategies within a comprehensive framework, and to relate strategic requirements to weapons systems and budgetary requests. In addition, he took steps toward enforcing a new code of ethics designed to eliminate any gratuities from individual contractors to Defense Department personnel engaged in R & D contracting, and toward reforming the instruments of R & D contracting themselves. Yet, in the final analysis, McNamara's reforms may have failed at the level which the technocrat perhaps cannot really understand — the level of politics. It is, therefore, the story of the political struggle within the context of technocratic reforms which is of most interest here.

Prior to McNamara, military planning and budgeting had been treated as independent entities, divided between the Joint Chiefs of Staff and civilian budget officials. While planning for military forces and weapons systems was projected over a number of years, budgeting was based on a single fiscal year, so that military plans were prepared without regard to limitations of resources, with little in the way of external controls.[30] The resulting military budgets represented compromises between the longer-range ambitions of the different services, rather than actual strategic requirements. As a result, serious imbalances in service capabilities developed, hampering integrated service deployment; e.g., while the Air Forces' strategic bombing capacity was highly developed, its capability for tactical support to Army ground forces was grossly inadequate.

McNamara attacked these deficiencies through a rigorous program of cost-effectiveness analysis. Fighting strength was reconceptualized in "program packages" which treated functionally related budget items as unit categories. Thus, Polaris submarines were considered part of the same strategic package as Air Force B-52's, Skybolts, and ICBM's. This made clear the strategic redundancy of some of the services' pet projects, and forced the military to calculate the cost and effectiveness of every available alternative, or to lay out R & D projects to help establish such knowledge. By defining each project in steps which spelled out the scope, technical requirements, and probable cost of given weapons programs at levels of commitment prior to full-scale development, premature commitment to redundant, irrelevant, or overly costly programs could be averted. In this way, the tendencies of run-away military technology, driven by service ambitions and rivalries, could at least be contained, if not halted.[31] Much, of course, depends on the character of the civilian leadership, particularly the defense secretary and the president, on the firmness of their commitment to technocratic control over service ambitions, and on the nature of their relations to Congress and other sources of political support in the society. Moreover, it should not be assumed that functional cost analysis and its contractual concomitants are a technically self-contained system. Like other governmental procedures, they are open to the pressures of domestic political interests and to changes in the international political situation, where the relaxation or escalation of crisis can provide opportunities either for strengthening or bypassing central controls over domestic military development.

The Problems of Central Control in the Contract State

The cost-effectiveness procedures introduced by Defense Secretary McNamara ultimately made possible the cancellation of a number of costly weapons programs, such as the Skybolt missile, the Dynasoar space glider, and the B-70 bomber, as well as a "bomb-in-orbit" proposal.[32] However, this came only after several years of determined political struggle and with some important changes in the domestic and international political context. As matters went during the Kennedy administration, a recalcitrant Congress was able successfully to bargain in the interest of its contractor constituents, using its traditional power over legislation and appropriations to dilute the impact of the defense secretary's policies. By the third year of Kennedy's term, when the delaying tactics of the Contract State interests began wearing thin, technological substitutes for programs subject to cancellation began to appear, such as the Manned Orbiting Laboratory (MOL), which reflected continuing Air Force determination to create military missions for outer space, and the luxury Supersonic Transport, which was aimed at satisfying aircraft contractor interests.[33]

Significantly from our viewpoint, it was not until after the Kennedy administration that McNamara's reforms began to show any sign of real effect. It should be recalled that Kennedy came to the presidency with a fairly sophisticated managerial orientation, was able to accept the implications of the "new economics" much more fully than his predecessor, and brought to Washington representatives of the technocratic mentality who would put these new economic and organizational perspectives to work. In addition, Kennedy explicitly put forward a pragmatic "end-of-ideology" position which pictured major political problems as being of an essentially technical nature and too complex to be settled by the clash of militant creeds, but ultimately yielding to the patient search for workable compromise by technicians and experts.[34] If any American president could, as of the 1960s, be said to express the technocratic orientation toward politics, it was John Kennedy. His successor, on the other hand, was the very image of the wheeler-dealer politician, trading favors and votes with aplomb, promising and cajoling, making alliances and creating a politics of "consensus" based on old-fashioned interest bargaining. Yet it was Lyndon Johnson, the traditional politician's politician, under whose regime McNamara's reforms finally were provided with enough effective political support to take hold, as reflected in estimated savings of over $4 billion in the Defense Department during 1964, which provided the model for Johnson's much publicized "war on waste," the government-wide cost reduction program instituted in October of that year. The great irony is that Johnson, as Senate Majority Leader during the 1950s, had been the key broker of the complex military-industrial-political coalition which emerged in the context of the opportunities provided by the crash missile programs of that decade, and which was nourished from the system of government contracting that burgeoned so rapidly in the military R & D sector. This was a role which linked up with similar roles played by Senators Robert Kerr, Clinton Anderson, Stuart Symington, and others, among whom Johnson became *primus inter pares*; moreover, it was a role which he maintained under Kennedy as head of NASA's Space Policy Board, which he had personally helped bring into being during the Eisenhower regime. In this role, Johnson was a central figure among the interests who sought to perpetuate and extend the system of the military oriented Contract State which took shape during the 1950s, fed by the panic of the nuclear missile race.

The first possibility of a break in the nuclear arms race came only near the end of the Kennedy administration with the signing of the nuclear test ban treaty. With the passage of the treaty, the context was provided for cutting-back on redundant strategic weapons development. Hence the series of weapons program cancellations over which Defense Secretary McNamara presided around this time. In addition, McNamara's managerial programs seemed now to have the possibility of going beyond the integration of the military services and the cutting of contract costs, to the control of the basic direction of R & D investments in strategic weaponry. Basing himself on the Bell Committee Report,[35] as well as on reports of the government's General Accounting Office (GAO), McNamara moved to rebuild government in-house capability and to exert greater control over contractor fees. In this way, the basis would be laid for switching from cost-plus contracts to open competitive fixed-price bidding for Defense Department procurement. In those cases where negotiated contracts might be unavoidable, the department would invite multiple-source proposals, and provide incentive fees, rather than the old system of fixed fees. If the contractor's performance was excellent, his fee would correspond with the maximum, or incentive figure; on the other hand, to the extent that he deviated from target costs, scheduling, or performance objectives, he would suffer penalties in the fee, down to a minimum figure.

McNamara scored some considerable successes with this program to reform the contract instrument. Cost-plus-fixed-fee contracts, for example, for building Titan III launch vehicles were converted to an incentive-fee basis; as a result, spending on the program was claimed to be one percent below the original cost estimates, entailing the lowest number of engineering changes relative to comparable procurements, and the program was unprecedentedly on schedule. In the case of the "Bull Pup" air-to-surface missile, introduction of a second contractor source for follow-on production led to competitive negotiated bidding and dropped the missile's price by about twenty percent, or over $40 million. The same procedure was then applied, with similar cost reductions, for procurement of the antisubmarine torpedo ASTOR, the air defense missile TALOS, and several other weapons systems.[36]

By the mid-sixties, McNamara's system had undoubtedly begun to have an important effect on contracting procedures and the resulting costs of procurement; yet the objects of the system, the agencies and their contractor constituents, were again beginning to find their way around it. Through a kind of collusion between agencies and contractors, contractors were nominally converted to the new system on the basis of grossly inflated cost figures containing provisions for rather unlikely contingencies. In this way incentive fee schedules tended to become safeguards against risk, rather than motives for quality performance. Furthermore, contractors soon realized that fixed-price contracts provided legal protection against GAO and Defense Department scrutiny, so that they could safely enter into such contracts, relying on the permissive attitude of contract officers and the lack of governmental yardsticks. In one case the contractor overran the negotiated target by almost $15 million, and was seriously behind schedule as well, yet NASA indicated that the final fee would be above the minimum, providing the equivalent of a performance bonus. The very instruments of the McNamara system — competitive procurement, incentive fees, and fixed prices — were turned to the purpose of the R & D contractors.[37]

While the contractors were learning to evade the new system of cost effectiveness, their congressional allies were busy attacking one of its major institutions, the General Accounting Office. Established by Congress shortly after World War I as a response to dubious contracting practices during the war, the GAO has functioned as a kind of inspector-general, with gradually expanding powers to examine records pertinent to negotiated awards and to suspend payments to contractors in questionable cases. Using these powers, GAO in 1965 detected the trend toward subversion of the McNamara reforms and reported a large number of cases in which conversion to incentive and fixed-price contracts had added millions of dollars of cost above what would have been required on the basis of the initial contract arrangements. As a result, Congress turned on its own creature and launched an investigation of the GAO in response to contract complaints about its rigorous use by McNamara as a management tool. The investigation, conducted by the House Military Operations Subcommittee, gave contractors testifying an opportunity to vent their displeasure with McNamara's reforms as well as the GAO audits which supported them. In these reforms, which were based upon a long series of GAO reports and recommendations, contractors thought they discerned a philosophy contrary to the rights of free enterprise, one which viewed them as regulated agents of government rather than private businesses. Underlying their complaints about this philosophy was the more mundane concern, in the words of Boeing's Howard Neffner, that

> the increasing number of audit reports, the scope and uncompromising nature of GAO criticism, and the efforts made to enforce its recommendations are already dominating factors in procurement policy and practice.[38]

While the subcommittee's members were openly friendly to the contractors who testified, making cordial invitations to them to move their businesses to their respective home states, they acted more like adversaries in relation to the GAO officials. Thus, even before the hearings had ended in specific recommendations for limiting the GAO's investigative powers, they served notice to the agency that the vigorous pursuit of its role would surely lead to further difficulties.

The expansion of the scale of the Vietnam War in 1965 brought with it an insistent clamoring for increased appropriations for defense contracts; often coupled with attacks on McNamara's "short-sighted," "penny-wise" attitudes, to which were attributed the nation's inadequate state of military preparedness. The congressional assault on McNamara's cost-cutting activities came to a head in the fall of that year, when it passed the Military Construction Act as a kind of congressional veto of military base shutdowns by the defense secretary. For the first time in his dealings with this Congress, President Johnson found it necessary to use the veto, signifying a breakdown of the formerly smooth working relationship between this master politician and his ex-colleagues. Again, as in the case of the GAO investigation, Congress served notice that it would defend the institution of the Contract State against incursions by the executive authority; the struggle over central government control was by no means over, and the Vietnam War has served as the context of a continuing conflict over the powers of legislature *versus* executive.[39]

As the economy's largest consumer today, government is no longer a passive referee of the rules of the economic game. The government contract, an improvised, inadequately understood, but basic instrument of the new political economy, has become an increasingly important device for intervention in the economy and in the larger society. In this chapter, we have explored some of its implications. We have observed that the government contract serves not only the ends of economic stability and growth; it becomes a basic means of achieving important ends of government policy, involving the allocation of major resources and the mobilization of manpower for specific programs of development deemed vital to the national well-being. Concomitantly, it has become an important means for the distribution of wealth and the reordering of social status and power in various states and regions of the country. As such it becomes the object of a new kind of political activity with important effect on the relations of public and private power.

Using the concept of "interest investment" we have sought to specify the key policy makers in postindustrial America and the binding relations between them, over and above their common interest in "maintaining the system." The government contract, by subsidizing major elements of the corporate economy and at the same time strengthening these elements as constituencies of the grantor agencies and their political allies, has achieved both the maintenance of the system as a whole and the satisfaction of the respective investing interests.[40]

Though the government contract has been important as a tool for the central guidance of both military and non-military economic development since World War II, there was until the late 1960s little general consciousness of this trend. The result has been a kind of covert economic federalism in which specially-privileged constituencies have participated, shielded from the surrounding society by a combination of political ambiguity and technical complexity. In the process, the allocation of government contracts to "private" enterprises and organizations has tended to blur the distinctions between private and governmental objectives, blending them into a system of interpenetrating corporate bureaucratic interests which stands beyond the critical scrutiny or control of the general public. In this power context, we have described how the role of the scientific-knowledge elite (one segment of Bell's "technocratic class") has proved to be subsidiary to the coalition of military agencies, industrial contractors, and political officials with interests in the development and application of the military and extra-terrestrial technologies of the new society. Finally in reviewing the establishment of NASA and the related actions of the Air Force we have traced an important instance of the way in which these interest relations have in the postwar era taken the shape of institutional arrangements best described as the "Contract State," over which the assertion of central governmental control was for a long time a difficult and uncertain objective. In the next chapter we describe the recent arrangements by which the federal government has tended to bring the defense-industrial sector under explicit central control, resulting in a new stage of development known as "Pentagon Capitalism."

CHAPTER V

Postindustrial America
and the
New Economy

In this chapter, we discuss the emergence of a new multisectored economy in postindustrial America, in which a military-industrial sector mingles with the private-corporate sector, and governmental and private objectives and interests converge in the production of civilian public goods and services as well as in the production of military weapons systems. This complex economy belies any simple theories of a "garrison economy"[1] and even offers the prospect of a "social-industrial" complex in the area of social services and facilities, displacing the military-industrial complex in overall economic importance. Yet it is by no means clear that an economy in which needed social services are effectively supplied through an expanding sector of nonprofit enterprise is in the offing. The "grand partnership" of corporate business and central government is still problematic in its economic as well as its political consequences, and this chapter seeks to identify some of the major questions which this new convergence of major power centers raises with respect to further directions of economic development.

Postindustrial America and Pentagon Capitalism

The most important theme which has recently been added to the discussion of the interlocking relationships between military, government, and industrial organizations in the defense sector, is that of "Pentagon

Capitalism." In his work by that name Seymour Melman carries the analysis of these relations significantly further than had preceding theories, by demonstrating how they have come to be crystallized in a major political-economic subsystem with social controls and dynamics of its own, yet closely related to the larger system of capitalism in America.[2]

As Melman indicates, what had been the "military-industrial complex" of the late 1950s has within the past decade been transformed into a formalized industrial management structure under central state management. This "state management" as he calls it, controls what is probably the "nation's largest network of industrial enterprises" from the office of the secretary of defense in the Pentagon. This formal central management office was organized by Secretary of Defense Robert McNamara under the Kennedy and Johnson administrations, with the aim of minimizing the uncertainties of defense procurement and research involved in reliance on private firms; in effect, the purpose was to "replace" the market with management. Melman contends that the result has been the displacement of the military-industrial complex, as a loosely defined market for "interest investment" involving various political-economic interests (including the economic interests of thousands of quasi-independent industrial managers), by a "defined administrative control center"[3] in the Pentagon. This governmental-industrial control center now functions explicitly as top management with respect to the defense industry managers, having at its disposal not merely the considerable economic powers of large-scale industrial management, but a combination of ultimate or "peak" powers of "economic, political, and military decision-making."[4] The broad scope and huge scale of its decision powers can be glimpsed by reference to the value of its product ($44 billion in goods and services in 1968) and the number of its administrative functionaries (15,000 in contract negotiations, 40,000 in management compliance); Melman estimates that today this is the "largest industrial central administrative office in the United States — perhaps in the world." At the same time, it "has also become the most powerful decision making unit in the United States government."[5]

From one angle, what has occurred is the further formalization and tightening of relations between government and industrial organizations, in what was formerly a relatively loose matrix of organizational interests. This has come about largely through the creation of a defined hierarchic structure bringing these elements into a rationalized system with appropriate managerial rules and controls. Overall this has taken the industrial concerns involved a step further along the road of "quasi-nationalized" to explicitly nationalized status, while incorporating numerous obstacles to *public* control, not least of which has been the frequent invocation of military-bureaucratic secrecy. In the process this has placed at the disposal of the Pentagon the kind of combined political-industrial-military powers which have typically been "a feature of statist societies — communist, fascist, and others — where individual rights cannot constrain central rule."[6]

By all measures, the magnitude of the decision power of the Pentagon "state management" is historically unprecedented. Thus the $44 billion worth of industrial output in goods and services under the control of the state management in 1968, was in the range of being 10 to 15 times greater than the net output of such leading American industrial corporations as U.S. Steel and DuPont as measured by their sales in that year, and twice as large as the super-giant General Motors. In fact not only does it dwarf the giant industrial corporations, its economic decision power today equals that of many modern nations.[7] Obviously all of this concerns Melman; but what is also of great concern to him is the prospect of the further growth of the military sector at the expense of other areas of the society. As he indicates, in the course of less than 25 years (1946-69), the U.S. government spent more than $1,000 billion for military purposes, and over half of this was spent from 1960 to 1968, during the eight years of the Kennedy and Johnson administrations when the "state management" was formally established.[8] Taking the work of C. Wright Mills as a point of departure, Melman notes that Mills in the mid-1950s pointed to the existence of a "three-part system of elites in the United States" and quotes Mills to the effect that the military had already in that period become "ascendant" with regard to the political and economic elites. Here Melman turns to Robert Heilbroner for at least partial confirmation, to the effect that "it is the military or the political branch that commands" (in the military-industrial complex); "the role of business in the entire defense effort is essentially one of jockeying for favor rather than initiating policy."[9] Pursuing this point, Melman emphasizes that if anything, the formal organization of the old military-industrial complex as a super-industrial management with its central office located in the Pentagon has even further enhanced the role of the state military agency with respect to the industrial sector. He is somewhat critical of the work of authors like John Galbraith and Murray Weidenbaum who emphasize the growing convergence of major military-industrial firms and government organizations (in which government assumes the "role of the private entrepreneur" while contractors exhibit the "characteristics of a government agency or arsenal") in the decade since Mills wrote.[10] For, in his view, the theory of convergence "does not specify which of the managerial groups" involved — governmental or industrial — "becomes more important than the other."[11] Melman seeks to emphasize not merely the blurring of the line between public and private activities in contemporary American society; as he puts it, "my purpose here ... is to underscore not convergence but the managerial primacy of the new managerial control institution in the Department of Defense," and the impact of this primacy on American society.[12]

What is involved for Melman then, is not merely a revision of the theory of the military-industrial complex, but a revision of the prevailing elite-pluralist theories of the society *as a whole*. This is so because the emergent powers of the state management have important implications for "the meaning of the various elite theories." While a diversity of elites in the society undoubtedly wield special powers "the elites are not equal." Some enjoy a relative "primacy in decision-power" as measured by "the extent of control over production and by the ability to implement policies whose consequences are favorable to some elites, even while being hurtful to the others."[13] Applying these criteria, Melman concludes that the state management is the dominant elite today, in terms both of the quantity of production it manages, and of the successful pursuit of its military policies, even to the detriment of the "decision-power" of other elites.

It is important to understand here that while Melman begins with the problem of the relative position of the elites in the military-industrial complex and underscores the continuing and increasing dominance of the military, or military-political, members over the business member in this elite complex, he ends with a theory of the relative position of elites in the *overall society*. Though we agree with his observation that the formalization and rationalization of managerial controls over industrial production in the Defense Department has enhanced its dominance over defense-oriented industry, and though we admire the careful tracing of these lines of control in his work, we consider it an unwarranted leap to assume from this that the military state management in the Pentagon is now dominant over either industry as a whole, or over the civilian political executive. That is, Pentagon Capitalism, while it has significant influence on the American economy, and particularly in regions where defense production and research are concentrated, does not describe American capitalism as a whole, but constitutes only a sizable yet limited sector of the larger political economy.

We emphasize the above distinction not because we are unconvinced by Melman's arguments that there has been a major transition from convergence of military, political, and industrial interests in the defense-industrial sector, to structural dominance of the Defense Department over the industrial interests in this sector. Rather, we feel that Melman, in generalizing this structure of dominance to the larger society, violates a major tenet of contemporary pluralist theory which is still true today, even in the context of the distorted elite pluralism of the time. This is what may be referred to as the principle of the limitation of the dominance of an elite to those areas or "scopes" in which it has special competence, resources, organization, etc.

Thus, while the Pentagon enjoys control over a larger industrial budget and administrative work force than any single American corporation, this in itself does not confer "dominance" over American industry as a whole upon this government agency. In the first place, the combined industrial outputs of only the handful of leading American industrial corporations which Melman himself names outranks the Pentagon's industrial budget by almost $10 billion; and the combined output of the top 100 corporations would outrank it by the scores of billions.[14] But even more to the point, the industrial budget of the Pentagon is highly concentrated in terms of its "scope," i.e., in terms of the areas in which it operates; as Melman himself notes, it is mainly the aerospace, electronics, and ordnance industries which "have developed primarily into suppliers of the military establishment."[15] In our estimation, the patterns which have been established in the relations between the Pentagon and the defense-industrial sector are undoubtedly pragmatically important in their wide economic impact for the economy as a whole, but this does not spell the dominance of the military elite either economically or politically.

While we agree with Melman that an understanding of the implications of the state management is "essential for a meaningful theory" of contemporary American society,[16] we believe that at a theoretical level the relations between the state management and the defense industry are significant mainly as structures of future possibility, rather than present typicality. In the absence of an explicit fascist-militarist takeover of the government, the possibility of their extension over the major part of the economy, i.e., the creation of a dominant "command" economy which produces at the behest and under the direct control of state agencies, is not highly likely. At the same time, this does not deny the enormous importance of the military state management as a factor in the contemporary American economy and polity. (See appendix at end of chapter on postwar public expenditures.) It simply seeks to keep in perspective the relative balance of power between the military "state management" and general corporate management in the determination of major policy by both private and public agencies in the American political economy. For "Pentagon capitalism" is only one segment of the larger system of American capitalism in the postindustrial era, not the whole, or even the predominating element; particularly so in a period when corporate conglomeration has just succeeded in increasing significantly the concentrated power of established privately managed corporate giants.[17]

Public-Private "Convergence" and the Pluralist Economy

In American society at present, relations between economic organizations and government agencies range over a spectrum which stretches from relative independence to "state management" (as in the case of corporations like Lockheed, General Dynamics, McDonnnell-Douglas, etc.). The approximate midpoint on this spectrum seems to be well described by the notion of "convergence" between private management and public agency, and many corporations are today on the move from more traditional relations of political influence to some kind of actual functional convergence with state agencies in their field of enterprise. At the same time there is little likelihood as yet that firms under contract to nondefense agencies, such as HEW or HUD, will come under the dominance of a "state management" in the near future, or even longer, for reasons we will elaborate later; thus far, even in the case of firms under contract to the Pentagon, only those which are reliant for most of their sales on that agency can be said to have come under its functional "dominance."

This is to say once more what has been frequently observed in the postwar period; the American economy is a "pluralist" economy, in that it exhibits a diversity of economic organizations and a variety of patterns of relationship between these organizations and the state.[18] Conceptualized with regard to their relation to public or private management we can view the sectors of the economy in terms of the range of possible relations between government agencies and private economic organizations. We have at one end of this spectrum, in the private sector, the typical profit-oriented firm (figure 1, I) which has relations of "mutual influence" with government through lobbying and like activities on its part, and from the government's side by way of the impact of general economic controls such as taxes and spending on the business activities of the firm. Such firms are under no direct government regulation of prices or profits, though government may regulate the quality of their product or the manner of their operations, and this can have indirect effects on prices or profits. The enterprises in this sector seek to pursue profits only within the limits set by their relative position in the market, and tend to resist direct public regulation of their profits. Further, such enterprises may range from single-owner proprietorships to multi-thousand stockholder corporations, all privately managed and profit-oriented. (Our main interest is in the larger corporate enterprises, though we do not exclude from consideration the smaller firms, particularly of the corporate form.)

Next, there are the private nonprofit-oriented firms and institutions (figure 1, II) related to government not so much in terms of patterns of

PRIVATE		Quasi-Public "Hybrids" (III)	NONPRIVATE	
Profit	*Nonprofit*		*Profit*	*Nonprofit*
Privately Managed Enterprise (I)	Private "Nonprofits" (II)		Pentagon "State Management" (IV)	Publicly Managed Enterprise (V)
Corporate Enterprise and Small Business	Hospitals Universities Research Institutes Service/Charitable Organizations Community Organizations Foundations	Public Utilities Government Subsidized Industries Early "Military Industrial Complex" Potential "Social-Industrial Complex"	Centralized Government Management of "Private" Defense Industries	Public "authorities" Government corporations Public Schools & Universities

Major Areas of
Current and Potential Convergence

FIGURE 1. *Postindustrial American enterprise by relations between public and private management* "mutual influence," as in terms of government's power to grant licenses, tax exemptions, or contracts which may enable their survival and growth. Here we have the possibility of developments in the direction of functional-managerial convergence, as "nonprofit" organizations grow increasingly reliant on government contracts to supplement or even supplant their relationship to private clients and consumers. These enterprise types usually have a fairly long historical background, rooted in the charitable, welfare, health, and education-oriented activities of private groups and voluntary associations. These privately managed enterprises have in the past not sought profits, because the purpose of their work derived from the original aim of helping some segment of the public. Here we find a mixture of hospitals, mutual insurance companies, religious, charitable and welfare organizations, community development agencies, universities, and research agencies, whose basic functions are connected with the areas of research, education, health, and social insurance or "welfare."[19] (As such, the existence and prospects for development of this sector can be viewed as highly important to the end-of-ideologists' theory of an evolving postindustrial "welfare capitalism.") Gradually these functions, with early roots in religious or philanthropic organizations, have come to be taken over either by public agencies or by privately managed nonprofit organizations. Owing to the strong interest of government in these functions, the next phase of development in this area may well involve increasing "convergence" between public management and private enterprise. It is in this light that we will examine the predictions of the growth of the not-for-profit sector as a whole (government plus private nonprofits) and particularly of its privately managed segment, to which the end-of-ideologists point as promising significant changes in American capitalism, particularly with regard to the satisfaction of various civilian public economic needs and demands, i.e., with regard to the provision of what are commonly referred to as "public services."

After this, we cross the increasingly hazy line into the sector which can be designated as "quasi-public" (figure 1, III). Here we have those profit-oriented firms which are effectively under dual management, with government having a critical role in determining the level of profits permissible. Though profit-oriented and formally under private management, such firms are in fact functionally and, in some respects, legally under the management of a combination of private managers and public officials. Such have been the defense-industrial firms; and such also are the enterprises known as "public utilities" and several government-subsidized industries, such as the maritime industry and aspects of the aircraft industry. Thus "public utilities" (enterprises in fields deemed publicly essential which enjoy natural monopolies in their respective areas, e.g., in power production, communications, and transportation), though privately owned, are directly regulated by government agencies with regard to both their prices and their profits. Much the same applies for government-subsidized industries, (e.g., shipping, or aircraft companies) whose profits are directly open to government regulation in several respects; and similarly for the "defense industries," whose profits and even survival have depended much less on open-market competition than on the terms of contract negotiation and the willingness of the Pentagon to pay for contract cost overruns.[20]

Common to these several different types of "hybrid" (i.e., public-private) enterprise is, first, the fact that while they are private enterprises oriented toward making profits, they perform functions deemed essential to the public welfare or the national interest. Consequently the control of their economic policies has not been left solely in the hands of private management, but is in various ways shared by decision makers in government bureaus. With the tightening and systematization of controls, some quasi-public enterprises, particularly those in the defense sector, can be said to have made the transition in the past decade from the status of more or less free-wheeling profit-oriented entrepreneurs to positions explicitly subordinate to the managerial control of the "state management," even to the point of becoming "disposable" Pentagon enterprises[21] (figure 1, IV). Finally, we have publicly owned, publicly managed organizations and enterprises, such as public schools, welfare agencies, and the TVA (figure 1, V). Significantly, under the Eisenhower and Nixon administrations, the trend has been to shift public enterprise backward to a quasi-public status, whereby the government contracts out a function such as postal delivery or the production of fissionable atomic materials to private contractors, who operate under its regulation as quasi-public corporations. (See figure 2, illustrating recent trends toward public-private convergence in several sectors of the economy.)

The overall picture we obtain then, is one of a continuum stretching from the more-or-less "purely" private enterprises which still make up the bulk of enterprise in total size of assets, employment, sales, etc., to the more-or-less "purely" public enterprises, which are still relatively few and far between in the American economy. At the approximate middle of this continuum are the quasi-public "hybrid" enterprises, like the public utilities, in which the goals and managerial activities of public agency and private enterprise tend toward "convergence"; flanked on one side by nonprofit private enterprises increasingly dependent on governmental "largess"[22] in the form of licenses, franchises, exemptions contracts, etc., and on the other by profit-oriented, quasi-public enterprises whose procedures and economics are no explicitly under the control of a "state management."

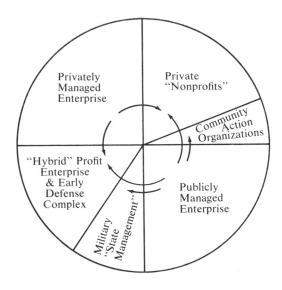

FIGURE 2. *Postindustrial American enterprise, em-*
phasizing mutual involvement in public-
private "convergence" (Arrows meeting
indicate contract, tax-exemption, or li-
ense relations between public agencies
and private management, typically involv-
ing public standards and controls; single
arrows indicate recent establishment of
public management in private areas).

What is, of course, most interesting and most indicative of contemporary trends is the growth of enterprise types at and around the center of
this continuum, which are neither clearly public nor clearly private in
their bearing. From the viewpoint of the end-of-ideology theorists of the
postindustrial society, the emergence and expansion of these enterprise
types is crucial to their theory because they express a solution to the
organizational problems of industrial society in terms which elude a clear-
cut ideological position either for laissez-faire or for state ownership.
This is the real significance of the "mixed" or "pluralist" economy and
of the support of the end-of-ideologists for it; not so much an economy
which mixes private enterprises with a growing number of public enterprises, as one which produces a "hybrid" type of enterprise in which
goals and management functions increasingly converge as between public
and private interests. For the end-of-ideologists, the crucial issue would
seem to be no longer the classic controversy over private *versus* public
enterprise, with the related issue of government planning as against non-

planning as a corollary, but the issue of what type of mixture of public and private interest and controls are most desirable *in the "quasi-public enterprise"*; i.e., what kind of "convergence" and, within this framework, what kind of planning to complement the pattern of "convergence" within enterprises and within the overall economy.

The Nonprofit Sector and the "Service Society"

Before going on to discuss the issue of planning, it is useful to discuss some recent developments in the private economy, both in its profit and nonprofit sectors. We will concentrate on the corporate organizations in these sectors, because of their scale and significance for the economy, touching on the behavior of smaller units only when considered in the aggregate or as important examples of further developments. This discussion will then complement our review of Melman's observations on the changes which have taken place in the quasi-public defense sector of the economy in the past decade; together they provide a picture of the important changes in the economy during the past ten years or so, and of probable trends over the near future.

As we have noted, from the viewpoint of the postindustrial theorists, the nature and prospects for further development of the nonprofit sector are of importance to their thesis of an evolving postindustrial "welfare capitalism." Essentially, they proclaim the emergence of a "service economy," with the implication that needed civilian services of various kinds will be generally available to the public.[23] In apparent confirmation of their optimism as to the development of this sector, we have the recent work of Richard Barber on the postwar development of the private corporate sector in America. Barber too uses the terminology of the "postindustrial society" and at several points virtually equates it with the emergence of a "service society" in which, as he notes, reminiscent of Bell, "most of the employed population is not involved in the production of food, clothing, housing, and other tangible goods"; moreover, this sector is particularly important today because most postwar expansion in jobs "has come in the service-government sector."[24] Government is here coupled with the service sector because characteristically, rather than producing goods, government enterprises produce services, from education and police to fire services to sewage and water and public health services. Since these services are provided for the public on a nonprofit basis, they most resemble those services provided by private or quasi-public nonprofit enterprises, as described earlier. Government enterprises and the nonprofit service enterprise are frequently classed together as a "not-for-profit" sector.

Today, the not-for-profit sector accounts for approximately one-third of total employment and for more than 25 percent of Gross National Product.[25] Roughly another third of total United States employment is accounted for by firms producing services for a profit (e.g., banking, business, and commercial services), and the final third by goods-producing industries (manufacturing, construction, farming, mining, etc.) which are mostly privately managed and profit-seeking. The enormous expansion of the service sector, both profit and nonprofit, in the past two generations leads the postindustrial theorists to refer to the United States as having made the transition from a goods-producing society to a "service society."[26] (However, while the services-government sector provides almost two-thirds of total employment, it accounts for only 40 percent of Gross National Product, as of the mid-1960s.)[27] This is largely due to the fact that the goods-producing industries, particularly manufacturing and refining, and to some extent mining and farming, are increasingly mechanizing and automating their production processes, thereby reducing their need for labor at a given level of output.[28]

Of further significance to the postindustrial theorists is the fact that "not-for-profit" service enterprises (i.e., government plus nonprofits) account directly or indirectly for the employment of about two-thirds of all professional and scientific workers. Within the not-for-profit sector the importance of nonprofits in particular (those nongovernmental enterprises producing services on a nonprofit basis for paying consumers), is as yet not so much quantitative as qualitative, since government jobs account for about three-fourths of total not-for-profit employment.[29] In particular, together with the universities, nonprofit research and consultative firms have a central place in the process of scientific and technical innovation today and therefore are of key importance to the development of the complex technologies of the postindustrial society. According to Barber, the crucial role of the nonprofits is "to develop ideas . . . new approaches . . . different techniques." In research activities for business, industry, and government the nonprofits and the universities have become "prime movers in basic and applied research," pointing the way for large-scale technological and social change.[30] Furthermore, while the goods-producing industries, as the characteristic enterprise type of the older industrial capitalism, have typically been profit-oriented, the service industries are a mix of profit and nonprofit enterprise. Hence there resides in the postindustrial theory some suggestion that the rise of a "service" society may carry within it the seed of a new "nonprofit" economy, oriented toward producing public and consumer services; at the very least the new economy is viewed as one in which the large profit-seeking industrial corporation "is likely to be overshadowed by the hospitals, universities, research institutes, government agencies, and professional organizations that are the hallmarks of a service economy."[31]

Looking at current trends projected over the near future, Barber points to a pattern of already high expenditure for services on the part of the individual consumer which promises to increase noticeably as early as 1975. While about 40 percent of personal consumption dollars went for services in 1969, almost 45 percent will be spent there by 1975, as against purchases of durable and nondurable goods. He concludes this could mean an additional expenditure of $135 billion for services by 1975.[32] Such spending would be widely distributed among a variety of services: part of it, such as health and education services, could be expected to be mainly provided by nonprofit agencies; the rest would fall under the category of personal services, such as recreation and hotels, basically produced by profit enterprises. In addition, Barber notes that government's role in expanding demand for services promises to be a large one. Currently government expenditures for both goods and services amount to over 20 percent of Gross National Product. While much of the federal dollar goes to the purchase of military goods, state and local expenditures are heavily devoted to the purchase of public services, and these expenditures, already at an over-$100 billion level ($112 billion in 1969), are expected to rise to over $180 billion by 1975. (In such areas as health and education, state and local dollar expenditures by the mid-1970s should multiply by about six times, as compared with the mid-1950s, i.e., from $12 billion to over $70 billion in education, and from $3 billion to almost $20 billion in health and hospitals).[33] Barber argues that unless defense expenditures rise at a comparable rate (about 70 percent from the early to the mid-1970s), there promises to be significant change in the mix of government expenditures by the mid-1970s. In the first place, there should be greater emphasis on spending at the state and local levels, and secondly, most local spending will probably go to such areas as health, education, and community renewal and will probably flow increasingly to nonprofit enterprises such as hospitals, universities, and research agencies.

One serious gap in the argument of theorists of the "service society," such as Barber, owes to the fact that they do not explicitly estimate the specific share of *nonprofit* enterprise in the expanding service sector. To the limited extent that they discuss its current share in some specific areas such as Research and Development, as well as the future general prospects of nonprofits, however, they raise some interesting qualifications about the notion of transition to a nonprofit public-service economy, which their work implies. Combined federal and private support for research and development activity to universities, to nonprofit research agencies, and to industrial research has skyrocketed from an annual level of a little over one-half billion dollars during the war years of World War II to $5 billion during the mid-1950's, prior to the beginning of the missile and space race, to about $25 billion by 1969.[34] Most of this rise has been the result of rapidly increasing government expenditures, amounting to about 3 percent of Gross National Product in 1969 (a higher proportion of government expenditure than for any other country in the world).[35] As of 1970, the federal government contributed about two-thirds of total outlays for R & D, somewhere near $18 billion, approximately 10 percent of the federal administrative budget. Yet contrary to "service society" expectations, little of this money has been going to fund the work of nonprofit research agencies, or universities involved in basic research on a nonprofit basis. Only about 10 percent went to universities and colleges proper, with about another 5 percent to university-related research centers directly under federal contract, and a final 4 percent to nonprofit institutions.[36] By far the main emphasis has been on the development of products or processes relating to defense needs, the missile race, the space race, etc. In the decade from 1958 to 1969, the $125 billion spent by the U.S. government on R & D went mainly toward the development of aircraft, missiles, electronic systems, nuclear devices, and the like, with most of the money going to the programs of the Defense Department, NASA, and the AEC (about 80 percent of federal R & D funds went to these three agencies annually as of the late 1960s). The emphasis on development activities has accounted for roughly 70 percent of federal R & D expenditures, with another 20 percent going to applied research often tied closely to a specific development aim; typically, only about 10 percent of funds have gone toward the performance of basic research undertaken solely to advance fundamental scientific knowledge.[37]

The picture we get is one in which universities, affiliated research centers under government contract, and other nonprofit research agencies have indeed enjoyed significant increases in federal support in the postwar period, but this support has been considerably smaller than that extended to private defense-related industry, and what the not-for-profits have received in the way of government contracts has directed them toward a relatively narrow band of inquiry, mainly militarily concerned.

Despite his enthusiasm for the expanding government funding of R & D activities, Barber's own figures indicate the very narrow concentration of government support for R & D, with most of its R & D work in that area being done by a handful of industries heavily dependent on government support. At the close of the 1960s just two industries (aircraft-missiles, and electrical communications) accounted for 60 percent of annual research by private companies, while federal funds paid for over half of all industrial research.[38] "For *most* companies in *most* industries the role of the Federal research funds is extremely limited."[39] Together with the strong emphasis on applied research and product development in industry today (about 75 percent of industry R & D goes to development of new products and cost-cutting production techniques, with another 20 percent for applied, product-oriented research; only 4 percent is for basic research), and this raises many questions about the "scientific explosion" about which Barber and other "postindustrial" theorists have made so much.[40] This promising-sounding development of the postwar period has actually been a rather contained "explosion," and its government support has focussed on producing new, improved types of military and space-related hardware, rather than the balanced encouragement of work on fundamental problems and processes in the various areas of physical and social science.

The Social-Industrial Complex and the "Grand Partnership"

Another major thesis of Barber's, central to much of the thinking of the postindustrial theorists, is that government and business are on the way to developing a "grand partnership," in which government provides a market for various public sector-related goods and services; in turn, business either through profit or nonprofit enterprise has the potential for entering this market and contibuting to the solution of various pressing social problems. Thus Barber at several points stresses the considerable sales opportunities which await business enterprise in the public sector and particularly in its services aspect, as against the established product-oriented, military-industrial sector.

As Barber indicates, there is a new business-government partnership emerging, not as the product of any preconceived ideology, but more likely as a pragmatic "coalition" in areas deemed important to government policy. This partnership first functioned in the areas of defense and space, and is now broadening into current civilian problem areas such as education, health services, job training, housing, urban planning and renewal, etc. As a consequence, business is becoming increasingly involved in areas long considered appropriately the province of government. Moreover, the particular manner in which this joining of private economic power with public political power is being effected, has meant an increasing delegation of governmental responsibilities and governmental powers to business managers beyond the reach of public scrutiny or control; a problem to which we will return. The new interdependence of private and public power has brought to the surface and made explicit what might have been thought to be traits peculiar to the defense sector, such as the interchange of personnel and information at high executive as well as staff levels with bearing on the making of policy in the civilian political economy as well. Today the executives of large enterprises are "deeply involved on a continuing though usually informal basis in the highest decision-making levels of the Executive Branch . . . in a great realm of issues."[41] The exchange of top management personnel flows as well from government to business, and besides improving communication between the wielders of public and private power, has entailed a new managerial understanding that the problems which face the executives of large modern organizations are much alike, "whether they happen to bear a 'public' or 'private' label."[42]

In this context there are emerging new signs of interest in utilizing the capacities and resources of private enterprise for an attack on contemporary social problems. Among these are expressions of interest by influential businessmen, such as George Champion, chairman of Chase-Manhattan Bank, in the prospects of private business for participation in "socio-commercial enterprise"; what others have termed the "social-industrial complex." Of course businessmen will participate in this new sector of enterprise to the extent that they feel they can protect and enlarge their sales and profits; with continuing disengagement from Vietnam, various businesses have begun looking to nondefense contracting to replace the part played by defense production in their sales.

Despite the ostensible benefits which might follow from government enlisting private enterprise in current efforts at solving social problems, there are several serious drawbacks involved. Once again, despite his own enthusiasm for the economic benefits which can flow from such a coalition (booming economy, expanded sales and profits, etc.), Barber notes that a full-fledged business-government partnership of the kind we have described tends to "tear at the very roots of our established political culture." What troubles him in particular is that the new partnership seems to be crystallizing simultaneous with "a vast conglomerate merger movement" in the corporate sector, which is placing increasing economic resources in the hands of a small number of powerful corporations. In his view, the simultaneous merger of power within the private sector and between it and the public sector is mutually reinforcing, and can yet produce "a unique brand of corporate state" linking government and private sectors "in a way that could be antithetical to democracy itself."[43]

Interestingly this comment is made in connection with the observation that previously countervailing forces in the economy and government are today coalescent in a grand elitist alliance which may have enough power to decide basic policies "quite independent of the customary processes of popular democratic participation."[44] It is useful to compare this observation with the implications of Melman's work on the changing relations of government to the industries of the defense sector. Briefly, Melman's contribution has been to detail the developments which have changed the status of the defense industries from formally autonomous but economically dependent enterprises in a "military-industrial complex" to formally and economically subordinate units in a structure of "state management." In our conceptual framework, these units can be considered to have moved from the position of "hybrid," regulated enterprises whose goals and interests converge with those of the government agencies granting them contracts, to that of subordinate elements in a hierarchic management system. In both positions, there exists a condition of functional and interest convergence between the government agency and the particular enterprise; in the state management situation however, there is created a condition of structural subordination of the enterprise to the military agency. In turn, this implies a shift in the locus of defense policy making to the institutions of executive government itself, i.e., a shift from bargaining between military, political, and defense industry elites as approximate coequals (*via* the "bureaucratic subsystem" described earlier), to direct negotiation between the budgetary representatives of the military agency and the political executive regarding military policy and budget, with the final resolution by the chief political executive himself.[45] Then the policy agreements worked out between the agency and the political executive are translated into production and research programs and related budget to be parcelled out in a coordinated manner to managerially subordinate units in the state management system. As Melman indicates, such a relationship closely resembles that typically existing in totalitarian statist regimes between government agencies and economic units in a "command economy."

In contrast, the image Barber presents of the development of a "services society" in which both private and public services are abundant is one of a relationship between government and economy which is not quite so "advanced." Here the significant transition is from the traditional "adversary" relationship between government and business, to one in which business increasingly responds to market signals from a network of government agencies making "interest investments" through contract awards, and in which business comes increasingly into the council of government at the initiating levels of policy formulation. This is a shift from the classic separation of public and private power to the convergence of these powers, through quasi-public organizational linkages which are not yet entirely clear. The political market structuring of government-economy relationships which Barber describes as possibly emerging in the services area in the near future (with heavy emphasis on public-related or social services") bears a strong resemblance to the interest investment relationships which were typical of the military-industrial complex in the 1950s, prior to the establishment of the "state management" and its central control system. What we are witnessing

then, may be the early stages of the development of what has been called
a "social-industrial complex," comparable in the structure of its political-
economic relationship to the original "military-industrial complex." Theoretically, it might be hypothesized that this relationship may yet pass
through the same stages as those described in the transformation of
the military-industrial complex to a state management; yet predicting
such an outcome at this early point seems not only premature, but even
in the long run rather unlikely. That is, there seems a greater likelihood
that the relationship of government and private enterprise in the social
services sector will remain limited to one of functional and interest convergence (i.e., one of "partnership" or coalition) rather than evolving
into one of "state management." The limiting factors have in several
respects probably been generated by the experience of the military
state management itself.

At this stage, we may expect to find crystallizing some of the complex
of government-economic relationships which marked the earlier emergence of a military-industrial complex. In the first place, there is presently
a large existing and potential market in such nondefense areas as education and health, which have received significant increases in government
funds since the mid-1960s;[46] in addition there is an important potential
market in such areas as urban housing, transportation, and pollution.
Areas like these can provide employment in a variety of service occupations, from research and planning to teaching, medical services, and
sanitation work; in addition, they can provide jobs in such goods-
producing fields as construction and allied industries.

Currently education is probably the largest of the fields attracting business interest. By 1969 the nation's educational institutions (from public
and private elementary schools through college and university level)
spent about $50 billion per year for goods and services; by 1975, it is
estimated they will spend about $70 billion. Since costs per pupil for
education are escalating (Barber estimates $530 annually per elementary
school pupil in 1968 *versus* $700 per pupil in 1975), owing to increasing
costs of staffing and supplies, there are strong inducements to employ
computers, closed circuit TV, and related electronic hardware to reduce
overall costs. According to estimates quoted by Barber, expenditures
for such equipment may rise from one-half billion dollars as of the late
1960s to between $5 and $10 billion annually by the mid-1970s.[47] It
should be noted that this trend tends to once again qualify Barber's
predictions about the involvement of private enterprise in the public
service sector; what private corporations will probably be supplying may
well be mainly educational hardware rather than services or "software"
such as systematic information and organizational skills.

In the area of health, Barber is optimistic that growing discontent with the fragmentation of health services, which are currently divided between doctors, researchers, hospitals, and drug companies, will open the way to basic reorganization of these services. In particular, he sees great opportunities for firms with systems-management experience to enter this complex and heterogeneous field and contribute significantly to the integration of its various elements — profit, nonprofit, and government organizations; independent professionals and large bureaucratic institutions —in some orderly fashion.[48] Thus the capabilities of firms with experience in the design and application of information systems and computer technology could provide an improved means of linking doctors with patients on the one hand and with the full-scale diagnostic and treatment facilities offered by hospitals on the other.[49]

Over the past decade, Congress has apparently been less interested or willing to provide funds for urban housing and redevelopment than for education or health. Partly this may be owing to the relative absence of an influential, articulate middle-class constituency in the deteriorated slum and ghetto areas most in need of renewal, and partly to the considerable powers of the real estate lobby. In any event, in 1960 outlays for community development and housing (exclusive of funds expended for maintenance of the housing market) amounted to about $200 million, in 1964 to $350 million, and in 1968 to $2.1 billion. Though this represented an overall increase of about ten times, expenditures in this area have been significantly lower than for education or health, exceeding $1 billion only since 1966; this despite various estimates of the need to spend from upwards of $10 billion per year over a ten-year period to eliminate substandard housing.[50] In this area of enterprise, owing to lack of government funding, business will probably have the major role in supplying the working capital, rather than relying on government contracts to supply it. Under these circumstances, President Johnson in 1968 asked Congress to support a program to utilize the capacities of private enterprise in the housing of low-income families "through the creation of a federally-chartered private, profit-making housing partnership."[51] In particular, what he sought was the establishment of privately-funded partnerships which would "join private capital with business skills to help close the low-income housing gap."[52] Besides providing working capital and taking responsibility for construction, private firms would also act as management for the housing built. In return, government would provide rent supplements to low-income tenants, thereby bringing rentals within their reach (and indirectly guaranteeing profitable rental levels to the builders); in addition, government would provide investment incentives in the form of tax exemptions, federally guaranteed low-interest loans,

etc. In effect, this federally chartered, privately managed corporation
would provide capital, construction, and management skills; the government would provide an array of financial subsidies to help insure the
profitability of the venture.

In addition, government at the local level might lend its powers of
eminent domain, useful in assembling specific building sites by vesting the
powers in the enterprise through state charter, as in the case of the New
York state-chartered Urban Development Corporation. Congress implemented these basic proposals with the passage of the Housing and Urban
Development Act in 1968, which created a National Housing Corporation to serve as principal investor and as general partner and manager
in low-income housing projects across the country. The corporation
can expect an initial capitalization of $200 million from investing cor-
porations; another $4 billion may be borrowed through government-
guaranteed loans. The corporation itself will thus be able to provide both
capital and management for the annual construction of approximately as
many low-income units as are currently being built through all existing
public housing programs (approximately fifty thousand). The Corporation's relations with the local construction and real estate firms, to whom
it will contract out details of specific projects, will be structured along
lines similar to those between prime contractors and subcontractors in
the defense industries, with overall production and management responsibility vested in the Corporation, and it may be assumed there will be
general review of its activities and progress by the Department of Housing and Urban Development under the provisions of the Housing and
Development Act.[53] However, since the Corporation will serve as the
primary source of capital with which it works (either through interested
investors or bank loans), rather than the government providing invest-
ment-capital grants through its contracts, the Corporation will probably
enjoy relative managerial autonomy, as compared to the current managerial subordination of firms in the defense industry. What we expect to
see here then, is a kind of "trade-off" of managerial responsibility for
capital to the quasi-public corporation in those areas where government
seeks to stimulate functionally rationalized economic enterprise but is
unable to provide capital for investment in such enterprise. Indeed, it is
likely that private firms induced to invest in the public sector will ask
not only relative managerial autonomy but also guaranteed minimum
profits, in exchange for their willingness to invest in an area of public
need.

In Barber's view the Housing Corporation "represents a hopeful way
of tapping private capital and mobilizing industrial organizational techniques." What is "especially interesting," however, is the fact that "it is
not a charity or not-for-profit operation"; through the tax benefits which

it offers, "business investors in the Housing Corporation should realize highly respectably earnings."[54] This is indeed interesting, in light of Barber's earlier emphasis on the significance of government funding in the public sector to the growth of *non*profit enterprise. These events to date seem to contradict the trends predicted by Barber; or at least to indicate that expansion of private profit-oriented enterprise will be stimulated by government spending in the civilian public sector as much as will nonprofit enterprise, and possibly, in terms of absolute increase, a good deal more.

Now it might be objected that Barber is really referring mainly to the stimulation which government public sector investment is currently affording to nonprofit service-providing enterprises in such areas as health, education, and research, rather than to goods-providing enterprises such as those in the housing industry. Yet here too, Barber suggests that profitable market opportunities await private corporations which have the facilities and the skills for applying "systems analysis" or "systems techniques" to the problems involved in coordinating the contributions of the various participants in the particular field. As he puts it, with regard to the health services area, the "growing dissatisfaction" with the fragmentation which presently exists in medical care, with the uncoordinated and overlapping participation of doctors, drug companies, hospitals, government, etc., opens the prospect of "great new markets," particularly for those corporations with developed systems analysis and management capacities.[55] Here is Galbraith's "mature corporation," applying to the social environment (and notably in the production of social services as well as socially demanded goods) the information-processing and planning techniques it has developed in the course of its own development into a technically sophisticated, advanced industrial enterprise. In this way, the distinctive informational and planning capacities of the advanced industrial corporation become the anticipated means for moving *beyond* advanced industrialism to "postindustrialism"; i.e., beyond "mature" corporate industrialism to the postindustrial "service society."

This theme is again picked up and expanded upon in Barber's discussion of "Systems Techniques and Civilian Problems," in the chapter on "Business's New Frontier: Social Problem Solving."[56] Here Barber notes that the "systems analysis" and management capabilities developed by large technically advanced corporations promise to be of use in the outlining and administration of solutions to important social problems, on a large scale. A number of large corporations, mostly aerospace companies, are already beginning to apply their advanced capabilities for "organized problem solving" in such service areas as transportation, crime prevention, data handling, and waste management.[57] Moreover, while these aerospace companies are currently moving into this area, the field is by no means presently or potentially limited to their efforts. In fact, there are fairly clear indications that firms like the aerospace companies, which have been spawned in the defense sector, feel most secure functioning in that area, continuing to use the experience they have accumulated in the various aspects of defense contract work, rather than moving whole-scale into civilian "problem solving."[58] The likelihood is that as the markets associated with the public sector expand by virtue of increasing availability of government funds, it will be large, "mature," privately managed, profit-seeking corporations like General Electric — less fully committed to defense work than the aerospace firms, yet possessing highly developed systems-analysis capacities — that will tend to move furthest into large-scale provision of research, planning, and management services to the public sector.

While it is entirely appropriate to speak of the "rise of nonprofits" in conjunction with expanding government allocation of resources to the civilian areas of the public sector, it is misleading to emphasize the *dominance* of such enterprises in these areas,[59] in view of the prospects for their relative displacement by much larger, better funded, private corporations in this new market, in the supplying not only of desired goods, but also services, on a large scale. On the other hand, though non-profit enterprises will not likely maintain current positions of dominance in supplying the needs of large-scale public service markets, indications are that they will continue to play a vital role in this area. As Barber suggests, their most important function has actually been that of technical and organizational innovation but he does not explore this beyond linking various nonprofits (universities, government-funded research centers, and private agencies) to research activities in the defense sector, or mentioning their role as planning consultants to private corporations. However, it is precisely their role as innovators in the area of "social problem solving" which is perhaps most fascinating, and which seems to indicate a highly important aspect of their future role as an innovative force in the economy.

Social Innovation and the Nonprofit Organization

In their recent work on post-war development in the structure of American society, Bensman and Vidich approach the question of the social-innovation role of nonprofit organizations within the framework of the developing relationship in the "service society" between public and private "philanthropy."[60] (By philanthropy they mean the provision of services by public or private organizations to their clients either free or significantly below cost.)[61] They point out that public philanthropy tends to be modelled along modern industrial lines, insofar as government seeks to purchase and distribute services on a mass basis. Typically government begins by purchasing services from small suppliers (e.g., the individual psychiatric counselor), and then tends to encourage the standardization and rationalization of these services (e.g., group therapy, mental hygiene programs, chemical and drug therapy) by virtue of the large scale of its programs. In this process, private, nonprofit, philanthropic organizations like the Ford Foundation play a critical role. The private philanthropy, having relatively less public accountability, is freer than government agencies to scout the public service terrain, discovering or developing new needs for services or new arrangements for delivering them. This accomplished, the government agency steps in either directly to provide the services involved, or subsidizes their delivery by way of contracts to private service enterprises. In effect, in the division of philanthropic labor, "private philanthropy is historically a research and development agency," generally moving "in the direction of further innovation at the expense of ongoing services." Thus, "private philanthropy is a significant economic institution in that it provides a perpetual mechanism of expansion"[62] for service activities and programs.

Since the market for services, as against that for industrial goods, is potentially unlimited (depending ultimately on the imaginativeness of the service agencies and their foundation scouts), the continuing expansion of services presents itself as a possible solution to the problem of over-production which industrial and advanced-industrial societies have never fully resolved.[63] As Galbraith's work makes clear, advanced-industrial society requires vast engineering and scientific programs to fully engage the enormous productive capacities of its industrial technology. Thus far, however, only defense programs and the space program have seemed to offer major outlets in the American economy for the channeling of otherwise un- or under-utilized industrial capacity. Moreover, in *The New Industrial State* Galbraith appears pessimistic that any significant portion of that industrial capacity which has been directed toward defense programs can be successfully diverted to any conceivable large-scale, nondefense program (e.g., urban renewal), other than the space program.[64] The innovative role of nonprofit foundations like Ford, in finding possibilities for private investments in the service sector, thus assumes an aspect of potential importance to the overall national economy.

According to Bensman and Vidich the Ford Foundation is outstanding among the nonprofit organizations for the manner in which it has systematized its role in the research and development of social service programs, specializing in pilot social programs financed on an experimental basis. Once proven in the field test, the given program is typically turned over as a prototype for mass application by the relevant government agency. Among social programs devised and tested by the Foundation are community action programs, school decentralization and urban education programs, manpower training and development programs — all with a heavy service emphasis — as well as urban renewal programs, which often include sizable service aspects (e.g., planning, community organization, code enforcement, and sanitation).[65]

The work of several recent authors, writing on the interest of the private corporations in the economic development of the black ghettos, tends to corroborate the observations of Bensman and Vidich. Citing the comments of Henry Heald (Ford Foundation president in 1965) to the effect that privately supported organizations are best fitted to develop new techniques and procedures as models for utilization by other institutions, Robert Allen notes particularly the role of the private foundation "as an instrument of social innovation and control in areas which the government has not yet penetrated, or in areas where direct government intervention would draw criticism."[66] As an example in the field of "social welfare," he points to the Foundation's grants to antipoverty pilot projects in six locations around the country (including Boston, New Haven, Oakland, Philadelphia, and Washington, D.C.) "well in advance of federal efforts in this field." In the related area of community organization, he cites the Foundation's later grant in 1967 to the Cleveland chapter of CORE, for job training, voter registration, and economic development programs, as well as for improvement of civil-rights program planning.[67]

As we understand Allen, the overall aim of such efforts is essentially twofold: first to quiet the black community and reduce the possibilities of massive violence by providing opportunities for political expression through established institutional means; and second, to channel the energies of the community and particularly its militant leaders, into various community development programs, including the development of local "black capitalism," intended to tie the community's economy to the larger white-controlled corporate system, as a subordinate appendage.[68] Complementary to the efforts of private foundations, such as Ford, in this area, Allen also mentions the role of long-established, nonprofit service organizations, such as the Urban League, in linking up the needs of the community with the resources of government, industry, unions, and foundations. Through such efforts it helped almost fifty thousand blacks find or improve their jobs in 1967 and set up on-the-job training programs in three dozen cities. Illustrating the support the League had garnered from established white-led foundations was the announcement in 1968 of plans for spending five million dollars in a two-year period to help black businesses in almost one-hundred cities.

Significantly, "funds for this project were to come from the Ford, Field, Carnegie, and Rockefeller Foundations."[69]

Finally, alongside the efforts of established service organizations such as the Urban League, there emerged in the late Sixties, particularly after the major Detroit riot of 1967, several alliances and coalitions of corporate businessmen, government officials, union leaders, foundation heads, and church leaders, seeking to link the resources of their respective institutional areas to the task of economic development and social problem solving in the black community. Most significant to the scale of this undertaking has been the effort to link the resources of the federal government to the enterprise of corporate business in pursuit of these goals.

John Gardner, Chairman of the National Urban Coalition (established in August 1967 and consisting of some 1200 business, government, and other leaders) spoke in terms of a $200 billion government housing investment over the next generation to solve the urban crisis. The National Alliance of Businessmen, organized under the Johnson administration in 1968 with Henry Ford II as chairman, also sought to facilitate large-scale government-business cooperation in urban development programs; by acting as a "one-step service for businessmen in dealing with several government agencies at once," it was to help bypass Washington's bureaucratic red tape.[70] Again the scale of operations projected for the organization was large — finding a half-million jobs for hard-core unemployed in 1971 (one hundred thousand by June 1969, and two hundred thousand in the summer of 1968 for youngsters out of school). In return for the efforts of the businessmen associated with NAB, the Johnson administration pledged $350 million to cover "extraordinary" costs involved in training and supportive services. At the same time it also sent to Congress the bill proposing the National Housing Corporation discussed above, which Allen observes was "designed to subsidize the construction industry by enabling the federal government to charter construction consortiums and grant them tax concessions to bring their returns up to the level of other forms of investment."[71] Though the National Alliance of Businessmen was itself essentially a nonprofit service organization, one of the major effects of its activities was to clear the way for government support for profitable investment in a field in which many of its members had a direct interest.[72]

In our discussion in this chapter we have noted the importance which the postindustrial theorists attach to the emergence of a not-for-profit sector in the new American political economy. In the context of their comments about the rise of a society in which public resources are purposely allocated on the basis of communal concern rather than business interest, their readers may be led to believe that the public or quasi-public, nonprofit or not-for-profit enterprise is the model for economic activity in the new society. However, our examination of the relation of the nonprofit organizations to the private profit enterprise sector leads to quite different conclusions. Rather than representing an independent force in the society, these organizations, from private foundations to quasi-public service organizations, today serve both as innovative explorers for government-supported military R & D, and for private investment in the public sector, in both its nondefense and defense segments,[73] as well as channels whereby government subsidies and guarantees of profits for such investment are first arranged and tested. The inverted image of their actual role which the "postindustrial" theorists of the "service state" suggest is but another instance of the functioning of that theory as an ideology of progressive change, rather than a critical analysis of contemporary developments.

Appendix

to

Chapter V

Military versus Civilian Government Expenditures in the Postwar Period

The conventional measurement of the impact of defense spending on the nation's economy has been to compare it to total national production (GNP). On this basis defense can be said to have absorbed "only" 10 percent of GNP since the early 1950s. As a percentage of GNP national defense expenditures grew from about 5 percent in the immediate postwar years (1946-50) to about 12 percent during the Korean War (1951-54), and since then have remained at a roughly constant 8 to 10 percent.[1] However, when measured against the total federal budget, defense expenditures accounted for 82 percent of purchases of goods and services by the federal government from 1946-67, as against 18 percent for nondefense expenditures. The total federal expenditure for defense purchases came to over $1,000 billion between 1946 and 1969,[2] with an average annual expenditure of $32 billion for 1946-55; $51 billion for 1956-65; and $70 billion for 1966-68. For 1969-72 direct defense expenditures had further risen to an estimated average of $79 billion.[3] As Lyle Fitch has observed, federal expenditures from 1960-66 for housing and community development amount to less than $2 billion, while spending for the space program amounted to over $25 billion, and defense and the Vietnam war received over $380 billion.[4]

Now, it might be argued, in response to those concerned with what they claim are inadequate expenditures for the civilian public sector,[5] that in fact since the mid-1950s these expenditures have risen to the point where they now surpass the total funds devoted to noncivilian expenditures (national defense, space, and foreign affairs). Budget estimates for fiscal 1972 place total civilian expenditures at a level of approximately $120 billion overall, or slightly more than six times the 1955 level. An estimated $84.6 billion was earmarked for "income maintenance," (an increase by a factor of almost 6 from 1955), and roughly equal to all noncivilian expenditures for 1972.[6] What, then, is the complaint of those who write of a "depleted society," and of large-scale "unmet social needs"?

Closer examination of such figures and their component elements, however, helps to explain the persisting concern of critics of government military spending regarding the misplacement of emphasis in our budgetary priorities. For example, while expenditures for housing and community development rose from under $0.5 billion in 1955 to an estimated $4.5 billion for 1972,[7] an increase of almost ten times, they were still more than $10 billion short of the estimated cost of a five-year program of replacement housing for substandard dwellings in existence in 1966; by 1972, it may be assumed that the gap will have been widened by the addition of other housing to the substandard category due to continued aging and overcrowding, particularly in ghetto and slum areas.[8]

In addition, it should be kept in mind that "community development" includes urban renewal programs, which have since the mid-1950s left a net deficit in dwelling units. The backlog of need in areas such as housing is so great that even the considerable increases in outlays of the 1960s fall far short of providing a program which will produce significant change in a short enough period to yield more than a mere shift in the locale of slums, and their subsequent deterioration. Since programs such as housing have in the past been funded at relatively low budgeting levels (under a billion dollars), the addition of several billion dollars means a 100 percent or greater increase in funding, without coming anywhere near the real level of need, which itself owes partly to prior long-standing budgetary neglect. Moreover, as any number of observers have commented, the provision of low-cost housing on a large scale could be enhanced by technical innovations in the building industry; the high costs and risks involved in R & D tend, however, to work against private R & D; yet total estimated expenditures by HUD for the conduct of research and development in 1970 amounted to about $20 million, as against approximately $8 billion for the Defense Department's military R & D, $4 billion for NASA, and about $1.5 billion for the AEC.[9]

At the same time, budgetary increases of less than 100 percent for items such as defense can mean added expenditure of sums as much as ten times the size of newly expanded civilian programs. Compare the approximately $35 billion increment in the defense budget during the Sixties with the $2 billion increment in housing-community development for the same period;

or with the $6 billion increment for education and manpower programs, or the $2.5 billion increment for health resources.[10] Furthermore, despite an increment of over 500 percent relative to the 1960 level, when measured against Melman's estimates the 1970 level of spending for education-manpower combined ($7.8 billion) falls over $15 billion short of what is needed to conduct education alone at an acceptable standard.[11]

If we direct our attention to the largest single item in the civilian budget, we find that "income maintance" grew by over 150 percent during the 1960s, from $25 billion to almost $65 billion.[12] In this case, the absolute size of the increment ($40 billion), as well as the percentage increase, are somewhat larger than the comparable figures for defense. However, we must take note of the fact that the greatest proportion of "income maintenance" consists of social security payments out of trust funds, and does not represent government purchases of goods or services in the civilian economy. Indirectly, of course, these transfer payments tend to stimulate the civilian economy, through discretionary purchases by recipients acting as individual consumers; *but in their present form they cannot be applied to the economy in any coordinated manner* for the purpose of development under any specific program, as, for example, federal programs specifically funded for development of educational or health services or housing, employment, or antipoverty action.

One important factor which has frustrated attempts to frame programs specifically directed toward developmental objectives in the civilian sector has been the structure of the federal budget itself. While total civilian expenditures as of 1970 had risen to slightly more than $90 billion (for income maintenance, human resources, physical-industrial resource development, and housing and community development), only about $20 billion of this amount was open to annual review and reallocation between programs. The other $70 billion, or about 80 percent, consisted of "uncontrollable" items not reviewable annually, such as transfer payments financed through permanent appropriations to individuals from social insurance trust funds or to states from highway trust funds; or "fixed charges" determined by basic statutes, e.g., public assistance, or veterans' benefits. This means that only a minor part of civilian expenditures can be re-allocated without major legislative changes. On the other hand, the currently more than $80 billion budget for defense is based on annual appropriations, and hence at least potentially "controllable."[13] (Despite this, little attention has been directed in the generation since WWII to close critical review of Defense Department budget requests. Of the approximately 500 personnel of the Budget Bureau only about 50 are assigned to review the defense budget, while the other 450-odd personnel scrutinize the $20 billion of "controllable" civilian budget items.)[14] A cut of only a little more than 10 percent of the defense budget would provide the estimated funds required to bring all households above the poverty level; while it would   require a cut of over 50 percent of civilian "controllables" to accomplish the same.[15] (Senator Proxmire cites the statement of the editors of *Congressional Quarterly*, based on interviews with Pentagon and industry officials, to the effect that the 1969 defense budget, for example, was heavily padded with inessentials, and that "$10.8 billion could have been cut . . . without in the slightest way impairing our level of national defense.")[16]

As Kenneth Boulding has pointed out, the adverse effects of the defense economy fall upon both the present generation and future generations. In the present generation they involve a relative withdrawal of goods and services from the domestic economy, such that from 1929 to 1969 the average household has been deprived of about 15-20 percent of "total potential purchases," while direct expenditures for defense have risen from 1 percent to 10 percent of GNP.[17] Even more serious than these effects on the consumer economy (which have been accompanied by inflationary pressures on prices and wages), has been the effect on the "grants economy" through which government has provided resources to vital areas such as education or industrial research and development. In Boulding's estimate, funding for education "needs to expand very rapidly in the coming years," partly because of the increasing cost of transmitting an expanding stock of knowledge, and partly because the productivity of education tends to rise very slowly. In regard to industrial R & D, "spillovers" from war industry to the civilian sector "are quite inadequate to compensate" for the drain of engineers and scientists into the defense sector, as evidenced "in transportation, in building, even in many of the areas of general manufacturing."[18] Thus whether the focus is on the welfare of the "poverty-class" or basic needs of the general civilian economy such as education and R & D, expenditures which preempt over 80 percent of the "controllable" segment of the federal budget will logically become the object of increasing attention and concern.

CHAPTER VI

Postindustrial America
and
Technocratic Planning

The problems which have led to the various conferences, coalitions, and commissions seeking solutions to the urban crisis are in many respects problems of planning. A complex set of interrelated developments has marked the first decades of postindustrial society as it has taken form in America, and found it in various ways relatively unprepared. Several structural transformations have occurred simultaneously, creating serious strains and conflicts in the social system. These include a major demographic transformation, involving both the growth and urbanization of total population, and the concentration of nonwhite population in the country's major central cities;[1] and the transformation of the occupational structure, resulting in the downgrading and displacement of unskilled and particularly lower blue-collar labor, and an emphasis on the training and reward of a new knowledge-oriented technocratic class capable of manipulating the "intellectual technology" which is the hallmark of the new society, as well as the rapid expansion of service occupations employment, relative to employment in the goods-producing industries. One of the problematic results of these trends has been the concentration of low-skilled, high-unemployment minorities in central cities, separated from access to whatever industrial growth has been taking place (increasingly located as such growth has been, in the developing suburban ring since the 1950s),[2] and unqualified for the newer service and professional-technical occupations even more in demand in urban centers. As a result, the growth of the "technocratic class" has been accompanied by the growing concentration in urban centers of a poverty class, producing serious pressure on social services and deterioration in the basic quality of urban life, as well as a pervading atmosphere of racial crisis. Despite the attractive possibilities of a purposively planning, future-oriented, "communal" direction for the "postindustrial" society, these potentialities seem to have been largely unrealized, fully two decades after the opening of the postindustrial era.

The Postindustrial State and Technocratic Planning

Since the early 1960s, the basic framework for social policy and planning has been the "new economics" of Keynesian derivation.[3] Economically this has meant that government would use its considerable taxing and spending powers to supplement total market demand when it was too low to support "full employment" (no more than 4 percent unemployment, based on the 1946 Employment Act), and to reduce total demand when it was so high as to create inflationary pressures. The immediate background to the acceptance of the "new economics" was the low rate of growth of Gross National Product and the rising unemployment which characterized the Eisenhower administration following the end of the Korean War in 1953, but particularly after 1956 during the second Eisenhower term.[4] Both the low growth rate and high unemployment of this period have been traced to the reduction in demand in 1957 and after, due mainly to the working-off of the early backlog of consumer demand in the decade after World War II, and the decline in industrial demand associated with the end of the Korean War. The net effect was a sharp decline in business investment; by 1962 business investment had "barely struggled back to its level in 1956."[5]

By the beginning of the 1960s various economic studies expressed concern about rising unemployment, increasingly frequent recessions, and the slow economic progress of the decade; in short, the major issue of domestic policy was now defined as economic growth.[6]

One of the major criticisms of the economic policies of the 1950s was that government had failed to take steps that would make possible the full utilization of the technological potential of the economy; as a result the actual performance of the economy had lagged behind its full performance potentials. In response to these findings, the Kennedy administration moved on a number of fronts to stimulate the growth of output and the reduction of unemployment, though with uneven success depending on the particular program. Measures enacted in 1962 provided investment credits and increased depreciation allowances to the business sector, the effect of which was probably felt in accelerated capital goods spending by mid-1963.[7] A variety of manpower training and guidance programs were initiated, aimed at reducing structural unemployment among the unskilled, the young, the elderly, and minority workers; however, "the distribution of unemployment was little changed." In addition, the existing pool of "highly skilled labor was not augmented significantly."[8] Several area and regional development programs, such as the Appalachia programs, were launched, providing increased sums of money for federal public works; however, this was "spread too thin over too many areas," and the focus of local development programs shifted to the urban ghettos, where their outcome was equally uncertain. At the same time, however, government expenditures for technological research and development grew rapidly, with the Kennedy administration accelerating the trends initiated after Sputnik in the late Eisenhower years. Most of this funding was for defense and space R & D, but its impact on total capital investments in advanced technology was great, accounting for over half the cost of all physical research in the nation.[9]

Yet, the really decisive economic step taken by the Kennedy administration was the major tax cut enacted in 1963. Though recovery from the recession of 1960-61 seems to have begun by mid-1962, the economy gave signs of stalling again. The choice before the Kennedy administration seemed fairly clear: either a signficant tax reduction to stimulate business investment as recommended by the Council of Economic Advisors, or expanded government spending as proposed by Professor Galbraith, Kennedy's economic advisor at large. The choice of the tax cut seems finally to have been grounded in political considerations, such as the lack of congressional support for increased domestic nondefense spending, coupled with the opportunity to induce Congress to accept tax reform in exchange for always popular tax reduction.[10]

Theoretically, the only difference between a tax cut and an increase in government domestic spending is that in the first case, increases in purchasing power and in investment capital are made available *via* tax savings to private consumers and business firms, while in the second, government uses tax resources it has collected from the private sector to provide economic stimulus through expenditures for public programs. In either case, aggregate demand should increase, stimulating increases in Gross National Product and reducing unemployment toward and even beyond full-employment levels.[11] While fiscal policy can thus be employed "to regulate the volume of investment and effective demand" the specific social impact will differ with the choice of the particular policy of demand management. This is fairly clear with regard, for example, to the tax policies of the Kennedy-Johnson administration, which aimed at converting American business to the "new economics" (thus breaking its long embrace with the Republican party) [12] largely by way of government subsidization of investment through credits, tax reductions, liberalized depreciation allowances, and government contracts, leaving the basic investment decisions essentially in private hands. Undeniably, the result was the stimulation of aggregate demand, rising earnings for corporate business and rising employment, wages, and salaries for semiskilled and professional workers (though the inflation of the past few years has tended to cut into the real incomes of these workers). At the same time, however, these new governmental incentives to private investment spurred goods-producing industries, such as mining and manufacturing, to intensify their programs of labor-saving capitalization. In return, this further cut their need for low and semiskilled labor, thereby increasing problems of manpower displacement and unemployment at these levels of the labor force, even while overall employment grew during most of the Kennedy-Johnson era.[13] The irony is that governmental policies designed to stimulate economic growth have contributed to employment and disemployment patterns which fostered increasing social inequality (particularly as manifested in urban racial conflict) in the absence of programs sufficient in scale to correct these social byproducts of the "new partnership" of business and government.

Compounding these problems was the fiscal policy of the Johnson administration during the middle and later years of its involvement in the Vietnam War (1966 through 1968). President Johnson's budget for fiscal 1967, submitted in January 1966, underestimated defense spending by about $10 billion, and again the budget estimates for the following fiscal year were low by at least $5 billion.[14] As one major economist notes, "the excise taxes would not have been cut in the summer of 1965 had there been advance knowledge of the war's economic impact." In this view, the appropriate manner in which to finance the war at that point "should have been a broad across-the-board tax increase" by early 1966. However, "taxes were not increased because the President could not get the American people to pay for the war."[15] Resistance to a tax increase was sufficiently strong to delay the tax surcharge obtained in mid-1968 by about a year. In the interim, "demand became excessive" and inflation boomed, while international financial crises multiplied. This whittled away at the postwar economic gains of all groups, but was apparently felt most sharply among lower-income groups[16] and probably intensified the reaction among the white working and lower-middle classes against "anti-poverty" programs apparently constructed mainly for the sake of the black poor, one rung down the economic ladder). Once again, as in the Kennedy administration, fiscal policy was not determined simply on technical-administrative considerations. In pursuit of business support for his administration, Kennedy had resorted to a tax cut favored by business circles and their congressional allies in order to stimulate the economy; Johnson, seeking, if nothing more, at least continued acquiescence for his Vietnam policy, resorted to massive governmental borrowing, rather than to increased taxes, to fund a growingly unpopular war. (The result was first an enormous government deficit, followed belatedly by measures taken a year later aimed at correcting the deficit *via* the surcharge tax of 1967-68, and second, a growing inflation which persisted through various deflationary measures taken by the Nixon administration; the latter having as one effect the increase of unemployment up to and beyond the 6 percent rate, and as high as 15 and 20 percent in the black ghettos.) The political context, in Congress and in the public, was directly relevant to these economic decisions, and it also influenced the relative emphasis placed upon the funding of domestic as against military public sector programs. Put in terms of the postindustrial theorists' formula, the direction and social impact of technocratic planning in the Sixties came to be seriously modified by the politics of influential interest groups, ranging from corporate management to "state management." However, this took the form less of a clash between two irreconcilable modes of governmental decision making — planning *versus* bargaining — than of an interpenetration and complex synthesis between them.

The unevenness of this synthesis between interest bargaining and modern administrative-state planning has long been apparent in the work of the "new liberals" of the postwar period, and is fairly clear in the evolving thought of a theorist like John Galbraith. Galbraith in the mid-1950s suggested that the mechanism of "countervailing power," when combined with conscious support from government to disadvantaged groups, would assure a reasonably equitable distribution of the social product.[17] By the mid-1960s, however, Galbraith's emphasis had basically shifted from the relations between group interest bargaining and "countervailing power" to the emergent role of the administrative state in assuring a healthy economic climate for the productive activities of the "mature segment of the corporate sector." In this perspective, Galbraith viewed the new industrial state as one in which there exists an informal but significant working partnership between government and the technocratic industrial system, with government providing a series of vital services for industry, such as the regulation of aggregate demand, the underwriting of advanced technological research and development, and the subsidy of the educational system which supplies vital skilled manpower to the economy. This amounts to a major departure from the notion of "semiautomatic balance" suggested by the earlier countervailing power theory.[18] The automatic balancing of the claims of diverse groups upon the society's economic product becomes less important in the expanding techno-industrial state than the growth of gross economic product; government's role becomes less one of insuring a relatively stable balance between different interests, than of actively fostering overall economic growth through stimulation of the corporate and military sectors; and with this, its role in the economy becomes more direct and more conscious than ever before.[19]

By the mid-1960s a certain amount of practical experience with regard to fiscal management of the economy had been acquired. To that point, the major policy questions which could appropriately be raised had to do largely with the stimulation of aggregate demand. Should such stimulation be approached through tax cuts and investment credits for the private sector, or through increased spending in the public sector;[20] and if the latter, what should be the orientation of government spending with respect to emphasis on military as against nonmilitary programs? In addition to these questions a new set of policy issues was at the same time being raised through the work of social critics and social scientists concerned with the problem of persisting poverty under conditions of relatively low total unemployment. This discussion was directed toward the problem of deeply-rooted geographic and structural pockets of poverty, and the seeming inability of conventional Keynesian demand stimulation to reach these hard-core unemployed and bring them into the labor force.[21]

Technocratic Planning and the Technology Commission

Perhaps the best example of the response of pluralist-technocratic planning to these questions is represented by the Report of the National Commission on Technology, Automation, and Economic Progress, published in February 1966.[22] This report is revealing for the emphases it strikes, and the blind spots it overlooks. The central theme adopted is that of the remarkable contemporary acceleration of technological innovation and diffusion. In its wake, technological change has brought new products, new services, new occupations, and new industries, and with these the benefits of abundance, innovation, and leisure. At the same time, however, technology has had a harmful impact on various aspects of environmental and community life, ranging from pollution and congestion to the depletion of natural resources. But the one most pressing concern, "perhaps the one most responsible for the establishment of the Commission," involved the connection of technological change with the emergence of a "substantial and persistent unemployment," in the decade preceding the publication of the report.[23]

Technological advance resulting in advancing mechanization of industry and agriculture had been clearly reflected in the high productivity of the postwar labor force; measured in output per man-hour, productivity in the private economy since shortly after World War II had been increasing at a three percent annual rate as against two percent annually over the preceding 35 years. In addition, the postwar growth of population had meant a growing labor force; together, increased productivity and increasing labor force spelled the need to substantially expand the creation of new jobs to achieve and maintain full employment. In connection with the basic aim of full employment, the Commission was concerned with the impact of technological change on production and employment, such as "new job requirements and the major types of worker displacement ... likely to occur during the next 10 years."[24] In order to satisfy new requirements for jobs and to remedy the effects of labor displacement, the Commission recommended innovative combinations of public and private effort under government leadership at federal and local levels, with important roles to be played by universities and nonprofit institutions.[25] Precisely what forms these public-private combinations would take were not spelled out in the body of the report, though some of the annotated comments by particular Commission members identified the broad forms these might involve.

Basic to the Commission's perspective was the observation that occupational displacement "is implicit in the natural history of economic development,"[26] from "primary" production of basic materials such as food, minerals and fibers, to "secondary" production of manufactured goods, to "tertiary" production of a widening variety of services; and that the main reason for the change in the structure of the American labor force is probably "the rapid growth of those industries — education, finance, insurance, health, and business services — which employ predominantly white-collar and professional workers."[27] As in the estimates cited by Barber, the requirements of the goods sector were projected as declining from about 40 percent of total employment to about 35 percent, while the service sector was seen as rising from about 60 percent to 65 percent over the period 1964 to 1975.[28] The Commission projected a relative decline in the need for blue-collar laborers and factory workers, while the largest increases in employment requirements would be for white-collar workers and particularly professional-technical workers.[29]

The favoring of highly skilled white-collar occupations in the developing trends of employment will probably have serious negative effects on nonwhite employment; for "if non-whites continue to hold the same proportion of jobs in each occupation as in 1964," i.e., with the highest concentration in low and semi-skilled jobs, "the non-white unemployment rate in 1975 will be more than five times that for the labor force as a whole. . . ."[30] Equally disturbing (yet given relatively little emphasis in the Commission report or in discussions in the public media), was the estimate that already unsatisfactory employment opportunities for younger workers (ages 14-24) will be shrinking as we move to the mid-1970s, assuming that "all occupations have the same composition by age in 1975 as in 1964."[31]

In brief, technological change leading to a "postindustrial," services-oriented society is intrinsic, and hence inevitable, in the developmental processes of advanced society. Such changes bring certain material benefits and potentials for further abundance, but at the same time involve the displacement of certain older categories of labor located in the primary and secondary industries, and the opening of opportunities for newer categories of labor in the tertiary sector.

How shall American society deal with this mixture of potential social-economic opportunities, costs, and benefits? The Commission had a number of substantive recommendations, which it put forward under the heading of "creating an environment for adjustment to change." With respect to employment and income policies, it recommended that the government continue in its role of managing total demand for goods and services, and assumed that this would suffice to provide "ample job opportunities and adequate incomes" for "those with reasonably attractive skills and no other serious competitive handicaps."[32] Though it made no specific recommendation for the *direction* of fiscal and monetary policy in the way of priorities in spending, the Commission suggested "some combination of tax reduction . . . and increased public expenditure"[33] with a target of no more than 3.5 percent general unemployment by early 1967. For those in the labor market "less able to compete," they recommended the creation of public service jobs in medical, educational, and welfare institutions, as well as in urban renewal and environmental services. In these various areas, the Commission estimated a potential of about 5¼ million jobs, many of which would be "in the State and local sector of the public economy."[34] Funding and overall administration would come through a federal agency created for the purpose, and wages paid would be no lower than the federal minimum. The program could be coupled with training and counseling for improving the skills of its employees and upgrading them occupationally.

None of these several aspects of the Commission's economic program were very original. The demand-management proposals were essentially an abstraction from governmental experience of the preceding decade in the use of fiscal policy to adjust overall economic demand; while the public service proposal had for its precedent the public works programs of the New Deal.[35] The major innovations of the Commission's recommendations regarding problems of employment or economics lay in another area; that of income maintenance. Here, beyond suggesting improvements in wage-related social insurance programs (such as increasing coverage, benefit levels, and benefit periods), the Commission broke new ground with its recommendation for a "negative income-tax" program which would assure a minimum annual income as a "floor" under family income for those who "cannot or should not participate in the job economy." This recommendation was made in light of the fact that public assistance programs reach less than one-quarter of the persons living in poverty; moreover, that they discourage work incentives by, in effect, placing 100 percent tax on additional family earnings above the allotted assistance. The negative tax proposal could be designed instead to preserve work incentive by only partially reducing the income allowance in line with a formula related to increases in earned income. The total cost of such a scheme for income maintenance could vary widely, between an annual level of $2 billion and one of $20 billion, depending on the income "floor" established. A "medium-cost" program, which would eliminate 50 percent of the gap between family income and the currently defined poverty level for the aggregate of families below the poverty line, would cost "between $5 and $8 billion per year."[36]

As the Commission report indicated, the minimum-income allowance is intended as one prong of a two-pronged attack on the various "unmet needs" which arise in a "predominantly private enterprise society."[37] Minimum income maintenance addresses itself to the "private needs of low-income people who are unable to buy housing and necessary services"; the other set of needs are "the public needs ... not readily available in private markets." These needs are related to the growth of a densely settled urban environment and its collective requirements and problems, ranging from pollution, transportation, and crime, to health, education, and housing. "Why have not these needs been met?" inquire the Commission members, and their response is itself interesting for the clues it gives to the social technocrats' strategy for action. Ostensibly, the failure to meet these needs follows *not* from any lack of a basic political consensus on them; the Commission was quite explicit in its assumption (stated without any accompanying evidence from sources such as public opinion studies) that there already exists in the public a "general consensus" on the appropriateness of addressing these various "human and community needs."[38] Nor did the Commission consider the problem essentially one of basic technological obstacles; in support of this "conviction" the report points to the "spectacular achievements in military technology and our success in the conquest of space."[39] The real problem, from the Commission's perspective, is to translate into specific technological-administrative programs the assumed general agreement on meeting civilian public needs; this will involve the development of "criteria to recognize which technologies can give us adequate performance," together with identification of remaining barriers to technological change and the finding of "technical strategies" with which to overcome them, in areas ranging from health to pollution to urban transit.[40]

Of particular interest here is the related concept of a national system of "social accounts" which would supplement the present system of national economic accounts. Such a system would set up "performance budgets" as yardsticks of accomplishment in a variety of public sector areas, and would incorporate indicators of social mobility and economic opportunity to analyze the status of various groups in the society, particularly members of disadvantaged minorities. It would also seek to assess, through the appropriate indicators, the social costs and benefits of technological changes, as well as the costs of social problems to the society.[41] In this respect, the Technology Commission's Report dovetails with the social indicators "movement" which was percolating and coming to the surface at about the same time, just as the Johnson administration moved into mid-term.

Technocratic Planning and "Social Intelligence"

Like the social indicators movement, discussed earlier in chapter 1 in our review of the notion of a politics based on advanced "social intelligence," there is a tendency in the Commission's work to assume that "postindustrial," "technological" society, because it has the technical means to monitor its own performance, can feed this information back to crucial institutional decision points so as to correct economic, political, and related social behavior and thereby assure the achievement of a variety of societal goals.[42] This notion of the postindustrial society technically self-guided on a stable course of progressive expansion — a society whose sociopolitical controls are set, in a sense, on an "automatic pilot" which quickly and accurately corrects for deviations from course — follows from the original technocratic premises of the postindustrial theory.[43]

Perhaps the most significant projection of the Technology Commission's report is that future technological progress "will come not only from machines, but from what has been called the 'intellectual technology'," based on computerized techniques of systems analysis, simulation, operations research, cost-benefit analysis, etc., all of which taken together are referred to as "the systems approach."[44] This approach implies "comprehensive planning," employing actual performance criteria rather than preexisting models, and seeks the optimum mix of facilities and resources to solve system problems. The report emphasizes that none of this is really "radical or new"; that the systems approach has been employed in the Department of Defense "most effectively" for several years; and that "program budgeting," which is an application of the systems approach, has already been successfully employed in "the reorganization of defense forces."[45] Once again this is reminiscent of Daniel Bell's notion that the "technical decision making" developed in the military agencies would inevitably spill over into and usefully affect the nature of decision making in the civilian public agencies.[46]

How shall we approach the chain of assertions and assumptions embodied in this report? One might take up and discuss each one, point for point, but this would be a tedious and ultimately unenlightening task, since considered in and of themselves, i.e., within the given framework of recommendations for technical self-correction of the operation of the political economy, the list is at least "reasonable." Though we will comment on a number of specific points, what is more important is the problem of the political framework in which "comprehensive planning" is to take place, and the question whether in fact such planning is comprehensive and from whose standpoint.

In an essay reviewing the experience of the Technology Commission, published shortly after the release of its report in 1966, Bell provides us with some insight into the political context for such planning, and some clues as to its possible limits. After discussing the report's substantive recommendations he goes on to note several aspects of the recently expanded role of such government commissions. Today, "as mechanisms of the Executive Branch," they "provide a means for the direct representation of functional constituencies in the advisory process." This is appropriate to the "increasing tendency for the American polity to be organized in functional terms" reflecting the interests of particular occupational groups.[47] Furthermore, government commissions, such as the Technology Commission, serve as media for exploring the limits of action within the context of various political bodies and as public relations channels, much like the "independent" citizens groups of yore "which served as 'fronts' for government-desired policies." Finally, they serve as forums for "elite participation" in formulating government policy; in fact, the "distinctive virtue" of such commissions is the "specific effort to involve the full range of *elite or organized opinion* in order to see if a *real consensus* can be achieved."[48]

These comments help clear up the nature of the Technology Commission as well as some obvious contradictions in its report. We can now clearly recognize that the commission was a consciously constructed instrument of elite-pluralist discussion and policy exploration. Put another way, it was a pluralist forum for the shaping of elite consensus between representatives of different organized functional or political pressure groups; counting its chairman, the commission was composed of five representatives of business, three of labor, four from the universities, one civil rights spokesman, and one representative of the liberal professional community. Interestingly, the only civil rights representative — Whitney Young — came from an organization (Urban League) which has traditionally specialized in providing services to the black community, rather than playing the role of political representative. Leaders of even relatively "established" political pressure organizations, like NAACP and SCLC, were absent, not to speak of the more "militant" organizations such as CORE and SNCC. The linkage to the executive elite was provided by an "interagency advisory committee" composed of ten government agency heads, including the secretaries of Commerce, Labor, HEW and Defense.

Particularly interesting from our viewpoint is the fact that even among this fairly carefully chosen collection of leaders and representatives of established organizations, none of whom could be seriously described as a current day ideological "militant," there were evidences of basic disagreement, particularly with regard to long-term recommendations concerning technological development and its social impact. At the very outset, in the comments appended to the first chapter on "The Pace of Technological Change" and its consequences, the committee split between business representatives on one side and union leaders and civil rights-liberal professionals on the other; with the academics (a group including Daniel Bell, then of Columbia) and relatively "liberal" business leaders (Watson of IBM and Land of Polaroid) refraining from comment. The representatives of labor and their civil rights and liberal co-commentators complained that "the report lacks the tone of urgency" required with regard to job creation and full-employment programs.[49] In these comments, the "functional group" leaders, who spoke particularly for blue-collar workers and ghetto dwellers, expressed endorsement of aggregate-demand policies for expanding private sector employment and of public sector policies which could supplement aggregate-demand policies. Their argument was that public service employment could provide jobs and income for those workers who had "fallen out" of the private labor market due to low skill, discrimination, age, and like factors. At the same time, it would provide needed services and facilities to urban centers, particularly to low-income areas in need of improved housing, health care, educational services, etc. In their closing comments, they emphasized the belief that economic means exist for solving the problems connected with technological change and that "the obstacles to their solution are essentially political," owing to a lack of urgent commitment comparable to that involved in our military efforts.[50]

Two of the business leaders, on the other hand, complained that the report "fails to give adequate emphasis to the positive contributions of technology," and reminded the reader of the role of technological progress in bringing the United States "the highest standards of material welfare . . . ever before . . . achieved.[51] What they were driving at was the reassurance that further mechanization, and particularly automation, "represents a logical extension of this 200-year-long history of technological progress. . . ." They tended much more readily to accept as inevitable the *fact* of occupational dislocation while refusing to acknowledge the "inevitability of the *hardships* of dislocations" which they felt could be adequately cushioned by programs of *relief* for individuals affected by technological dislocation; through such programs, they hoped that "resistance to change can be reduced and further technological progress promoted."[52]

In this exchange it is the business leaders (particularly the more conservative two on the committee, Sporn and Haggerty) who endorse "postindustrial" technological development, specifically in the form of automation, and accept the likelihood of large-scale reduction of employment in the goods-producing industries, without an equal emphasis on expanding services-related employment. Apparently, they are content that between fiscal demand-management and some "vigorous programs" of relief ("income maintenance" in the Commission's terminology) the income needs of the growing labor force can be met. (It is in this light that we interpret the trend of Nixon administration domestic policies toward an underwriting of a minimal income maintenance program, together with considerable reluctance to endorse the principle of government as an "employer of last resort" through the provision of public sector jobs.)[53] The other leadership groups, representing the interests of inner-city and working-class populations (whose social class and occupational base are still linked to the industrial system now undergoing such rapid change), place their first emphasis on the provision of employment and income-via-employment, and would like to strengthen the hand of the public sector in providing employment to a new "public service" working class.[54]

The nature of the differences aired in this debate, and the subsequent fate of those Commission recommendations on which there did appear to be consensus, should caution us against any simplistic image of a technocratically guided, automatically self-correcting society. Even though the Commission omitted from the main text of its report several recommendations for stimulating employment favored by its more liberal members, its report was considered too controversial for the Johnson administration to identify with, and was "brushed . . . temporarily under the rug," according to Bell's own later account.[55] Despite Bell's apparent expectations that this would be only "temporary," the report remained buried throughout the later part of the Johnson administration, as the problem of aggregate demand was relieved for the private sector, and the focus of attention shifted to the inflationary impact of spending on the Vietnam War.

Under the Nixon administration, the proposals for expanded public service employment were accepted only with great hesitancy after an earlier veto, under pressure of unemployment going beyond a 6 percent level. (Proposals for public works programs, on the other hand, were kept on the shelf ostensibly because of the relatively long time lag involved in their impact on employment.[56]) Moreover, this administration, apparently prepared to accept a higher stable level of long-term "hardcore" unemployment than the 3.5-4.0 percent discussed by the Commission, rejected full employment measures resembling those proposed by the Commission. Instead, it identified itself with an income maintenance program as its major response to long-term unemployment, thus pursuing a policy line like that of the conservative business leaders on the Commission. Yet even here all did not go smoothly, since under the pressure of severe unemployment coupled with persisting inflation, Nixon finally opted for a tax cut to stimulate private investment; at the same time, showing concern for the possible inflationary impact, he ordered sharp cutbacks in government spending. As a consequence, the income maintenance program, apparently the most dispensable of Nixon's major domestic policy initiatives, was put back on the administration's program calendar by a year, and even the revenue-sharing program, his prime creation, was slated for a delay of at least several months.

Contrary to Bell's optimistic notions about the technocrats' ability to "invent the future," the flux of politics often tends to pick up this proposal or that program from the context of a reasonably coherent set of recommendations, and carry it on to be legislated and somehow implemented, while leaving the rest on the shelf or "under the rug." The technocrats (at least at this point in history) propose their plans while the play of important interests disposes of them, constructing through legislation and executive action a fragmented *pastiche* which reflects the resolution of a series of changing crises with shifting foci of attention, rather than the coherence or comprehensiveness projected by technocratic planners. Even the pluralist "consensus," based on bargaining between organizational elites which these planners take as premise for the representative "democratic" character of their planning, falls short of its ostensible representativeness. As organized labor follows agriculture into the position of a subsidized interest-elite with a narrowing base (unless and until it can organize white-collar and public sector employees on a scale to compensate for the incursions of mechanization and automation upon its predominantly blue-collar rank and file),[57] the field is left open to a new kind of political-economic partnership between business and government which may replace even the elite-pluralism which the technocratic theorists equate with liberal democracy. Out of mutual interest, these new partners seek to create a controllable quasi-public sector which can progressively augment the private service sector in taking up the slack of the traditional goods-producing industries as a source of jobs and markets.

Among other things, it appears that what remains to be worked out for the near future is the balance between the size of the military as against civilian segments of the new public sector; in good measure, this will depend upon the respective technologies and political weights of contending corporate interests, and the degree to which these diverse interests can be satisfied by government investment in military R & D and hardware as against civilian public services. However, at this point, the technocrats' projections of a rapid growth of public service employment in the context of public or "nonprofit"' institutions serving the public sector seems less likely of early realization than arrangements in which private enterprise is induced by offers of tax credits, write-offs, and other incentives to enter neglected public services or facilities areas at a profit; or, if not so tempted, to wait patiently for another military crisis and expanded defense spending.

Technocratic Planning and "Liberal-Pluralism"

In the light of our review of the recommendations of the Technology Commission and the political obstacles to their implementation, it seems entirely illusory for technocratic administrative-state liberals to pretend that "comprehensive planning" or even comprehensive cost accounting can proceed, except in very small and restricted areas, under these circumstances.[58] The fact is that despite the faith they place in social indicators, program budgeting, executive-government commissions, and the "systems approach," interest group claims and conflicts are very much alive, though taking on new forms. The attempt of academic liberals like Bell to overcome the "failure of liberalism" (as he put it in a recent article)[59] by way of gathering superior intelligence about the system and providing government with more sophisticated models and plans for managing and developing it, seems bound to run up against the pluralist interest core of American liberalism which was crystallized earlier in this century and still persists today.[60]

In order to more fully appreciate the implications of this conflict of political modes, it is helpful to turn briefly to the work of Robert Dahl and Charles Lindblom, published in the early 1950s, concerning the relations between modern pluralism and the emerging possibilities for planning.[61]

The political point of departure for the work of Dahl and Lindblom is similar to that of Bell and Lipset, i.e., the observation that in matters of the organization of the political economy, "the 'great issues' are no longer the great issues . . . ," and the problem of social reform is not one of a choice between "grand alternatives," such as socialism or capitalism, planning or nonplanning, but rather one of a choice of "particular techniques" as devices of social policy.[62] Furthermore, like the end-of-ideologists, what the authors perceived in the early postwar discussions of social planning and social reform was "an emerging agreement on appropriate social techniques," among conservatives, liberals, and socialists, "of extraordinary significance for the social sciences and for the possibilities of rational politico-economic action."[63]

Despite their strong emphasis on the importance of techniques, these theorists were keenly aware of the need to take into account the realities of the political situation. For the mere discovery of new social techniques is not in itself sufficient to insure their utilization; application of techniques clearly is "a matter of politics."[64] Thus, "whether a nation can achieve rational politico-economic organization depends not only upon the particular economic techniques it employs but upon the political and economic literacy of its citizens, their faiths and attitudes. . . ."[65] The limits to rational policy making are a function not merely of the imaginativeness of the social technician, but also of the general nature of the political culture in which he works. The political culture and the institutional structures which it reflects and influences are prior conditions to the social techniques that are themselves prerequisite to rational planning.

In the case of the American political economy, Dahl and Lindblom identify the capitalist competitive price system,[66] bureaucratic administration ("hierarchy"),[67] democratic controls ("polyarchy"),[68] and interest bargaining[69] as the major dimensions of political-economic relationships which set the context for social policy making. These "central sociopolitical processes" affect both the social calculation and the control of the various resources required for implementing any given social policy or program. What these authors emphasize is that the *key* mode of arriving at political consensus in a pluralist society is interest bargaining between the leaders of organized groups. This in turn has historically set limits to the kind of social planning which could be undertaken in twentieth-century America, since in a political context characterized by interest bargaining, planning can only be a piecemeal affair of "making relatively small adjustments in existing reality,"[70] or what is known as "incrementalism." However, this limitation is quite acceptable to these theorists since incrementalism, as a policy mode which seeks to remain within the limits of the predictable in making change, reflects a "basic commitment to rational calculation"; by contrast, "holistic," "utopian" change, which is large-scale and encompasses the entire system, is by nature the "antithesis of rational calculation." Large changes (such as the reforms of the New Deal era) are made by incrementalists only as "calculated risks" and only under the pressure of severe crisis.[71]

For Dahl and Lindblom, writing in the postwar period when the gap between the public and private sector had already been bridged through various government programs and various forms of advisory policy contact between government and the business community, politico-economic "techniques" essentially meant experimentation on a limited scale with new organizational arrangements of a "mixed" or public-private type.[72] Writing in the period just prior to the revolution in "intellectual technology" and the rise of the "systems approach," which are both related to advances in computer development and application, these authors could have no idea of the possibilities which such technology would present with regard to the objective of comprehensive planning. Though they represent a sophisticated culminating statement of modern liberal-pluralism, the bases of their position are relatively simple compared to the expectations and visions of the postindustrial theorists regarding the application of computerized "social intelligence" to social planning. While both Dahl-Lindblom and Bell-Lipset can certainly be described as sharing the perspective of the "end of ideology," and specifically, the expectation that public problems can be resolved through "mixed" public-private arrangements, they are far apart on the possibilities of even a partially comprehensive system of national planning in a democratic society. For the liberal-pluralists Dahl and Lindblom, skeptical of either the possibility or desirability of large-scale national planning, the central problem is how far the hierarchic principle of bureaucratic administration connected with the modern state can be allowed to modify the principle of social pluralism, in the interest of arriving at new integrative social forms in a dynamically expanding large-scale society.[73] For the end-of-ideologists, on the other hand, far more confident of the possibilities for planning, the focus of concern, and the specific ideological element in their work has been their interest in

joining sophisticated social technique and intellectual technology with
authoritative central administration in the formulation of social policy,
since they view central administrative decision making as both more
rational and more politically representative of the general public interest
than traditional pluralist processes. As contemporary discussions of planning make clear, essential elements required for social planning include
the intellectual calculation of resources with reference to societal needs
and goals, and the corresponding social control of resource allocation.[74]
In part then, the strategy of the end-of-ideologists is to strengthen the
framework for planning by fostering the new postwar intellectual technologies which facilitate the translation of political decisions into quantitative, economically useful terms.[75] What is complicating in their position, however, is the fact that, despite their attachment to "rational
planning," as liberal-pluralists they also advocate the incorporation of
organized interests *directly* into administrative policy making; this, it
seems, would even further complicate the already complex problem of
structuring into the administrative planning process a communal "welfare
function" which adequately reflects the public interest. The direct incorporation of the most powerful private interests into the planning mechanism would only add to the tendencies toward "corporatism" which have
been developing at least since the New Deal in the relations between
government and private interests; and the new trends toward government-
business "partnership" in particular have to be understood in this light.
Most clearly in the area of domestic, nonmilitary policy making, interest
group liberalism has tended to favor the parcelling out of the powers
of government to established, organized, and powerful private parties. In
effect, modern twentieth-century "liberal-pluralism" has worked out the
institutional structures and the theoretical sanctions for providing powerful private interests direct access to central administration, both in the
making of policy and in its interpretation and execution. In the process,
it has denied its own roots as a system of equal protection for individual
rights, particularly the social-economic rights which are the distinctive
development of the twentieth century,[76] and has become an ideology
which rationalizes the technologically sophisticated corporatist sharing of
power primarily between postindustrial governmental and business elites,
and secondarily between these elites and the residual elites which derive
from key interests of the preindustrial and industrial periods, such as
farmers and industrial labor. We will discuss some of the institutional
structures intended by technocratic planners as mechanisms for "system
guidance," and examine them with regard to their latent function as instruments for corporatist policy making, in the following section and as
relevant points in chapter 8.

System Guidance and the "Active Society"

As we have noted, the end-of-ideologists, as theorists and ideologists of technocratic planning, seek to foster the application of scientific method to the design and development of social organization and policy in government agencies, local communities, and the society as a whole. Apparently, these technocratic ideologists tend to place ultimate faith in the ability of central state administration, equipped with comprehensive knowledge about the society and its institutions, to function authoritatively *vis à vis* private interests in the political arena. Such knowledge can be obtained from the systematic collection and analysis of "social indicators" which measure social conditions quantitatively, and which can be utilized in the planning process for the design or re-design of organizational structure or resource policy with respect to given social units. Supposedly, a system of administrative state planning using social indicators is both practical and persuasive because it is based on objective measures of the impact of social policies stated in terms of quantitative criteria of actual system performance. In this sense, then, in the statistically oriented society of later twentieth-century America, the political strategy of the technocratic planners is based upon a "politics of statistics." These statistics will be "social indicators," purposively chosen to accurately reflect the gap between the impact of particular social policies and specific social targets and goals. In this way, using complex information on the state of the social system and of its subsystems, policy makers can orient their decisions as to future investment of resources and design of programs. As a number of proponents of such a scheme have stated, a system like this would aim to avoid being one-dimensional. In particular, it would seek to go beyond merely economic measures of performance, and look to the social qualities of the system in relation to economic variables, on one hand; and to the special cultural interests and needs of sub-cultural groups, on the other.[77]

Several recent models which incorporate the resulting notion of "social systems accounting," are those of Daniel Bell, Bertram Gross, and Amitai Etzioni.[78] Bell's model tends to confine itself to the nature of the accounting system itself, in terms of the kinds of information which it would be desirable to collect through such a system. His discussion of the political-administrative system which would utilize this information is implicit and scattered in various writings; we have touched on it in part in our examination of the notion of "government by commission" and the concept of a "systems approach" to be pursued in the operations of governmental agencies. These are, however, only elements, not explicitly an integrated system of social action based upon social information. The work of Gross and Etzioni, on the other hand, does look to the problem of creating an explicit model of the systems into which social accounting would be incorporated and utilized as a basis for social action.

Gross's work is helpful in that it specifies the components of a system of consciously guided social action in terms of presently existing, somewhat familiar social interests and institutions; it is a pragmatic theory which begins from society at present and looks to negotiating the passage into the future, through the conscious construction of change-oriented planning institutions.

The social subsystem which Gross specifies as necessary for integrated system action on social information is what he calls the "guidance system." This is a "special subsystem with responsibility, authority, and power for system guidance." Very generally, this corresponds to what we know as the modern state; however, Gross seeks to be more specific, and identifies the societal "guidance system" with an idealized model of "the central control system of central government."[79] This system would be composed of a "complex cluster of interrelated subsystems," roughly as follows: (a) "General Leadership Roles," including the chief political executive and his planning advisors, together with a national planning authority and some executive organ through which key interest groups would be directly represented; (b) "Financial Management Roles," including fiscal and monetary policy managers, plus accounting and auditing managers; (c) "Critical Problem Roles," divided between military services management and program management in problem areas such as unemployment or utilization and development of natural resources; (d) "Special Staff Roles," such as staffs analyzing social trends and making policy recommendations; and (e) "General Staff Roles," involving "consensus building," communications with interest groups and between guidance subsystems, and expediting the flow of work between these elements.[80] Some of these roles already exist in the society-in-transition to self-guidance, others may have to be further developed, or created anew. Despite the formalization of these roles which is suggested by explicitly differentiating them on paper, Gross observes that they will inevitably be "associated with a variety of informal, ritualistic, or ceremonial roles,"[81] and that some actors in the guidance subsystem will play several roles at once, while others may specialize in a given role. This kind of contrast will probably describe not only the difference in role repertoire between general and special staff roles, but also between general leadership roles and the more purely financial or problem-management roles.

Perhaps because he is a realist about the informal side of formally conceived management roles, Gross does not do much to specify precisely how these several role clusters will relate to one another in his "guidance system." What he does indicate is that these relations will probably, "as with any system," be marked by "both integration and conflict."[82] He does not assume that administration and politics can be set against one another as opposite or opposed modes of behavior; politics is pervasive, within central administration as in any other subsystem of the society, and the social analyst will do well to take account of this. In answer to the "inevitable problem" of "who shall coordinate the coordinators?" within the central guidance system itself, Gross shuns the simple answer of "hierarchy," or control by top executives, as inadequate to the complexity of this multifaceted system. The internal controls which are required are less formal and more spontaneous, and will depend on the kind of informal understandings which come about only quite gradually between the "highly competitive and politically sensitive" subsystems of the overall guidance cluster. In discussing the relations of the central "guidance system" with other subsystems in the society, Gross again acknowledges some basic realities of contemporary executive policy making; particularly the tendency for close informal relationships to develop between the executive bureaucracy and key interest groups of the society as a means of circumventing formal political representatives such as the Congress and developing direct lines of communication with various social interests, as well as facilitating the acquisition of "feedback" on the results of government policies.[83]

It is in this light that we can understand both the governmental commissions (as a link to specific organizations and interests), and the community action agencies (as a link to various communities and their change-oriented actors). The result of developing these direct linkages, unmediated by formal representative bodies, is "to recreate within the central guidance cluster the group conflicts and value conflicts within society as a whole."[84] In this way, executive-technocratic politics tries to assure itself the vital elements, not only of information, but also of a forum for interest bargaining among key social groups, by building into itself a replica (albeit with considerable distortion) of the most important and influential interest configurations in the society.

For another interesting perspective on "societal guidance" we may turn to Amitai Etzioni who provides us with an abstract and suggestive model which bears close examination for its similarities and differences to that developed by Gross. Etzioni describes the major components of such a system and their functions in the language of automatic electro-mechanical self-regulation, "cybernetics." We have first the "cybernetic overlayer" or "command post,"[85] consisting of a center which sends guidance signals to the "controlled underlayer" or "work units."[86] In Etzioni's model, the subsystems which perform the functions of the cybernetic command center are the institutions of the state at its various levels in contemporary society. Within the cybernetic center or "overlayer" the major distinction is that between the knowledge-producing units and the policy-making units. The knowledge-producing units include not only government experts, but also organizations outside government, such as universities, research agencies, "think-tanks," etc. Connecting the controlling cybernetic overlayer to the controlled underlayer, or "societal units" (i.e., the rest of the society outside of the state), are lines of communication which carry instructions from the command centers in the cybernetic overlayer to the work units of the controlled underlayer, and supposedly bring information and response back up to the overlayer. Civil service, press, radio, and television are assumed to function as "two-way communication lines" between the cybernetic state and the guided society (although these are not generally noted for their effectiveness in carrying public responses back to elite message centers, with the possible, rather limited exception of the press). As further means of communicating citizens' "values and needs" back to the controlling overlayer, Etzioni also mentions "votes, letters to congressmen, petitions, and so forth."[87]

In the interest of "effective societal cybernetics" Etzioni clearly prefers the building of societal consensus on policy issues to the use of coercive power as a basis for cybernetic action by the controlling overlayer. This is to be accomplished through the communication of interests laterally among citizens and social groups and then vertically to the controlling cybernetic units. "Societal guidance" is a combination of the two basic processes of "cybernetic control" and "consensus building," and it incorporates social information and political-economic controls as integral aspects of these processes.

What Etzioni has constructed here tends to suggest the "machine à gouverner," referred to by Norbert Weiner as a utopian possibility in the 1950s, at the very beginning of the cybernetic era.[88] However, unlike Weiner (whose work in the field of "cybernetic control" he refers to as "basic"), Etzioni apparently regards this utopia quite positively as a societal goal, for in several of his discussions of the notion of the "guided society" he refers to it as a "utopia" in the sense not merely of a society nowhere yet existent,[89] but also as one both capable of being created, and moreover well worth creating, one which "will promote broad, effective participation in politics" and "will advance social justice."

Assuming that the societal guidance elements indicated by Etzioni can be assembled and linked together according to specification, what kind of planning would be most appropriate to the resulting guidance system? How would it differ from the piecemeal, crisis-oriented planning of modern pluralist society in response to the pulling and hauling of diverse social interests, which tends to be closer to "muddling through" than to any distinctive kind of planning? In the first place, argues Etzioni, planning would be more comprehensive, more "fundamental," more encompassing. It would not merely make marginal, incremental decisions leading to small adjustive changes; it would also consider the overall context for policy making and make decisions which establish "basis directions." Such fundamental decisions would actually seek to head off social crisis by taking into account in an orderly way the effects of rapid technological change and the results of previous nonplanning or misplanning; thus the process of fundamental decision making which has been resorted to only *ad hoc*, by "incrementalist" decision makers under the pressure of crisis, would become a regularized, precrisis decision mode.[90]

Secondly, this combination of fundamental and incremental decision modes, which Etzioni calls "mixed scanning," would not only be more comprehensive than pluralist-incremental decision making, it would also be more socially equitable. For decisions reached in a partisan pluralist context, in the absence of any "regulatory center," tend to overrepresent the more powerful interests in the system and underrepresent the less powerful, even to the virtual exclusion of the weakest (the poor, the minorities, etc.). As Etzioni suggests, the pluralist "incrementalists" tend to accept this outcome because of their strong opposition to centralized rationalistic decision making, which they believe is intrinsically statist and "undemocratic." Since for them, democracy is synonymous with pluralist consensus, they prefer the unequal outcome of consensual decisions to equality achieved *via* state decrees over the objections of dissenting private interests. Much of this argument is already familiar to us from the contemporary controversy over federally enforced integration. But not only does incrementalism tend to neglect the underprivileged; it also fails to explore significant social innovations. As the decision mode favored by established interests-in-consensus, Etzioni pictures incrementalism as essentially conservative, seeking to maximize the security of these interests rather than exploring basic new policy directions. In effect, according to the incrementalists, "all reliable knowledge being based on the past, the only way to proceed without risk is by continuing in the same direction."[91]

As we have noted, Etzioni associates incremental decision making ("disjointed incrementalism") with pluralist-democratic society; at the opposite pole he places the master planning of totalitarian-centralist societies. Totalitarian planning seeks to be comprehensively rational, i.e., to encompass simultaneously all major system requirements in an authoritative manner; but the intrinsic limitations on the capacities of societal decision makers for making rational decisions are such that this is impossible.[92] In practice, some interests must be relegated to low priority, and since the system's various interest groupings have no established recourse to decision makers, the latter will likely run roughshod over some of them.[93] As opposed to both the insensitive coerciveness of totalitarian planning, and the confused "muddling through" of incrementalism, Etzioni offers the strategy of "mixed scanning." This strategy provides a middle way, both socially and intellectually, in two major respects. Socially, it not only respects private rights but also actively seeks to comprehend the needs of all interests in the society, and to make provision for substantively meeting those needs, even when they represent politically weaker groups. Intellectually, it does not attempt an impossible comprehensive rationality in which all details as well as major directions for action are specified (as in totalitarian planning, where, in fact, black markets and other subterranean modes for incremental adjustment function alongside the ideal model of the comprehensively planned economy). Instead, it explores major alternatives by way of a general overview, or "scanning" procedure, and then through a process of successive elimination narrows the field to that policy alternative which involves the least major disadvantages or "crippling objections." Choice of this course of policy is a fundamental decision which sets the context for subsequent scanning and review of lower level policy alternatives, in descending order. This policy procedure recycles periodically, to again review at an encompassing level the overall state of the system, even though no crisis may exist; thus, the "trigger" for engaging in encompassing overviews which lead to fundamental decisions is normalized, and becomes a crisis-anticipating rather than crisis-responding procedure.[94]

Like incrementalism and comprehensive rationalism, "mixed scanning" is the expression of a distinctive social system and can only be fully achieved under such a system, which Etzioni identifies with countries that have been governed by Social Democratic parties, such as the Scandinavian countries and Israel.[95] Such societies have multisectored economies that include various mixed forms of public-private regulation, in which the state provides "contextuating control for privately managed and owned enterprises,"[96] alongside more purely private or governmental enterprise sectors. Thus the economy as a whole is "mixed," and its distinctive sector, that in which public and private management converge, is itself "mixed." Though such managerial "mixing" is often regarded as transitional towards higher degrees of state control, e.g., toward "state socialism," Etzioni regards it as a "permanent feature of the post-modern society."[97]

For Etzioni, attainment of the "active society" and of the relatively encompassing yet flexible and adjustmental planning which he describes, means in practice the achievement of a social-democratic order characterized by a "mixed" economy and by change-oriented, technocratic-cybernetic planning, rather than "state socialism." In the context of contemporary welfare-capitalist America, the agenda of change which he prescribes as necessary to make this an "optimum responsive" or "active" society would involve increasing social egalitarianism without creating overbearing state power, accompanied by a rise in the state's effectiveness as a planning and change agent.[98] He views this transition as having already begun in countries like Britain, and being well under way in social-democratic societies like Sweden and Israel. Ideally, it will involve "an expanding welfare state, government guidance of the economy . . . and mobilization of weaker collectivities."[99] In the welfare capitalism which characterizes contemporary America, however, he sees so far only a "post-modern extension of modern capitalism . . . without a basic change of structure."[100] Yet he views the transition to an actively planning, change-oriented, social-democratic society as entirely possible in America, given two major conditions: first, the likelihood of lower resistance to the prospect of a "mixed" and flexibly "guided" economy than to a fully state-owned and planned economy; and second, the possibility that underprivileged groups can be mobilized politically and that American society can be made to change in an egalitarian direction by virtue of such mobilization. Of course, these are both large assumptions, particularly the second, and Etzioni himself is unsure whether in itself further political mobilization of minorities, e.g., the poor, for conventional political participation will be sufficient to "tip the balance in favor of a transformation to an active society without a showdown, or will lead to a showdown. . . ."[101]

In reviewing his work, it becomes clear that Etzioni's ultimate concern is with the relationship between the social structure and the particular mode of social policy making which "postmodern" society pursues; hence his correlation of pluralist, totalitarian, and social-democratic societies with distinctive kinds of planning (incrementalism, encompassing rationalism, and "mixed scanning," respectively). Gross, on the other hand, is mainly concerned with the development of a social accounting system and of a societal guidance unit in government which will ultilize the accounting system for effective planning and policy making. His basic questions are, "How can we best appraise the state of a nation? How can we outline the major elements in any broad program or plan for the future of a country?"[102] Their work is essentially supplementary, with Gross giving us a relatively detailed picture of the components of the guidance system, and Etzioni a picture of the structure of the overall society and its linkages with the guidance system. One interesting point of difference between them has to do with this difference in focus; that is, Gross's interest in making improvements in the societal guidance system *per se*, as against Etzioni's concern that such changes will either not be possible or not have their intended meaning in the absence of other accompanying political changes in the larger society, particularly the mobilization of a political movement which will support structural change aimed at increasing the political-economic equality of the groups in the system. This is reflected quite clearly in their contrasting attitude toward interest group representation in the guidance system. Gross accepts the practice of direct representation for key interests through a representative council located in the guidance agency itself, in order to facilitate communication, planning, and implementation of official plans. Etzioni seeks a more egalitarian representation of interests than now obtains, and envisions the representation of interests through more traditional intermediate structures which would insulate the guidance system from being overly influenced by any particular interest group. In this respect, Gross seems to be less concerned about transcending the existing society, and content to improve the effectiveness of planning within the structure of a welfare-capitalist society, whereas Etzioni would like to see the structure of that society also changed, as well as having its planning mechanisms improved.

Though Etzioni views this dual set of changes as a realistic option of the postmodern period, he does not believe it can be pursued fully merely through the application of recent developments in intellectual technology to the government planning process. Achieving the option of a socially responsive planning mechanism depends also on the political support for such planning in the larger society, and ultimately on the degree to which the social-political structure is egalitarian in practice. If some key groups are significantly more powerful or privileged, there will be little advantage to them in shifting from a conservative incrementalist strategy to a change-oriented activist strategy in official policy making; besides improving the absolute minimum standards of disadvantaged groups, active-responsive change could also enhance their status relatively, hence reducing the relative status of currently privileged groups. Resistance may therefore be expected from privileged groups on this account, as well as on account of their uncertainties about the degree to which government would encroach on their managerial powers in the economy of an "active society." Accordingly, Etzioni indicates the importance of mobilizing the weaker groups to help supply the political force for making the transition to a society in which active-responsive planning would actually be implemented.

Etzioni's position appears to be that no real break with incrementalist policy making can be expected to occur without the mobilization of the weaker collectivities, probably in coalition with egalitarian planning-oriented intellectuals and others; that in the absence of such political mobilization, the hold of established key interests on the planning and policy process cannot be broken, and they will tend to block the further evolution of the machinery of planning out of concern for the possibility of its use against their own interests. In Etzioni's strategy, the transition to an active-responsive society would be effected gradually by using the existing machinery of planning to expand the national product and to use the new resources thus created for the "upgrading" of the weaker collectivites, i.e., the Keynesian "fiscal dividend" is to be invested in programs for social-economic development of the underprivileged collectivities. In this way, less resistance will be engendered in the society than by attempting to directly reallocate assets from the relatively privileged to the relatively underprivileged.

Etzioni theorizes that upgrading would tend to make the state more neutral in its responsiveness to the plurality of the various interest groups in the society since it tends to reduce the gap in their power assets. Ultimately, upgrading is the product of improved societal guidance, since it is a function of the capacity of sophisticated "cybernetic" controls to raise GNP through full employment policy and to distribute the output increment primarily to the least-privileged groups. Thus for Etzioni, as for the other postindustrial theorists who identify themselves with social-democratic goals (e.g., Bell, Lipset, Heilbroner), the *deus ex machina* which provides the means for resolving their political problems resides in the new capacities for planning economic growth and channeling its product to groups in need *via* complex and sensitive social "guidance" and accounting systems. In this way, the technocrats of the welfare-capitalist state, using "mixed-scanning" policy techniques which incorporate various social indicators of group status, believe they can effect an evolutionary transition into a social-democratic, flexibly planning society.

There are, however, some serious problems with this analysis. First is the assumption that powerful interests will simply resist the further development of mechanisms for system guidance, unless this receives wide support from a politically mobilized underclass. The record of development of Keynesian mechanisms for planning indicates strong support for their development by important segments of the business sector, at least since the Second World War, and even before. Of course, it is true that segments of business, including corporate business, are cautious and defensive about providing government with powerful machinery for central planning, so that even the proposal for a continuing commission simply to observe and report on technological development and associated social problems at the federal level met with sharp opposition from the more conservative business members of the Technology Commission.[103] Yet for some time, support has been building in the business community for national economic analysis and forecasting on a long-term basis, and currently a fairly wide consensus has developed in the business sector (as represented by the prestigious Business Council itself) in support of a governmental system of wage-price controls.[104] All of this indicates the willingness of a significant segment of key interests to accept active state planning for the protection and enhancement of their own interests, and their readiness to provide government with ever more powerful instruments for economic stabilization and development to this end. *Within these boundaries,* these interests find it entirely reasonable to develop an "active society," mobilized to insure the stability and prosperity of the business sector, though it is certainly far from the "active-responsive" society pursuing egalitarian goals envisioned by Etzioni.

Second, Etzioni assumes that "have" groups will allow the "upgrading" of "have-nots" to proceed to the point where the political-administrative planning mechanism becomes as responsive to the latter as it has been to the former, and to produce programs for further upgrading, followed by further equity in responsiveness, further upgrading, etc., until a substantially egalitarian society has been achieved. While we do not believe the business community will mechanically block the further development of mechanisms for active government planning and for the provision of relief to underprivileged groups, it seems highly dubious to assume that the "have" group will allow the process to go any further than the granting of minimal or token concessions to "upgrading." These concessions leave the have-nots feeling "that progress has been made," but keep the status distance between them and the "haves" as great as ever, since allocations out of the increment in economic output, over and above token concessions, can still flow primarily to the "have" groups.

The assumed cycle of social-political development whereby upgrading leads to power equity, which leads to further upgrading etc., can probably be broken without much difficulty by the resort to tokenism on the part of the most powerful elites; in particular, by elevating a limited segment of the black community to middle-managerial positions connecting the ghetto economy to the larger corporate economy.[105] This relates to the second objection to Etzioni's argument: the state is not the only unit which is "neutralized" as a result of "upgrading"; but the "upgraded" collectivity itself is neutralized (more specifically, its mobilizing leaders are "co-opted," satisfied by concessions, and generally drawn into implementing programs of development whose ultimate design and control lies outside their own community). In fact, this is probably the basis on which the state becomes tolerant to the "have-not" collectivity's demands — that they are canalized and moderated relative to more extreme demands for radical change. Thus the political "neutralization" of the state does not simply owe to the "upgrading" of the underprivileged collectivity, but to the collectivity's own political neutralization in consequence of upgrading, which leads it to moderate its demands, so that these become more tolerable to the policy-controlling elites in the state. This, however, is actually a formula for no more than incremental concessions, rather than the fundamental social restructuring which

Etzioni began with, and his argument for the possibility of basic social change collapses into the possibility of a violent "showdown" between the "have-not" collectivities and privileged elites already enjoying high access to the state and its policy mechanisms. (Mobilization for a "showdown," even short of a violent clash, will probably involve militant ideological politics of a sort which the "end-of-ideologists" oppose. At this point Etzioni would have to part company with these other theorists of technocratic system guidance, consistent with his differences with them in seeking to definitively transcend contemporary "welfare capitalism.")

Despite some differences "at the limit," there is much in common and supplementary between the work of Etzioni, Gross, and Bell. In each case central state structures are envisioned as utilizing complex social data collected with an eye to responding to both qualitative and quantitative concerns of social-technocratic planners about the society and its subgroups, on a nationwide level. However, since the system of planning envisioned by the social-technocrats is not totalitarian, its goals are not set solely by them. A major part of the "feedback" which they seek to provide to their planning subsystem is to be obtained from representatives of group interests, either directly or in a structurally mediated fashion, through intermediate organizations, communications media, government commissions and advisory councils, etc. Probably where Etzioni differs from other proponents of active planning most sharply is in his emphasis on the need to expand the technocratic guidance system to include, in the planning and policy process, group interests which have previously been relatively excluded owing to their political weakness. As already noted, this will require the political mobilization of such groups, which in turn (besides threatening the relative status of groups already possessing strong representation) will also tend to complicate the planning system. To the degree that such mobilization actually occurs, planners will no longer be able to simply plan "from the data" without seriously taking into account demands articulated by group leaders whose judgment they have traditionally regarded as untutored and hence less qualified than their own. It will no longer be possible to bracket out the demands of formerly unmobilized groups in determining what is the best policy compromise. In effect, Etzioni's work points up that in a pluralist-technocratic system, though knowledge by central planners probably increases with regard to all groups in the society, responsiveness to their interests and demands increases only in proportion to the extent and degree of their political mobilization. Knowledge which is not backed up by group power remains an abstraction, at best a factor in the ideal projections of the planners, but not a working element in actual social policy.

CHAPTER VII

Technocracy
and the
New Pluralism

As we have observed in the preceding chapter, a stated aim of the social technocrats is to transcend through sophisticated social-economic planning and administration the uneven distribution of power among diverse groups, in order to enlarge the total economic product and improve the overall society. However, politics even in the postindustrial era does not become easily transformed into a mere matter of technical administration; political conflict goes on, taking various and often confusing new forms, so that the transcendence of such conflict in the service of the public interest itself requires a base in effective political power. This base the social technocrats appear to have located in the new partnership of "mature," "enlightened" corporate business and the central state. However, the implications of that partnership for democratic pluralism are highly problematic, as indicated in this chapter by tracing the development of corporate-state relationships since the New Deal up to the present day. Corporate influence on government policies, ranging from regulatory policies and granting of contracts to taxation and income redistribution, remains great in an era of increased government reliance on business initiative in social problem solving for the public sector. Powerful mechanisms for exerting this influence, through top-corporate advisory groups, such as the Business Council (which has shaped government policies from the days of social security legislation to the recent establishment of wage-price controls), bear further investigation.

At the same time, the image of "professionalized social reform" produced by the social technocrats, in which the poor and minorities are viewed essentially as client-recipients of programs designed and administered by social service professionals rather than as participating political actors, gives us the other main aspect of the technocratic program. The minimal role allotted the poor, as against the close and numerous channels of access provided to the postindustrial business elite in the shaping of government policies relevant to their respective interests, stamps the two sides of the technocratic coin. Together, these aspects of the technocratic perspective provide us with the image of a program for the professional engineering of social welfare and reform for heretofore neglected interests, ultimately grounded in a political position of "elitist pluralism." The present chapter concludes with an analysis of this variant of contemporary pluralism in relation to several alternative pluralist configurations.

Technocracy, Pluralism and the "New Politics"

Much has been written in recent years about the emergence of a "new politics" in American society. To some, stunned by the breakup of the Johnson era's politics of consensus, the riots in the ghettos, and the militancy of antiwar students, the new politics has been one of irrationality, extremism, and infantile rebellion against authority. In this view, the new politics has been essentially an antipolitics.[1] To others, the new politics has been one in which the emerging educated middle class is central; it is the politics of a new majority ready to listen to reason and fact, without the ethnic and racial prejudices of earlier majorities, and less concerned about economic issues than about environmental questions, particularly about the quality of metropolitan life, considered as a social-physical environment.[2] To yet others there is a new politics of "backlash," based on a reaction against the increasing militancy of urban blacks, which seeks to reunite the traditional white Protestant majority of smalltown (and now increasingly suburban) America in a neoconservative politics, along with conservatively minded members of the white ethnic minorities.[3] The partial and one-sided nature of these different perspectives on American politics today suggests that they can be understood and reintegrated as different facets of the same underlying sociopolitical reality, only if that deeper reality is itself adequately recognized and interpreted.

In part we have described some of the major elements in the changing American social structure in our discussion of the emerging "hybrid" economy, and of the rise of new military, scientific, and governmental elites which apparently challenge the established business elite descended from the industrial era. What must be recognized as the key to the "new politics" of our time is the new role of the state in American society, as a stimulant and regulator of the activity of the overall economy, and as distributor or underwriter of contracts, grants, franchises, insurance, and other forms of largesse and security to businesses, universities, and research agencies as well as to states, cities, families and individuals. Since the State is the Great Institution of our time, what this means is that underneath the familiar, but diverting, politics of group interests, there is a politics of institutional relationship, conflict, and accommodation, involving the State in its component units, and the institutions of business, the universities, the unions, the farm organizations, the research institutions, etc.

The several forms of contemporary interest group politics, as expressed through political parties and through the more fluid forms of contemporary "movement" politics can be understood as the politics of marginal groups seeking entry into more desirable positions in the new political economy (e.g. the blacks); of formerly established groups reacting against being pushed to the margins (e.g. the white rurals and small-towners), or the anticipation of being pushed out or displaced in importance (e.g. the white industrial workers); of ascendant new groups taking up positions close to the active center of the new system (e.g. the new educated middle class); and of a minority of the latter (e.g. the radical students) reacting unpredictably against the institutional values, commitments, and politics involved in moving into functionally central positions.[4] Though this vigorous interaction appears to be basically a struggle among groups, its stakes lie in the relations of these groups to the major institutions of our time, foremost of these being the State. Thus contemporary politics is less a struggle between clearly divided opposing interests, such as labor *versus* capital, and their political and ideological representatives, as it is a contest between different claimants for the largesse and support of the institutions of the State.[5] With the multiplication of functional groups, as well as the cultural revolution among minority groups proclaiming their distinctive identity, the result is an increasingly complex kind of pluralist politics, a politics of proliferating claims upon the state involving friction between groups at and around the claimants' table and those pushing toward it, and vociferous reaction by those groups thrust away from it.

This situation has developed as the State has moved from being a meeting ground of different group interests within which differences could be resolved in a context of orderly, channeled conflict (i.e. a focal point for the peaceful resolution of structural conflicts), to the State itself playing key functional roles, first as regulator of the national economy, then as defender of the national security, and finally as supporter and guarantor of the national welfare. This is reflected in the fact that between the Civil War and World War II, the three new cabinet posts established were Agriculture, Commerce, and Labor, each "created to represent a major economic estate of the realm, and to make sure that its interests were protected."[6] In contrast, the new cabinet departments created since World War II — Health, Education, and Welfare; Housing and Urban Development; Transportation; and the somewhat special case of Defense (consolidating formerly separate military-service departments) — were established to enable government to perform functions deemed important to the society, rather than to represent particular economic interests. In the version of the New Politics put forward by the end-of-ideologists, this shift by the modern State from structural interest accommodation to functional role performance for system goals means the liquidation of the political position of the leading interests of the preindustrial and industrial eras (farmers, business, labor), and their replacement by politically neutral and economically disinterested agencies working to fulfill the societal functions of economic growth, military defense, and social welfare, in a manner transcending any narrow economic interests.[7] However, this version is a highly selective simplification of the complex politics of adaptation by key economic interest groups, and particularly of corporate business, which have been able to retain major political influence because of the enormous resources they command (including advanced managerial technology and scientific knowledge) and the importance these resources have to the postindustrial State.[8]

As any number of observers have noted, the critical point of transition for government-business relations was the Second World War, out of which came a distinctive new "partnership" based on a mutuality of interests in such areas as research and development, and fiscal stabilization and stimulation of the economy. As a third partner came the universities and the research agencies, providing the new vital commodity of the postindustrial period — advanced theoretical knowledge and its producers, physical and social scientists, and "scientific administrators." In return for this knowledge came contracts, subsidies, appointments to government committees with some leverage on the budget for science, and the suggestion of a chance to rationalize and civilize government policy in areas of overlap between specific scientific and general human concern such as atomic energy. Since government was now function-oriented (and no longer simply group-oriented), wherever institutional arrangements for satisfying its emerging functional interests did not exist, it took the step of creating them. Where government had sought reliable information which would help it guide policy and development in some vital functional area such as defense, it had moved to create "hybrid" knowledge-producing organizations which would supposedly be free of the possible conflicts of interest that might be engendered in directly contracting to private research agencies. (This is not to say that it has always gotten the "uncontaminated" value-free information it was seeking as a result, but at least the ritual of exorcising private interests was performed.) In the process we have seen the creation of a spectrum of privately managed, but publicly funded, nonprofit organizations such as MITRE and RAND, created for purposes of research, alongside quasi-public service-producing enterprises of a regulated profit nature, such as COMSAT, or goods-producing enterprises such as defense industries.[9]

In the scientifically oriented, postindustrial society the result is a new pluralism in which the old separation between the roles of government and private actors has been removed, and politics becomes "a process of bargaining and negotiation among public and private agencies in which politicians and private leaders function as brokers and overseers in the effort to apply science and technology to social concerns."[10] Some have sought to rationalize these arrangements by drawing an analogy with the traditional principle of political federalism, which delineates the division of political powers between the states and the federal government, and have coined such phrases as "federalism by contract" or "creative federalism" in describing this new phenomenon. However, others have pointed out that this analogy is faulty, in that "federalism by contract" actually tends to parcel out powers specifically reserved to government, by vesting them in private or "quasi-public" enterprises. Further, they maintain that the resulting system amounts to a "new feudalism," or "corporatism" in which control powers formerly reserved to central government have been shared out to private interests by the effective incorporation of these interests at the executive policy levels of the governmental system.[11] It is at this point that interest group politics is joined with institutional politics, the point at which powerful groups in control of well-organized institutions bargain with and against other institutional groups and with the governmental elite for policies of benefit to their institutions, and derivatively to themselves.[12]

In response, some have suggested that, unlike medieval corporatism, the new corporate-pluralism pursues "positive ends" of general societal utility; and others like the end-of-ideologists have stressed the powerful social-technical capacities of these new political-economic arrangements as the best hope for the solution of current social problems, and for the stable management of contemporary society and its economy. In relation to such claims, probably the most significant current set of rationalizations for these corporatist arrangements has to do with the new mystique of science. In this image, postindustrial society is identified as "scientific" society, in which major decisions are appropriately made by key functional elites— political, military, industrial, educational, scientific— located within or closely connected to the central state through political, administrative, and specialized-knowledge relationships.

In their encounters as decision makers, these elites function "as a surrogate for an absent and incompetent democracy," and in the process become incorporated into the interior decisional mechanisms of the administrative state. Their access to central power is justified on the basis of their superior technical knowledge and competence in the development and management of new scientifically based technologies and social organizations.[13] Theirs is a politics of "pragmatic consensus and . . . the rational resolution of competing claims," rather than the political-ideological confrontation of ideas, and they share the common intellectual and managerial perspective of "systems analysis," which functions for them as a binding ideology, and which may well be identified as the "ideology of scientific society."[14] As Sanford Lakoff observes, "In scientific society, ethical controversies are compromised and economic reasoning is generalized to serve as a universal instrument of policy making. This, at any rate, is what systems analysis amounts to and as such it is the closest thing we have to a successor to the ideologies generated by industrial society."[15] If the postindustrial society of the "post-ideological" era has an ideology, it is the ideology of systems analysis and systems management, which we have referred to more generally as the "technocratic ideology."

Significantly, systems analysis emerged and found its first major applications in governmental military planning during the Second World War, and became the regular basis of defense planning thereafter. From there it has been projected to the civilian agencies in order to stimulate a more explicit kind of planning, in connection with the detailed articulation and comparison of alternative agency program strategies and their costs and benefits. Thus systems analysis has several manifest functions, as it has been applied in government agencies. In the first place, these include greater economy and effectiveness of government programs; i.e., greater governmental program efficiency through improved techniques of relating goals to resources. At the same time another manifest function of systems analysis is to provide a counterbalance to the tendencies toward fragmentation in a highly specialized, multifunctional group society. By setting "objective standards" for overall system functioning and for specific system targets, the technocratic systems planners hope to overcome the diffusion of power which could paralyze the system under the circumstances of the "new pluralism," if it were left to run unchecked. However, the task of quantifying and objectifying complex multidimensional social goals is formidable simply as an intellectual enterprise; mixed with the realities of political influence in goal definition and the obstacles presented by entrenched bureaucratic and clientele interests to implementation of new techniques of program and budgetary review, it promises to be a long time in perfecting.[16] In the interim, the latent function of systems analysis could be to provide a rationale for government programs aimed at satisfying some of the newer functional interests in the system (e.g. universities, hospitals, research organizations), while challenging some of the older ones (e.g. agricultural bureaucracy, Army engineers). Accordingly, the ideology of the technocratic class would serve to bolster the distinctive emergent institutions of the postindustrial society, with which it has associated the new scientific rationality.[17]

The New Pluralism and the Corporate State

Amidst the various current claims and counterclaims regarding the role and character of the postindustrial state and its relation to private organizations, it is well to keep in mind that "positive government," the administrative state exercising its powers of political-economic action, has for some time been accepted by the "haves" as well as the "have-nots"; by conservatives opposed to the extension of welfare programs to the underprivileged as well as by liberals seeking an improvement and expansion.[18] Both political factions have come to recognize government as an extremely useful instrument for the channeling of various kinds of benefits to the groups in which they are interested, from military contracts to public assistance. In fact, contrary to the frequent assumption that government action means intervention in favor of the groups most marginal to the system, examination of public policies according to their effect on privileged *versus* underprivileged interests reveals that "government is most effective and most frequently employed when something in society has been deemed worthy of preservation." The frequently conservative nature of government programs with respect to established interests leads such an observer as Lowi to note that "the notion of 'maintaining public order' may be a more suitable definition for contemporary government than any current liberal is prepared doctrinally to accept."[19] Programs whose initial intentions may have been liberal-egalitarian, seeking to level down class differences or mitigate their effects, such as the social security system, have tended to safeguard the established social structure (in this instance acting as a countercyclical economic stabilizer) rather than work any significant change in it. A similar point can be made regarding the application of income taxes, which in the case of the American tax structure allow "fast write-offs, depletion allowances, hosts of 'Louis B. Mayer Amendments,' privileges on real estate transactions," etc.[20] Programs for business regulation such as antitrust have long since seen the regulatory agencies become instruments of their business clients; and government policies toward monopoly have in practice been expressed through legislation in restraint of competition such as "basing point laws, fair trade laws, etc."[21] Farm price-support programs, initially aimed at restoring agriculture to its pre-World War I levels, have succeeded in maintaining considerably more farmers than are actually economically supportable.[22] Recognized interests of the pre-New Deal period such as business and the farmers have been protected by government programs; while the subsidization of groups such as labor in response to the crisis of the thirties has itself further contributed to the stabilization of a system of capitalism dominated by large enterprises and modified by a frequently regressive system of social insurance and public assistance, referred to with unconscious irony as "welfare" capitalism.[23]

In addition, direct participation by interest groups in government programs has been encouraged and legitimated through a doctrine of self-administration which identifies itself with the older theory of "local self-government." Such self-administration has been justified as a technique of governmental decentralization; and federalism, which was intended as a division of powers between different levels of government, has itself become a symbol for the parcelling-out of governmental powers to private interests.[24] Thus, the emergent postwar notion of a business-government "partnership," frequently enunciated by the Republicans under Eisenhower, and then picked up and elaborated by various liberal Democrats under Kennedy and particularly Johnson, has become another item of the underlying common public philosophy of interest group liberalism shared by important "centrist" segments of both parties.[25] As Arthur Schlesinger, an eminent spokesman for modern liberal Democrats, has stated, a "multi-essence administration" (the aim of Kennedy, and the accomplishment of Johnson in his capture of business support in 1964) implies that "the leading interests in society are all represented in the interior processes of policy formation — which can be done only if members or advocates of these interests are included in *key* positions of government. . . ."[26]

As Lowi indicates, the practice of interest group participation in government programs has a history which can be traced back at least to the New Deal, with a number of programs, particularly in agriculture, that resulted in bringing interest groups directly into the administrative process of government.[27] Somewhat more dramatically, at about the same time these programs were established, the Roosevelt administration attempted to set up machinery to allow the nationwide self-regulation not only of agriculture but of industry as well, through the establishment of the National Recovery Administration (NRA) in 1933.[28] Under NRA, government was asked, in effect, to set aside its antitrust laws in order to secure business cooperation for industrial planning. (The model for government-business cooperation which underlay these proposals was the WWI experience of the War Industries Board in which such practices had first been adopted on an emergency basis.) The legislative package embodying these proposals was the National Industrial Recovery Act, which contained something for every major interest, including guarantees to labor of the right to collective bargaining and minimum wages, concessions to recovery planners who won the demand to have government license business participation in NRA, and official sanction of the business practice of drafting anticompetitive codes for the conduct of business.

Within months there was mounting criticism of NRA, much of which was centered on favoritism to big business interests; in particular, the charge that the codes promoted monopoly and actually slowed recovery "by permitting price rises and cutbacks in production."[29] Studies by several committees confirmed that similar monopolist practices were being sanctioned by the codes, and maintained that "giant corporations dominated the NRA code authorities and squeezed small business, labor and the public."[30] Under growing criticism and pressure from avocates of competitive enterprise (not least of whom were small businessmen and their associations), and of consumer interests, the codes were gradually tightened and began to be more scrupulously enforced. This led to disenchantment among larger business interests resentful now not only of the provisions concerning wages and working conditions, but also of the new scrutiny by government personnel brought in specifically to enforce the codes. Finally the NRA was declared unconstitutional in 1935, and "many businessmen gladly went back to clandestine collusion, happy to be rid of legal cooperation under the glare of unfavorable publicity and with an ever present threat of unhelpful governmental interference."[31] The end of NRA, however, did not signal the end of the incorporation of interest groups into the processes of government administration of policy making.

The principle of the interest-incorporative or "corporate" state was firmly established through the agricultural programs of the New Deal, and then spread to other areas, particularly the newly emergent defense industry, under the pressure of subsequent World War and cold war emergencies. As we have indicated, the incorporation of group interests was closely connected with the notion of group self-regulation, of which the NRA provides an outstanding early example. However, rather than being merely an agricultural version of the NRA (which provided interest representation by industry on a nationwide scale), the farm programs of the New Deal tended to be essentially locally based due to the dispersion of agricultural production and the government's desire to avoid the appearance of central control.[32] Operating under the umbrella of the omnibus Agricultural Adjustment Act, independently administered programs of extension services, credit, price parity, education, electrification, forestry, and conservation were established. The major initial aim of this system was to bring farmers to reduce production by voluntary contractual agreement (in return for government payments bringing commodity prices up to par with prices in a normal period), as well as to provide credit, education, technical aid, and other services added later. To this end, a complex parallel system of federal-local "cooperation," amounting to administrative self-government by locally elected farm committees, was devised in each program category, with county committees meshing with the farm bureaus of Chambers of Commerce on the local level, with state farm bureau federations at the state-wide level, and with the American Farm Bureau Federation at the pinnacle, on the national level.[33] As a result of the autonomy of the programs from one another and from the central agency, each administrative system of agricultural interest representation has tended to become a political domain in its own right, linked through the local agriculture committees to the Agriculture Department on one hand, and to the Congress on the other, where they operate as local lobbies for privileged sectional or national farm interests.[34]

Between the ten or so separate programs associated with the Agriculture Department, a budget of almost 90 percent of the Department's annual expenditures (about $5.6 billion of $6.7 billion as of 1970) is administered, plus a comparable amount in federal loans.[35] As Lowi observes, each of these autonomous programs has become a political-administrative system possessed of "institutional legitimacy" such that they are shielded from effective regulation by the "central sources of democratic political responsibility"; from the executive, where Agriculture secretaries have vainly tried to effect coordination of related programs; from the Congress, where they have enough influence to stalemate or veto regulatory legislation; and from the general public, which is largely unaware of their activities and influence. The result is a decentralized uncoordinated cluster of administrative subsystems providing official channels for narrow interest representation, independent of overall government economic policy, which Lowi characterizes as a "new feudalism."[36]

Comparing Agriculture with the Departments of Commerce and Labor, it has been observed that the three are unique among cabinet agencies in that they all relate to some specifiable interest segment of the economy and are required by law "to develop and maintain an orientation toward the interests that comprise this sector."[37] Unlike the other Cabinet departments which are organized around some governmental function, this trio of "clientele agencies" are organized around specific economic interest groupings. Like the prewar German and Italian Councils of Corporations, these departments provide "functional representation" to specified interests, in contrast with the provisions for geographic representation in Congress under the Constitution. In particular, the Commerce Department has actively fostered the organization of trade associations, taking the initiative just before WWI in providing official government endorsement for the integration of local chambers of commerce into the U.S. Chamber of Commerce in 1912. Going a step further during the war years, the Wilson administration gave sanction to the official representation of trade associations at the executive level of government; during the 1920s, Commerce Secretary Herbert Hoover spoke in favor of normalizing such arrangements during peacetime, stressing the slowness of legislative action in responding to economic change, in contrast to what he viewed as a "great moving impulse toward betterment" among economic associations.[38] Under the New Deal, along with the abortive attempt to establish self-regulation under NRA, came the less dramatic but more lasting establishment of the Business Advisory Council by the first secretary of commerce under Roosevelt,[39] with the declared intention of providing guidance to the Department on matters of mutual interest to it and business groups. Later, under Kennedy, this became the Business Council, and it remains to the present day a basic channel for communication and negotiation between influential business interests and the executive branch.[40] As Richard Barber indicates, the Council is "a veritable *Who's Who* of big business"; its active membership consists of over sixty business executives, and three of its four officers are top corporation presidents, heading firms among the largest one hundred manufacturers. Moreover, "the Council meets regularly with top government officials"; in fact, within less than a week after his inauguration in 1965, President Johnson had invited a gathering of business leaders "most of whom were members of the Business Council" to the White House.[41]

Modern war, as waged in the twentieth century between industrial powers, has meant an important intensification of these business-government contacts. We have already mentioned the War Industries Board of WWI, which brought business representation directly into the making and administration of wartime economic policy, and its role as a model for the later organization of NRA. Once again during WWII, the underlying philosophy of the War Industries Board was pursued by bringing industrial leaders directly into policy councils, thereby seeking to enlist their cooperation in the war effort from the highest levels down.[42]

Initially, though, growth of the influence of industry on government administrative policy was perhaps most significant at middle and lower policy levels. Because of the need for industrial expertise as well as support, a complex network of Industrial Advisory Committees was established, in which each committee served as the representative of its respective industry. The manifest role of the committees was "advisory only" but as McConnell notes, "The committees met before programs had crystallized and their help was obtained in basic planning," so that industry was brought directly into the detailed formulation of government administrative policy with regard to itself.[43] Supplementing this device for obtaining industrial advice and support for war mobilization was the practice of bringing leading businessmen into high-ranking government agency posts as "dollar-a-year men," serving without compensation (WOC) from the agency, but usually kept on a retainer by their regular employers.[44]

The overall effect of the World War II experience of government-business cooperation was that "it perpetuated the dream that lay behind the now-defunct NRA" and revived notions of government authority being placed in support of business self-regulation. Lending weight to these visions was the establishment in the early postwar period of an industrial advisory network serviced by the Commerce Department's Office of Industry Cooperation. With the advent of the Korean War, the Defense Production Act of 1950 again authorized the utilization of advisory committees in enlisting industry support of the war effort. By the end of 1952, over 500 committees had been developed by the Department of Commerce through its National Production Authority. As during WWII the issues of representativeness and possible bias of the advisory committees were raised and resolved with little satisfaction. This time, labor was explicitly excluded from the advisory system, since its presence might "inhibit discussion" between industry representatives and government officials; moreover, if labor were permitted to participate, "other organized groups" might seek entry, and the like. Ostensibly the only function of the committees was to provide required technical expertise; accordingly trade association executives were officially excluded (though in fact, this rule was often flouted). However, the Celler antimonopoly committee found various committees went considerably beyond providing technical advice to establish pricing agreements or to formulate agency regulatory standards for their own industries.[45] In this way, the presumed objects of regulation themselves become the arbiters of regulation.

In late 1953, with the end of the Korean War, the Business and Defense Services Administration (BDSA) was established to carry on in place of the National Production Authority. The agency was set up only after "extensive consultations" as to its functions between Secretary of Commerce Sinclair Weeks, and corporate and trade association leaders. Though it would not "dictate Government policy," it would "approve or disapprove of the implementation of such policy and plans from the standpoint of their practical workability in everyday industrial operation."[46] Through a reconstituted network of advisory committees, the employment of WOCs, and the appointment of assistant administrators to the commerce secretary upon recommendation of each sector of industry, BDSA would carry out an inherently ambiguous mission. It would provide general services to business in dealing with the government; serving in particular to forward business views and recommendations directly into the policy process "while governmental policies are being discussed and formulated."[47] At the same time, it would pursue a variety of official aims with regard to industrial mobilization (such as materials allocation in military and atomic programs), as well as other economic programs, such as federal loan assistance, accelerated tax amortization, and stockpiling. In short, the agency would actively represent business interests at the same time it pursued the role of regulating them. The duality of agency function is perhaps best illustrated by the anomaly of conferences of industry groups every so often being presided over *for* the agency by WOC's *from* the participating industries. The conclusion of the Celler Committee was that "the organizational arrangements of BDSA have effected a virtual abdication of administrative responsibility on the part of the Government officials in charge of the Department of Commerce in that their actions in many instances are but the automatic approval of decisions already made outside the Government in business and industry."[48]

With the Republican administration of the Eisenhower years, the utilization of business advisory committees in the executive branch tended to mushroom, the number going to between five and six thousand by 1956, as compared to the level of about 500 in the earlier Office of Industry Cooperation and its successor the National Production Authority, both creations of the Truman Administration. However, though quantitatively unprecedented, the basic concept was by no means new; it was "little more than an adaptation of the devices used in the just-ended Democratic Administration and employed for many years in various parts of government, whatever the party in power."[49] What was new was that for the first time the notion of intimate business-government cooperation, originally derived from the mobilization for large-scale war, was being put into unhampered practice (unlike the ill-fated NRA) in a peacetime context. Of course it was an ambiguous context, this "Cold

War" situation, amounting to "mobilization without war" and it produced a "dual economy" divided into "peacetime" and "defense" sectors. Yet it is a point of basic importance that the machinery for business-government cooperation in the shaping of government policy was no longer limited to the requirements of mobilization for defense; it was also explicitly intended to pursue general governmental objectives in regard to "other economic activities," and to provide a variety of services to business "in almost all dealing with Government."[50] At the same time that the BDSA's advisory committees provided the veins and capillaries for the circulatory system of business-government cooperation so essential to the nourishment of the expanding complex of military-industrial contracting in the 1950s, they also served to "normalize" the corporative relations between business and government in regard to the civilian economy.

To this point it is clear that since the 1930s, as government involvement in the economy fostered by both domestic and military crisis has become more widespread and more detailed, cooperative-consultative relations between business and government, such as those facilitated by the medium of advisory committees, have proliferated and multiplied. Politically and structurally, what has been the result of these developments? Apparently the result has been an increasingly more fragmented organization of economic jurisdictions in government, owing to the rise of new business and industrial groups in the defense sector, and the ever finer technological differentiation of functional groups in the civilian sector, each with representation in the executive bureaucracy; many connected to the Commerce Department, most to Defense, others to Interior, and others to the Treasury Department, for example. Postwar developments would seem to point to a new, more complex, and more fragmentary pluralism in government-business relations, rather than to the creation of a monolithic business elite. At least it would appear so from observing the multiplication of the advisory committees and the spreading use of executives from all branches of business and industry in official agency positions.[51]

Yet such a conclusion has only limited validity. In the first place, the selective bias of the agencies toward larger firms — firms with greater market integration, advanced technology, etc., in the selection of membership for the advisory committees — has tended to produce an elite sampling of "representatives" from the industries involved. In its elite-selective effects, this has operated not unlike the "principle of leadership" pursued by the Agriculture Department which has resulted in the by-passing of smaller, marginal farmers. Thus the expanding functional pluralism of the advisory committees has been largely elite in character.

In this respect, the selection criteria for businessmen as WOCs in the more responsible agency posts has been consistent, with the leading firms being sought after for people to fill the top posts.[52]

Moreover, while technological and administrative differentiation has undoubtedly occurred, as reflected in the multiplication of industry linkages with government agencies, a countertrend toward integration is to be noted. For, the proliferation of business advisory committees has certainly not been the only important trend in postwar business-government relations. In this regard, the development of the prestigious Business Advisory Council since its establishment during the New Deal suggests the presence of significant countertrends. At its formation in 1933 just prior to the establishment of NRA, the Council served essentially in an advisory status to the Commerce Department, being composed of "leading businessmen...sympathetic to the attempts being made by President Roosevelt to deal with the Depression."[53] Since that time, however, its influence has been felt far beyond that Department's purvey, with current evidence of advisory contacts to such important departments as State and Defense, as well as to the Executive Office itself.[54] The membership of the Council has typically "been drawn from the world of large corporations," with a minor sprinkling of small and middle-size business representation.[55] In fact, within the "world of large corporations," it is the very largest which have been most regularly included on the council, with the core Council membership composed of the top manufacturers in such major industries as autos, steel, chemicals, electricals, textiles, oil, glass, and rubber. The representatives of these firms include nationally prominent businessmen who have functioned in other connections as public spokesmen and "statesmen" for the business community as a whole: men like Roger M. Blough, board chairman of U.S. Steel, or Ralph J. Cordiner, of General Electric, both of whom have served in recent years as Council chairmen.

Until 1962, the BAC was officially an advisory council to the Commerce Department, a government agency; nevertheless, the press and other members of the public were customarily excluded from its bimonthly meetings, held in exclusive vacation-type locales with expenses paid by private contributions. Typically high government officials would address the Council members and their wives with "confidential advanced economic information," in an "aura of secrecy." Besides the exchange of views which accompanied these meetings, the Council more or less regularly submitted reports to the Commerce Department, and apparently to State and Defense as well, on topics in every major area of government concern, including "labor policy, foreign trade, manpower mobilization, monetary policy, fiscal policy, and antitrust policy." (These reports as

well were usually kept secret.) In addition, the Council has become
known as a primary source of recommendations for business appointees
to high government posts.[56]

Apparently the Business Council is no ordinary advisory group con-
fining itself to a single functional-technical area, such as the pricing of
tungsten steel, or the regulation of product standards in pharmaceuticals,
but a group whose scope is broad enough to encompass all major policy
questions relating to basic directions of business policy and development,
over the relatively "long term" (certainly longer than the fiscal year, with
orientation toward the five-, ten-, fifteen-year span and even longer;
witness the wave of interest in "future-projection" and forecasting in
sophisticated business circles). In addition, this is a group with sufficiently broad scope and power to influence the several basic *types* of
government policy which can be identified, insofar as these policies have
national significance. The Business Council can affect both large-scale
"distributive" policy (e.g., major weapon system decisions such as ABM,
MIRV, stockpiling and allocation of scarce materials and resources) as
well as basic "regulatory" policy, insofar as this is framed with reference
to regulating the overall functioning of the economy (e.g., major decisions on tax cuts, "breaks," write-offs, depreciation allowances, and
other forms of broad fiscal stimulus and reward to business investment
as well as guidelines and controls on wages, prices, profits, interest rates).
In addition it can also affect major governmental "redistributive" policy,
such as broad decisions on social insurance and the use of taxation for
income redistribution[57] (both of which have in fact been drastically
moderated in their intended effects in response to business pressures, both
during and after the New Deal).[58] This is not to say that the Business
Council unilaterally determines these policies; it must respond to basic
governmental concerns, both foreign and domestic, which go beyond
the relatively narrower perspective of business interest, as well as to the
pressure of other elites with somewhat different perspectives (such as
the military branch of the executive, controlling its own capital resources
and managing many heavily government-dependent enterprises). It *does*
suggest that the Business Council stands high enough as an elite-
representative power to have sufficient perspective to formulate an encompassing policy agenda, covering issue areas from foreign to domestic
affairs of interest to various executive agencies and the central executive
staff, and sufficient power to command official attention to its perspective. In this respect the Business Council stands as one of a small number of policy-research and advisory organizations which, either internally
or in the aggregate, span the range of political perspective from liberal
to moderate to conservative, and which are interlinked with major corporations, universities, and government agencies at numerous points, thus

serving as basic channels in the process of policy formulation as it involves business and government today in connection with the knowledge-producing institutions of the postindustrial era.[59]

Our examination of the Business Council's structure and role in policy formulation is intended to suggest the manner in which major corporate organizations act to pool their political resources and perspectives, *via* policy-recommending peak organizations which seek to arrive at consensus among the range of policy orientations connected with their respective members. In this context, it becomes clear that the Business Council, like the other leading policy organizations mentioned, looms over the more ordinary advisory bodies to specific agencies whose power and perspective are limited to their functional-technological areas, though within the given area their influence may be great. This does not assume that the Council is a typical "peak association" which speaks with one voice for a given industry or for a viewpoint cutting across several major industries. Rather it embraces the likelihood that a body of over fifty business leaders, though predominantly representative of large and super-large private interests, will include non-negligible differences between consumer firms and capital goods firms, services and goods producers, banking, manufacturing, sales, and distributive enterprises; differences in section and locale, differences between older and newer industrials, differences in dependence on world market and overseas plant locations, etc.[60] As a result of these differences, we can assume that coalitions will form representing combinations of firms with interests most alike or at least capable of compromising their differences. We would not expect a highly unified ideological politics in this context, though we would expect in some issue areas, and particularly those relating to redistributive policy, a reduction of the number of different positions to several basic ones, related to and justified in terms of different ideological premises.[61] This is because redistributive policy most tends to challenge the class position of established elites such as those represented on the Council, and to evoke from some segments a basically defensive, conservative response, couched in terms of traditional ideological legitimations ("free enterprise," "self-reliance," "individual self-help") and from others a more pragmatic, experimental response to contemplated social changes ("modernization," "system-orientation," "corporate involvement"). Since these changes are likely to have a structural character, the politics of formulating redistributive policy in such an elite body is likely to exhibit certain ideological qualities, though the body does not support any one ideologically-legitimated position as an automatically unified elite.[62]

Against the backdrop of the "new pluralism" of an increasingly complexly differentiated society and economy, organs like the Business

Council in their own milieu play a role somewhat similar to the newly created institutions of centralization in the executive office of the government. Like the National Security Council and the Office of Science and Technology,[63] they bring together top functional elites in a manageable institutional context, speaking for key interests or perspectives in their respective institutional sectors, whether governmental, scientific-academic, or business. Within this context, there will usually be several different viewpoints providing a range of alternative courses of action as policy recommendations to the government agencies to which the elite advisory council submits its views. This range of alternatives strongly influences the shaping of the overall framework for "contextuating" policy having to do with large-scale decisions of wide impact at a national level, as against "incremental" policy which is typically shaped at the level of industry advisory committees incorporating a less inclusive range of interests, most usually in the areas of distributive and regulatory policy. (However, as distributive or regulatory policy may have bearing on major allocation of resources or major intervention in the economy, on a national level, it also is likely to then become a matter for deliberation by advisory organs such as the Business Council, transcending the competence of any single industrial committee or even a cluster of such committees.)

Despite the powerful drive toward centralization over the past two decades in the American political economy, pluralism still thrives according to the end-of-ideologists. Our own inquiry seems to confirm this, insofar as it demonstrates a new and more complex differentiation of interests connected with the technoeconomic developments of the postwar era. Yet this is a pluralism with a pyramidal structure, in which a new upper level of interest bargaining between favored elites sits astride the earlier system of bargaining among a variety of local and national interests, and rapidly supersedes it. What we are describing here then, is in a rather special and formal sense "pluralist politics," but it is an elite-pluralist politics of a very different sort than that which has been associated with the concept of pluralism over most of its history in the West, and certainly cannot be equated with democratic practices involving a conception of popular government or popular sovereignty in any very significant way.

The Social Technocrats and the "Professionalization of Reform"

While the social technocrats have shown their willingness to accommodate the interests of powerful corporate leadership at the very center of administrative planning, their attitude toward the general public and especially toward its less privileged, less politically influential segments is quite different. Though they profess a commitment to democracy as their "only bias"[64] the social technocrats have tended to actively disparage public involvement in the planning process.

In this connection, it is interesting to consider an article by Daniel Moynihan published in the first issue of *The Public Interest* (edited by Daniel Bell and Irving Kristol), titled the "Professionalization of Reform."[65] It is a fairly bald treatment of the process of technocratic planning, in which complicating contemporary political resistances to planning are essentially ignored. Far from being a description of reality, it is in effect a model of the operation of an ideal-type social-technocratic system, one which might go into operation with the clearing of the various existing conservative obstacles to planning, and this is precisely what makes it useful here. Writing in the flush of optimism that surrounded the social programs of the early Johnson administration, Moynihan observed that the antipoverty program, then in the early stages of operation, was "the best instance of the professionalization of reform yet to appear." He went on to predict that it would serve as a "prototype of the social technique of action" that would become even more common in the future. What was most gratifying to Moynihan was that the program, like the others in the Great Society package, had ostensibly been conceived by professional social planners essentially in the *absence* of the kind of popular political support and intellectual leadership that produced the welfare measures of the New Deal. The war on poverty "was not declared at the behest of the poor," who throughout had been silent as well as invisible; it was conceived by those officials of the Kennedy-Johnson administration "whose responsibilities were to think about just such matters."[66]

According to Moynihan it was the special expertise of the men who conceived the war on poverty that enabled them to perceive the worsening condition of minorities and the poor amidst the celebration of affluence which persisted into the early 1960s. This rare specialist capacity for analyzing the present and predicting the likely future now provides the basis for intelligent intervention in the area of broad social problems. The successes of the technocrats in management of the economy — the "econometric revolution"—provide not only the theoretical background, but also the financial resources for social planning: rapidly rising Gross National Product means that "the supply of resources available for social purposes might actually outrun the immediate demand of established programs,"[67] to the tune of $4 or $5 billion annually in the near future. Moreover, there is a positive need to turn these revenues back into the economy, lest their withdrawal from circulation impose a "fiscal drag," and slow down economic growth. The success of technocratic methods creates the conditions for their application on an ever-expanding scale.

If Moynihan's analysis is correct, we have here a conjunction of circumstances which opens unique opportunities for significant social planning. Indeed, these circumstances actually make it incumbent on the administration to devise new programs for expending public funds. This is the type of decision making that is increasingly engaged in by professional planners, working in the context of large organizations, which provide the facilities for the collection and analysis of the necessary data, and of the simulation of hypothetical programs of action. In fact, a veritable "industry of discovery," built around computer technology, is today developing in the social sciences, having earlier made its debut in the physical sciences. The special talents of the social technocrats in government, working with information provided by a combination of computer technology and opinion polling, make it possible for government to foresee the changing needs and demands of the public, and to respond in time with relevant social programs. The signal advantage of these postmodern techniques of data gathering, analysis, and projection is that they do away with the need for public political initiative; Moynihan emphasizes that "mile-long petitions and mass rallies" are no longer required for persuading modern government of popular support for social change. In his estimation, "the very existence of such petitions and rallies may in time become a sign that what is being demanded is *not yet* a popular demand.[68]

This kind of political action, which involves the massing of public pressure behind the political demands of organizations and movements, is rather different from the kind of client participation which Moynihan envisages as appropriate to the social-planning process. In place of the mass-movement politics which provided support for social change during the latter part of the modern era (roughly the first fifty years of the twentieth century), the techniques of "guided change" in the postmodern era call for the "participation" of client populations through what is in effect a panel sample of their leaderships. This is a highly qualified kind of participation, open to being circumscribed by manipulation of the criteria for "feasibility" of participation, as the disappointing experience of militant organizations of the poor has demonstrated in any number of cities in the past few years. Rather than a true amalgam of clients and assisting professionals, the local program boards which were supposedly vehicles for client participation have typically become a combination of the major professional, business and political interests in the community, plus the client representatives, so that the clients have often found themselves a minority element. Thus, instead of structures in which clients and professionals could meet directly to exchange perspectives about needs and resources of the community and the larger planning context, the community-action boards and their increasingly close relations with the local city hall have merely served to contain the underprivileged clients' perspective by reproducing the elite-pluralist structure in which they have traditionally found themselves edged into marginality. In this context, a significant portion of the client group's leadership has found it impossible to maintain independence from the board, or from other officially dominated "community action" organizations which are introduced into the community on the premise of "maximum" client participation. Integral to Moynihan's program for technocratic planning by professionals, then, is the co-opting of client group leadership:

> ... (T)here is rather a pronounced tendency for persons from such groups, when they do rise to the middle class, to settle into professions which involve work with the very groups they left behind. Thus, in a certain sense the poor are not so much losing their natural leaders as obtaining them through different routes.[69]

In such remarks, Moynihan exemplifies the paternalism of the full-blown technocrat toward the public clients of the planning process. He views the client group leaders mainly as social service professionals who can serve as a valuable information resource for the planners as well as a persuasive channel to the client community, but who will not primarily function as active representatives of a community which will exert pressure to insure that its perspectives on its own needs are not ignored or distorted in the planning process. Moreover, when client group leaders make it into the middle class, often into positions with "social welfare" or "reform" institutions, Moynihan pictures them as serving essentially the same leadership function as do "grass roots" leaders. There is not the least suggestion that his institutional position may involve serious role dilemmas for the technocratic "reform" leader, revolving precisely around the question of how far he can lead efforts at reform which could limit the powers of the institution *vis à vis* the client group which he leads. Which does he represent, to which does he owe first loyalty, the technocratic agency or its clients? This question, which has long been recognized as a dilemma of one degree or another for any agency worker, is not even hinted in Moynihan's discussion of the transplanted client group leader, for whom it may be particularly thorny. What is finally most disturbing, however, is Moynihan's suggestion of technocratic infallibility *vis à vis* the public; that technocratic foresight may in time become so perfected that "mile-long petitions and mass rallies" will have to be regarded as spurious because the computer has not yet produced indications of the popularity of their demands. In this view, the full range of democratic expression is, in the last analysis, an unwarranted interference in the work of the professional planners.

Moynihan's position seems ultimately to encompass a curious kind of technocratic egocentrism grounded in the notion that only that which can be measured by advanced techniques really exists; other manifestations of social reality, such as popular demonstrations, are illusory and misleading. This is an extreme intellectual expression of the subordination of what was once a culture of popular democracy to what is now increasingly a culture of managerially controlled technique in the advanced industrial society of the West. At the least it tends to lend credence to the occasional suspicion that the planners would like to become somehow a part of the "power elite," if not its leading or exclusive members.

Technocracy and Contemporary "Liberal-Pluralism"

Historically, a major distinction typically made regarding the development of the American political economy has been that between the classic "laissez faire" liberalism of the nineteenth century, and the administrative-state "welfare" liberalism of the twentieth. However, this simplistic distinction, which has been incorporated into the work of the end-of-ideologists, is misleading in implying that the historic political transition consisted merely in moving from a "negative state," a minimal order-maintaining, watch-dog state, to a "positive state," a regulatory, service-providing, welfare-oriented state. Our understanding of the history of American liberalism leads to another interpretation, that is, that as the major, over-arching political ideology and guide to political practice in American history, Liberalism in America has been forced historically to accommodate the claims of competing groups, of the privileged and underprivileged, the upper and the lower classes, and has therefore always been a complex system incorporating important internal conflicts. Thus, instead of speaking of a straightforward historical passage from laissez-faire liberalism to welfare-state liberalism, it seems more accurate to say that the strains within nineteenth-century liberalism (culminating in the contest of populist-egalitarian liberalism against laissez-faire business liberalism) were resolved during the first third of the twentieth century in the form of a complex mixture of interest group liberalism ("liberal-pluralism") on one hand, and administrative-state liberalism on the other. This took place essentially within the context of the political movement first known as Progressivism and then as the New

Deal which created the early structures of administrative-state social insurance, welfare programs, and business regulation, and fostered and sanctioned the practice of political bargaining between a plurality of interest groups, including the labor unions, on which is based the philosophy and practice of twentieth-century "liberal-pluralism."[70]

Our understanding of both nineteenth- and twentieth-century American liberalism is that these have been complex political-ideological systems concerned with interpreting and integrating a changing democratic-capitalist system. As this system has moved from Jeffersonian agrarianism to mass-industrial democracy, it has generated conflicts within the liberal ideology, rendering it a complex system of ideas and values in constant internal tension. However, the resolution of these conflicts has occurred through compromises internal to the system, rather than through any sharp break with it, as in the twentieth-century European revolutions which have led to Socialism, Communism, or Fascism. Accordingly, our conception of modern Liberalism is that it consists of a synthesis of several interrelated elements which are historical end products of the more than century-long history of American liberalism. Chief among these elements today, we can identify the established system of "interest group" liberalism, currently leaning increasingly toward corporatist interest arrangements with the central state agencies, and contemporary administrative-state liberalism as the other, tending increasingly toward technocratic planning and central "system guidance" for the public welfare and security.

The assumption of the pluralist-technocrats is that the system of interest-group liberalism can be preserved and brought under some kind of manageable control (planned for) if only adequate knowledge "for policy purposes" can be joined to the powers of the central administrative state. The crucial factor for them is the introduction of a powerful social-economic planning which would go beyond the limitations of gross Keynesian economic planning, to the more sensitive qualitative planning required in areas such as education, health services, welfare, and urban community development. (As Daniel Bell put it in an article which conceded many of the weaknesses and crudities of the early, "unrefined" end-of-ideology position which he held at the end of the 1950s, modern Keynesian liberalism had shown during the 1960s its incapacity to manage an economy "to order"; his conclusion was that the failure of contemporary liberalism is in good part "a failure of knowledge.")[71] However, they do not discuss how this planning is to go beyond satisfying the interests of the groups with prime positions of access to the planning units of the central administrative state. Thus, we are left with a liberalism holding in internal tension the aim of authoritative yet democratically responsive technocratic planning as against the special aims of interest groups capable of bypassing the legislative arena and moving into the core of the executive advisory and planning apparatus itself.

If administrative welfare state liberalism and interest group liberalism ranged against one another in internal tension constitute one axis of the crisis of liberalism today, then the other major axis of this crisis is composed of the opposing principles of what might be called "elitist" liberalism and "contemporary populist" or "participationist" liberalism, reflecting an emphasis on the primacy of established leadership in the making of institutional policy, as against the participation of nonelites in the policy process. To date, this difference has manifested itself politically in the struggle for reform of party procedures, in order to allow for wider membership participation, particularly in the Democratic party on its "reform" wing.[72] In the economy, it has demonstrated its presence as an important factor in the drive for greater influence on corporate policy making by consumers, stockholders, and the general public, as in the efforts of Ralph Nader and his associates.[73] Only by taking account of the mutual tension and interaction of these several elements in modern liberalism can we account for its peculiar contemporary development, and for both its ideological and "anti-ideological" qualities.

Historically, administrative-state practices, established at the state level in the urban-industrial states during the early 1900s, became codified at a national level through the New Deal, which thereafter exhibited *both* the face of the "broker state" and the "welfare state."[74] During the 1940s the development of the "welfare state" was halted owing to wartime involvement and a sharp attack on the welfare state concept in the immediate postwar Congresses; however, during the 1950s it appeared that this ideological position had become established under the new political consensus described by the end-of-ideologists. During this decade, as the end-of-ideologists have documented, the notion of the "welfare state" (one insuring at least minimal social standards for the bulk of the population participating regularly in the economy), became accepted by "conservatives" (i.e., classic "laissez faire" liberals) as well as "liberals" (i.e., modern "welfare state" liberals). The common ground between these groups was their political pragmatism and their acceptance of the principle of "interest group" liberalism, i.e., their willingness to bargain rather than wage ideological holy war, encouraged by the context of an "affluent" and powerful economy. At the same time, the principle of the administrative state intervening in the economy could no longer be resisted with the old conviction by groups now dependent upon it directly, such as industrial interests with defense contracts, or indirectly (the business community as a whole, *via* the economic multiplier effect which has stimulated business generally, or *via* the technological "spillover" effect, which brought new products, processes, and managerial techniques to the business community, offering new opportunities for investment and economies of management and production). As a result, business, as the most powerful contract-seeking interest group, and labor, as the group most concerned with the stimulation of employment through public as well as private measures, could now join in support of administrative-state interventions in the economy, in a way they could never quite manage in the context of the "welfare"-type programs of the New Deal, from which large segments of business had always hung back in revulsion. Until the rapid escalation of the Vietnam War and the explosions of the black ghettos, these arrangements seemed to provide the stable basis for the integration of welfare state liberalism and interest group liberalism in a single system. This of course was the core of the Kennedy-Johnson political philosophy and practice and it took the form of a growing military contract subsidy to industry, as well as fiscal policies favoring tax reliefs and incentives to private investment; simultaneous with a "War on Poverty" and Medicare programs seeking to extend the coverage of a minimal welfarism to politically numerous blocs of voters such as the blacks and the aged. Such was the essence of Consensus Politics, a blending of interest concessions to business, particularly corporate business, and welfare concessions to economically disadvantaged minorities.

In that context, amidst the ascending powers of the federal government and their exercise at home and abroad in a more decisive and dramatic way than ever before, the technocratic theory of postindustrial society made its appearance. In that theory, the Grand Consensus is joined by intellectuals and academics (members of Galbraith's Educational and Scientific Estate), who lend their special expertise to government in order to augment its political and economic powers with the guidance of postmodern knowledge. Hypothetically, this opens the prospect of simultaneously satisfying the interests of "action-oriented" intellectuals and power-oriented government executives while providing the beginnings of a "containment" policy toward a co-opted business elite, whose day of dominance is at last on the wane, owing to increasing dependence upon government policy and planning by business policy makers. In a sense, this is a new theory of "countervailing power," except it is a theory of counterbalancing political-administrative *versus* corporate-economic powers, rather than one located in the marketplace pitting countervailing economic organizations against one another. In its vision as an ideology, it foresees the development of policy-relevant societal knowledge (and of institutional bases for it in the context of the technoadministrative state), to such heights of competence that knowledge functions not only as a lens for the focussing of national power on chosen objectives, but as power itself on a nationwide scale; this at least is the dream of the technocratic ideologists. Beginning essentially as liberal-pluralists, they have advanced to the projecting of a postmodern "cybernetic" guidance system which can authoritatively program alternative futures of the whole society, ostensibly for the general welfare. At the same time however, their working model tentatively proposes the incorporation of the society's most powerful interest groups into the heart of the guidance system itself, as a kind of Grand Consensus of support for technocratic action. But as the drawing of powerful private interests directly into the executive circle of public policymaking becomes routine practice, it thereby increasingly circumvents such traditional liberal-pluralist arenas for the representation of social interests as the Congress. With private interest representatives of only partially representative functional groups like corporate business and organized labor brought directly into executive policy formulation, and the executive exercising preponderant initiative and powers *vis à vis* the Congress, this tends to become a recipe for a peculiar blend of technocratic corporatism, rather than a vision for transcending the politics of established interests for the sake of larger public goals.

CHAPTER VIII

Further Prospects
for
Technocratic Planning

To this point we have been discussing the end of ideology both as a theory of pluralist technocratic society, and as an ideology intended to fulfill that theory through providing an intellectual rationale for the acceptance of technocratic mechanisms for social planning in the society. Here we continue this discussion and go on to inquire what kind of system of technocratic management might yet be achieved by the pursuit of a strategy of consensus with corporate technocracy.

Intellectually, the major elements in the technocratic management of social development are information, coordination, and planning. However, from a political viewpoint, the question of effective central controls is fundamental; controls over manpower, resources, and productive units, without which the planning agency is unable to translate its intellectual perceptions into an actual process of development. In previous chapters, we have indicated some of the political impediments to the translation of social technocratic theory into operating governmental institutions with sufficient central authority to successfully initiate and execute planned development in the public sector. In particular, we have observed how the fragmented nature of the executive bureaucracy has made it possible for corporate enterprises to assimilate to their own purposes and interests segments of governmental authority. In the process, corporate management, not publicly accountable, has come to share considerable power over the allocation and disposition of enormous public resources with governmental bureaucrats who are themselves only indirectly accountable to the public. In this chapter we examine the directions which social planning may take under the conditions of co-operation between the social technocrats and corporate technocrats operating beyond the reach of public scrutiny or control. A comparison of French and British planning, with the state playing a respectively strong and weak role in the planning operation, provides a framework for our discussion of the possible directions for American planning.

Technocratic Planning and the Control of Private Power

In its emphasis on the likelihood of very rapid change based on technological innovation, with impact on institutional patterns, class structure, and culture, the theory of "postindustrial" society is one of revolutionary change. At the same time, there is great concern in the theory that change should not get out of hand, that it be predictable, controllable, manageable. In asserting the need for a kind of change which is manageable, but rejecting ideological prospectives as inappropriate to such change, the theory becomes, paradoxically, an "anti-ideological" ideology of managed change.

Since the thrust of the social technocrats' "anti-ideology" is essentially antipopulist and gradualist, the ideology of managed change sets as its goal the piecemeal strengthening of the state's authority over the development process and its executors in the private sector. Thus, it seeks legal-functional instruments, such as selective procurement policies, by which to persuade the corporations to cooperate with the government's designs.[1] As envisioned by Galbraith, it also seeks political authority to govern the operations of the corporations, consistent with public sector policies determined by a polity revitalized by the participation of humanist intellectuals and academics.

Certainly Bell's legalist pluralism and Galbraith's activist pluralism involve different strategies of action, yet their aims are quite similar. In both cases, the aim is the enhancement of *government* control over the "private" sector. In neither case is there much reflection on the implications of such a solution for the democratic system, or its appropriateness to meeting the current criticisms of this system.

In this respect, Bell and Galbraith are no better or worse than the elite-pluralist theory of democracy which has failed to come to grips with the general problem of public control over private power. In our present context, they have failed to deal with the specific problem of the inner government of the corporation except from the viewpoint of heightening its efficiency through development of technocratic methods and structures. As Peter Bachrach observes:

> Despite the growing complaint that the corporation way of life and values has sapped the political vitality of the middle class and has markedly contributed to the alienation of the faceless masses who man the factories and offices, democratic theory has remained aloof and unchanged.[2]

Both these liberal-pluralist theorists tend to leave the problem of democratic control over corporate power in the hands of government as a representative institution. However, this tends to overlook the remoteness and indirectness of accountability of the government bureaucracy itself with respect to popular democratic control. As Bachrach points out, there is a considerable difference between making the corporation accountable to the bureaucratic state, with little disturbance in its private oligarchic arrangements, and making the corporation accountable to the public, by establishing public control over it on the grounds of its role in allocating values for the entire society.

Ultimately at stake is the notion, official and unofficial, of elite-managed democracy itself. This theory, which views democracy essentially as a system of interest-representation by a plurality of organizational elites, tends to envision the control of private power in terms of the countervailing power of groups with different interests. In the past it was expected that balance would be established through the play of forces within the private organizational sector itself but the enormous growth in corporate power since the Second World War, aided and to a considerable extent promoted by government subsidies, has seriously reduced the possibility of sufficient countervailing power from private sources. Today government alone is viewed as having sufficient power to bring the corporate sector under control for social purposes. But the question remains as to what effect the vesting of authority in central government to accomplish this end will have on the system of contemporary democracy. In particular, can it be expected to significantly reduce the remoteness of the general public from the policy process, either in the corporation or the government bureaucracy?

In the second place, how effective can we expect government control over corporate planning to be in any event? Certainly we can foresee a greater degree of coordination between government and corporation in the name of purposes such as social planning, as well as the already popularly legitimated purposes of national security. But we have seen that the conduct of this coordination on behalf of the latter has been extremely dubious, and has in fact contributed to the expansion of the influence of the corporations on the government agencies, as well as enhancing their economic power. In this light, we must ask how the objectives of social planning will be defined, and by whom, in a system of technocratic planning. Once again, as in the case of planning for national security, we have the prospect of a system of coordination by elites, in the name of the public interest: on the one hand, corporation managers and technicians whose major interest, as Galbraith puts it, is in the expansion of output in order to secure the freedom to plan further expansion of output; on the other hand, government bureaucrats who are highly respectful of their corporation counterparts, and hardly invulnerable to the career opportunities the latter may have to offer, in the short or long run.

The history of unsuccessful attempts to regulate corporation power should give pause to us here. Commenting on the operation of the governmental regulation commissions, Grant McConnell observes:

> The outstanding political fact about the independent regulatory commissions is that they have in general become promoters and protectors of the individuals they have been established to regulate. . . .[3]

After an initial crusading phase, the regulatory commission typically loses its reforming zeal and settles down to the role of managing the given industry, "of course serving the interests of the industry."[4] In practice, this means that the commission serves the interests of the dominant enterprises in the industry while maintaining its own position as "the industry's recognized protector." McConnell attributes this assimilation process to the freeing of the regulatory commissions from presidential and party control, a circumstance which has left them free from popular politics, but not from "the politics of industry and administration." The effect of independent administrative status has been, therefore, to substitute the industry itself, a small and particularistic constituency, for the nation as a whole.[5]

In brief, McConnell's basic point is that the relative autonomy of the independent commissions from political and specifically presidential control has been a significant source of their one-sided responsiveness to powerful industrial interests. Yet he comments himself that the process of agency assimilation to the organized interests subject to administration "is by no means confined to the independent commissions; it is also familiar to veterans of active administration in many long-established governmental bureaus. . . ."[6] The commissions, apparently because of their independent status, have simply tended to attract more attention than the regular governmental "bureaus better hidden from public observation," whose direct accountability to the chief executive probably encouraged taking their operations somewhat more for granted. But this only serves to weaken the thesis that autonomy from executive and party control is what leads to bias in favor of the agency's clients. Even in the case of the regulatory commissions, there are many ways in which the president, the Congress, and the Courts can move to place limits on their independence: the president by means of various appointive, managerial and budgetary controls, the Congress through committee controls and investigations, the courts through the powers of judicial review and statute interpretation. It is in spite of such controls, not because of their absence, that the administrative agencies directly in the presidential chain of command, as well as the independent commissions, have developed especially responsive relations to their organizational clients.

Comparative Models for Technocratic Planning

Under the circumstances described the best that might be hoped for a system of "indicative" planning (the type referred to as a model by the Technology Commission's report) would be the placement at the disposal of the federal government of sophisticated instruments with which it might "persuade" both local governments and the private economy to take steps toward accomplishing social aims such as urban redevelopment, or employment and retraining programs, or transportation planning and development. It should be borne in mind that under such conditions the major corporations might succeed in bending the planning process to their own purposes, with the ideological and political help of the widespread political forces of localism. Whether this actually occurs will ultimately be determined through a struggle of forces involving a combination of political-economic power and technocratic intelligence, currently available not only to the federal government, but to the large corporations as well.

The National Technology Commission has explicitly ruled out government compulsion in any future system of planning, claiming to seek "a common framework of assumptions" for government and private organizations as a basis for "voluntary action" so that "decisions made in the public sector would tend to mesh with those in the private sector."[7] Yet the experience of the French system, the best developed to this date in the area of indicative planning, has been so far rather to the contrary. In the French case too, the proponents began by describing the planning operation as if it were essentially an intellectual confrontation through which the ordinary businessman with his customary short-term and profit-oriented view of those aspects of the market which affect him, would be converted to a longer perspective in time, as well as a broader one concerning the economy. The result would be decisions by the individual businessman more in tune with the requirements of the industry and the economy as a whole, as discerned by the planners. Deviations from these socially conscious economic decisions would produce "danger signals" from the planner, leading to consultation between the relevant circle of given industrialists and the relevant *commission de modernisation*. This in turn should lead to the appropriate coordination of action among the individual businessmen, setting matters right again.[8]

No doubt the voluntary character of this operation was emphasized in order to draw the widest possible distinction between capitalist indicative planning and the communist method of planning by decree. In the early phase of French planning during the 1950s, the typical expression of this contrast was to say that the Plan was "indicative," and never "imperative"; and to emphasize the central role of continuous "dialogue" between the planners and the planned. However, these simplified, basically intellectual conceptions of the process overlook the significant issue of motivation. Though the Plan did not involve direct compulsion, this did not exclude the government's use of its considerable resources to reward the obedient and persuade the recalcitrant. The government, as a political "investment firm," has at its disposal capital reserves in the form of tax revenues, and capital credits in the form of reliefs, greater than those of any individual firm, even the largest. It can and does use the fiscal powers of taxation and the granting of tax credits to obtain the cooperation its planners require of individual private enterprises. The fourth French plan lists eight major categories of tax relief which the economic planners can employ for these purposes, as instruments of official discrimination in favor of the enterprise which will cooperate with the plan by financing approved investment projects. In addition, there are a variety of other tax concessions on profits ploughed back for modernization or new investment. Finally, there is the financial triumvirate of the Treasury, the FDES (Fonds de Developpement Economique et Social), and the Caisses des Depots et des Consignations, the three main sources of public funds, which divide up among themselves the responsibility for the large items of investment in the Plan.[9] The Treasury is responsible for the use of all government funds outside the nationalized industries, and exerts a major influence over the flow of public capital into the private sector. While the FDES complements this through its control over the investments of nationalized industries, the Caisses, a semi-public institution, is the biggest bank in France, acting as chief underwriter for new issues of industrial bonds, thus constituting a major factor in the private capital market, since its approval is vital for any new bond issue.[10] Through these agencies the government exercises both direct and indirect control over a substantial part of the nation's economic activity, and uses this control to persuade private business that their economic decisions would be wisest if made in concert with the plans of the public authorities.

We can see then that in addition to the purely intellectual, "indicative" aspect, this sort of planning involves the utilization of considerable governmental powers over the level and direction of investment in the economy. As M. Masse, Commissaire General of the Plan, puts it, the Plan is "less than imperative but more than indicative."[11] Nevertheless, it would be entirely mistaken to assume that the pressures in the planning process are all one way, from the planning center to the private firm. In the first place, the large French corporations have accepted planning for a number of reasons. For one, we have the familiar reason, cited by Galbraith in his discussion of planning by American corporation giants, that they recognize planning as a means of reducing the uncertainties of investment and orderly market growth. In addition, the large firms share the goal of the planners with regard to the concentration of production, though for their own reasons. From the planners' viewpoint the smaller firms are difficult to incorporate into coherent planning, due as much to their numbers as to their technical obsolescence. The planners seek what they call the "80-20 ratio" — a distribution of output such that 80 percent of production comes from about 20 percent of the firms in the industry — significantly lower ratios such as 60-40 are considered unmanageable over the long run. Of course, small businessmen have reacted with suspicion, demanding that their trade associations be permitted to act as intermediaries for the individual firm. The planners have resisted such a system, since inevitably this would mean that the trade association would take on the role of spokesman for the attitudes of the average business, whereas the planners have sought to select above-average firms, usually large corporations, as allies in a given industry to help force up the general level of performance in the industry.

In France, large corporations for some time have welcomed industry-wide planning as a means of reducing investment uncertainty and securing orderly development of their respective markets. As vital allies to the planners, they have considerable opportunity to voice their ideas and exert their own pressure on the Plan, which in many ways reflects a compromise between their own collective wishes and the wishes of the government officials responsible for economic policy.[12] At this point, it should be noted that the "indicative" planning proponents' model of a direct dialogue between economic policy planners and private organizations is itself oversimplified. The "dialogue" also involves an intermediate layer of technical experts in the *commissions de modernisation*, who are intimately familiar with the details of what is happening in the given industry to which they are assigned, as well as the professional economists at the center, in the *Commissariat du Plan*, whose emphasis is on *cohérence*, i.e., an integrated, overall, generalizing view. The thirty-odd *Commissions* bring together groups of civil service industry specialists with representatives of the most powerful interest groups in the industry, including heads of firms, representatives of employers' organizations, and trade union representatives, plus independent persons from the universities and the professions. However, the policy planners in the *Commissariat* complain that the civil servants on the *commissions* do not merely become absorbed into the detail of the respective industries ostensibly under their tutelage; they often act as if they were in some way the representatives of the particular industry interests. As Andrew Shonfield, a close observer of the evolution of postwar French planning, has perceptively observed:

> There is no doubt that the activity of planning, as it is practiced in France, has reinforced the systematic influence exerted by large-scale business on economic policy. . . .[13]

Though the meetings of the modernization commissions themselves are held in the presence of union officials and cannot be used for explicit discussion of cartel arrangements or for making price agreements, they encourage an atmosphere of collaboration among businessmen who have come together for a number of years for the sake of coordinated planning. Thus both through co-optation of intermediary officials, and through increased coordination among themselves, the leading French corporations exert considerable influence over the planning process.

Now, the French model is actually the best currently available, from the viewpoint of the administrative power of the central government *vis-à-vis* the private corporations. Owing to the long tradition of centralization and administrative discretion that stretches back at least to the Revolution, the French government bureaucracy approaches the planning activity with a great deal of confidence and a real determination to bring about cooperation with its plans. The British, with a different governmental tradition, have tended to view the planning process in terms of their traditional ideology of absolute distinction between public and private power. Thus, development planning under a Conservative government is guided by a traditional policy of limited intervention by the state in the private sector while under a Labor government it has tended to lean in the other direction, toward outright nationalization of industries vital to development. Neither approach has been promising; under the Conservatives, planning has amounted to little more than a voluntary agreement between representatives of organized private power, with the state losing its opportunity to guide development from an overall national perspective; under the Laborites, the government has tended to conduct its planning activities without the active support of those with effective power in the relevant industries.[14]

The great advantage held by the French, besides their strong official bureaucracy, has been the existence of a network of mixed enterprise which is more inclined to communicate and cooperate with government than the ordinary private firm. Since the First World War this type of enterprise, a partnership of private and public capital, has been used to extend the range of industry in branches of production where private capital would not otherwise venture, e.g., oil and chemicals. This is an outgrowth of traditional governmental intervention in the economy, but in the Twenties the approach changed from the granting of exclusive concessions to firms willing to venture into risky areas, to the establishment of contractual relations with the given firm by which the state holds joint ownership in the assets. In some instances the state has no equity investment in the enterprise, yet appoints its top management in return for special privileges in the mode of raising capital as well as "the assurance of a great deal of governmental business."[15] This type of relationship is particularly interesting for the purpose of comparison with U.S. government contracting in the R & D sector. Though the function of venturing into an area of heavy investment at high risk is similar, the difference, until the McNamara reforms, lay in the absence of comparable government control over management. (Even then, such controls are much more formidable with regard to quasi-nationalized firms like Lockheed, which rely upon government support, than to truly "mature" private corporations like GM and GE.) Thus the French mixed enterprise is more truly a wedding of public control and private capital than the typical American case, which more nearly resembles the early continental device of granting exclusive concession to the venture capitalist in an area of risk important to the interests of the state. Through the instrumentality of the "mixed enterprise" the French have at their disposal a central core of major enterprises which are more responsive to the desires of the state than the ordinary firm.

Possibilities for American Social Planning

As between the French and British context for planning, current government-business relations in America resemble those of the British

situation somewhat more than they do the French, in a number of respects. If we consider American firms that do a significant part of their
business (e.g., over 15 percent) with government a species of "mixed
enterprise," the degree of governmental control over the "mixed enterprise" has been greater in the French case than in the American. And
the readiness to employ measures of direct economic intervention with
respect to individual firms, either through fiscal or managerial controls,
still appears considerably lower in the American firms in the nondefense
sector, than in the French; once again there is closer resemblance to the
British model, in which government has avoided the use of direct intervention, and relied instead on a kind of corporatist scheme for economic
management. In the British approach, the major interest groups — business, unions, farmers — are brought together for the purpose of reaching
agreement through a bargaining process concerning their future economic
conduct. The role of the state is that of general coordinator and referee
for these negotiations, but beyond that it has little more than the character of an additional interest group, much on the same level as the
others, rather than an authoritative architect of planning policies over
which there may be only a small margin for compromise, as in the
French case.

   In more highly modernized American industry, however, with its
greater organizational capacity for conducting large-scale planning, there
seems to be greater effective interest in industry-wide and interindustry
coordination among corporations than in Great Britain.[16] In the U. S.,
Shonfield notes, private corporate enterprise has developed a number of
devices for pooling information for the purpose of industry-wide economic forecasting, leading ultimately to a degree of intercorporate coordination. There are business surveys, planning associations, "statistics
users conferences," and the like, which have been operating for at least
a decade, compiling and distributing information on how firms view the
market and what their intentions are with respect to it. In addition, some
of these operations serve to collect data from government on its own
fiscal and investment intentions in a way that will allow incorporation
into long-range company planning. Shonfield notes the existence of a
kind of "intellectual underworld" in American business which, despite
antitrust laws, uninhibitedly exchanges ideas "on how firms see the future of the market and on some of the things that they are going to do
about it." Here Shonfield suggests that this kind of common economic
forecasting may lead to other forms of coordination between firms.[17]

   This interest and readiness to engage in, industrial planning, as well
as the actual development of a subculture of planning which continues
to grow and to influence the operations of the large corporations, is an
important consideration in approaching the question of whether a sys-

tem of national planning will develop in the United States, and what form it might take. Shonfield states that Gerald Colm, chief economist of the National Planning Association, doubts that a system of planning on the French model will develop here, in view of the "individualistic attitude" of entrepreneurs. But Shonfield regards this as more of an anachronistic myth about American business than an accurate reflection of the real sophistication of contemporary corporate enterprise in this country. He points to the strong tendencies toward consensus in the corporate community, which may well outweigh the urge to compete, particularly when the uncertainties engendered by sharp competition can be so expensive to firms with heavy long-range investments in specialized technology.

What Shonfield regards as the real remaining obstacle to national economic planning is not the competitiveness of corporate business, but the lack of direction from a federal government in which competing public agencies are able to assert their independence of decisions made at the center. As he observes, when central government is weak as against other public agencies, private firms will tend to be skeptical about going ahead on the basis of the government's "planned targets." In Shonfield's view, what is unique about the American situation in regard to central planning is the prevalence of a "competitive theory of administration inside the government, rather than any ungovernable competitiveness outside it. . . ."[18] At the same time that this constitutes a serious obstacle to coherent national planning — in which developments in one area must be coordinated with developments in related areas — it also allows private corporations cooperating with relatively autonomous agency bureaucrats to exploit their relationship to mutual advantage.

Michael Harrington, writing on the so-called "social-industrial complex," cites the remark of a federal agency executive to the effect that each government agency has built up a list of willing firms in its special field of responsibility, and is capable of providing the right incentives to get them to carry on its programs ("we know how to turn them on.")[19] In this connection, Harrington points to the experience of the military-industrial complex, in which such procedures (the cost-plus contract, for example) led to "private alliances between self-interested executives and ambitious bureaucrats." This tendency, he notes, "is already quite developed in the cities industry — where, for instance, real-estate men support rent subsidies as a means of attacking public housing — and, as the *Wall Street Journal* realizes, it is going to appear in education too."[20] In regard to education, he cites the case of a $2 million government grant to build a computer classroom for an Indian tribe in Wisconsin which would serve only sixty students of the thousand on the reservation. In the words of the *New Republic* article which he quotes: "The one substantive reason for financing this project is the government's interest in building up the education industry."[21] And the manner in which the corporation fulfills or fails to fulfill its contract — say in the case of running a Job Corps Center with inadequate teaching staff, employed under poor working and wage conditions, and with little voice in curricular policy (as a Rutgers University study documented in the case of the AT & T-run center at Camp Kilmer, New Jersey)[22] — is much less likely to attract the attention of the ranking congressional committee members charged with agency watchdog functions, than would the operations of an OEO research project or a Peace Corps institute run by a university.

It is interesting that Harrington closes his remarks on the "social-industrial complex" with some comments on the end of ideology. The theory of the end of ideology, he notes, in which the "new men" are the manipulators of the new computer technology, has been adapted to corporate purposes by business ideologists like Max Ways of *Fortune* magazine. The end of ideology, in denying that the current politics of the public sector bear any resemblance to the issues of the 1930s, has provided an "excellent rationale" for the ideology of the "social-industrial complex." Ostensibly the proper subjects for debate are no longer the sharply focussed political clashes of different group interests over the need for basic income redistribution, and the like, but the best technical means of solving a complex variety of remaining domestic problems. In this view, observes Harrington, "The corporation, as a neutral association of qualified experts, will, for a reasonable fee, promote the public good in an absolutely impartial and scientific way." However, as Harrington emphasizes, the image has little substance, for an examination of corporate practices in various areas of enterprise, from building a knowledge industry to redeveloping the urban downtown, clearly reveals that "the social-industrialists are, at every point, pursuing a private interest. . . ."[23]

In light of these considerations, it is significant that the planning-oriented majority of the Technology Commission, composed mainly of union representatives and university social scientists, seek the establishment of a system of "indicative" planning, like that most frequently identified with the strong central controls of the French system.[24] Apparently, they recognize the need for greater governmental control *vis à vis* corporate decision making, in order that the programs required for the implementation of public sector plans be faithfully and efficiently executed. At the same time, however, in order to achieve corporate acceptance of even the very moderate technical proposals they put forward, they find it strategic to include a "voluntarist" formula stipulating that this kind of planning would involve "no compulsion"; rather it would seek a "common framework of assumptions" for "voluntary action." On this basis "both governmental and private organizations would determine their separate policies and action." How this would lead to "decisions made in the public sector [which] would mesh with those in the private sector" is hard to see.[25] Whether indicative planning, especially in areas not of primary interest to the corporate sector, could succeed in the absence of adequate governmental controls is open to question; perhaps the American system, much more affluent than either the British or the French, could afford to provide adequate incentives for cooperation by that segment of the corporate sector which now styles itself the "social-industrial" complex, through cost-plus contracting in the public sector resembling that which has enriched the R & D corporations in the military sector.

However, despite the rapid growth of GNP, it would appear to be extremely difficult in the near future to satisfy the demands of both a military-industrial and a social-industrial complex. In fact, according to a study by the National Planning Association cited by the Technology Commission:

> Even with a four per cent annual increase in national products we would, in 1975, fall short by $150 billion a year of the possibility of satisfying all those goals [military and civilian] at the same time. Thus we will continue to face the need to set priorities and to make choices.[26]

Among the preconditions for the planning which this will require is the curbing of the political power which the corporations enjoy in the military agencies and Congress, and which they might as readily acquire as a "social-industrial" complex in the social agencies. Curbing their power, however, assumes the emergence of political forces sufficiently powerful to ensure the necessary legislative and administrative action. In the absence of a socially conscious labor movement, it will require a broadly inclusive political movement to make the ostensibly "private" power of the corporations significantly more available for public purposes than it has hitherto been. Such a movement is not merely unlikely; it would, according to the social technocrats, be undesirable as well, since it would certainly require, for the coalescence of the many different kinds of people seeking improvement in one or another aspect of the public sector, a unifying ideology as theory and rallying point.

In view of the above discussion, what can American social technocrats hope to accomplish in the way of a system of social planning? The range of possibilities seems to lie between the "consensual planning" of the British, involving the full representation of unions, professionals, farmers and other interests besides government and business in the planning councils, with relatively weak central controls, and the "collusive planning" of the French, with close, somewhat exclusive collaboration between big business and top-ranking government officials, and built around strong central controls.[27] Emerging government-business relations may yet promote development of a system of planning along the lines of the latter; however, major questions remain concerning the strength of central government controls which can, of course, affect the whole nature of the enterprise.

As we pointed out earlier, there already exists within the corporate economy a special economic preserve where private enterprise has been replaced by a tacit kind of planning between R & D corporations under government contract and the relevant government agencies. The essential point is that this planning goes beyond the market control which has been exercised by large corporations since the early 1900s, and represents a new era in corporation-government relations. We can see now that this phenomenon, which crystallized during the 1950s, was itself absorbed by the end-of-ideology theory then being formulated under the ambiguous rubric of the "mixed economy," and has lain conceptually dormant since. During the present decade, however, its operations have come to have an increasingly important impact on the larger economy, and particularly on the structure of the federal budget. As a result, its emergence and functioning have become the specific object of a number of recent studies. Whether referred to as the "Contract State" the "New Industrial State," or the military "State Management," we have here a nucleus of collusive planning that stands outside of public scrutiny or control. Within this state-within-a-state, favored corporate recipients of government largesse have been guaranteed a market for their military products, enabling them to plan the allocation of resources and investments over the long term with minimum risk.

In our present context, what is perhaps most significant is that these very corporations, and particularly the aerospace firms, which have been perhaps the most favored members of this internal "state," are now seeking to further protect their economic position by diversification into non-military, public sector areas. For example, in the name of preserving their "systems-engineering" capability, occasionally underemployed aerospace industrial teams have sought contracts in areas such as urban traffic management or water conservation. In the process, they have found allies among local and state government executives of California, who strong endorsed the handling of such problems from the "systems management" viewpoint. (Nelson Rockefeller, with his plans for a giant urban redevelopment corporation operating along these lines in New York state, is another example of the sophisticated technocratic executive in government who sees the government contract pattern as a useful

approach to providing the requirements of the local public sector.)
Former Governor Pat Brown, testifying to a congressional committee,
indicated strong willingness to put the areospace industry's talents to
work on public sector problems, and the state retained Aerojet-General
for preliminary studies. The implications are not limited to California.
As one aerospace trade magazine observed: "Other states and the federal
government are watching the experiment with interest."[28] Unfortunately,
on the basis of experience with federal contracting, there is real likelihood
that firms wihich win state contracts will actually tend to drain the public
sector in various ways, such as hiring technical personnel away from
state agencies, universities, and local research firms, or taking inflated
profits based on cost accounting that incorporates the cost of subcontractors' work. In addition, firms working on long-term state contracts,
and having established prime contract status, may well pursue a policy of
mergers and acquistions among subcontractors, thereby expanding their
own facilities and eliminating competition for further state contracts.[29]

In this way, the federally favored R & D corporation, already possessed
of enormous resources and decision-making authority, can also sink
deep roots at the level of the local public sector, producing a formidable
concentration of power there which is not merely economic, but also
political in a rather direct sense. In effect, the "private government" of
such a corporation would take on many of the features of a political
party in power, excepting those of public accountability.

> Like the conventional political party, the corporation will have acquired
> the ability to allocate state resources, to dispense job and financial
> patronage, and to insure profits for its investors from the tax resources
> of state government.[30]

In these circumstances, with some of the most powerful and respected
corporations in America already enjoying the benefits of the R & D Contract State and now reaching for the leading role in the development of
the local and regional public sector, unless the strongest safeguards are
erected, the "consensual" planning supported by the social technocrats
may likely prove to be in practice a surrender of governmental authority
over the developmental process and its goals to the managerial oligarchies
of our giant corporations. Once again, on a vastly expanded scale,
"what's good for General Motors," and Westinghouse, and A T & T, and
Chrysler, Ford, Socony, Firestone, and Philco will be "good" for the
nation, in the public sector itself. The outcome could be a repetition of
the pre-McNamara heyday of waste and profit in the R & D sector,
but this time on the local level, involving fifty state bureaucracies and
hundreds of city halls, rather than the relatively manageable three mili-

tary agencies over which McNamara was able, after years of effort, to impose some degree of restraint. Moreover, this time the product will not be removed in its impact from the day-to-day socio-physical environment (such as a missile to be shot off into the ocean, or a space probe to indicate conditions on the surface of some distant planet), but the human ecological and cultural environment itself; the roads we travel, the houses we live in, the schools we study in, and their visual, physical and psychological effects on the very grain and texture and rhythm of our experience. Will innovation in these areas be determined by the needs of the inhabitants, e.g., the often-expressed desire for opening up the living environment, in terms of space, variety, and design; or will it be the fancy, flashy outcome of the particular combination of technology and materials which the contractor is "pushing," from teaching machines to skyscraper apartment houses, from aluminum sidings to all-glass construction? Will the bureaucratic design and inhuman scale so typical of contemporary corporation headquarters and corporation-sponsored renewal projects become the prototoype of the supercity of the future, repeated a thousand-fold?[31]

At present, it appears that what the social technocrats have in mind as a means to gaining a measure of political authority over corporate development policy in the public sector are such devices as a national-goals commission made up of representatives of major interest groups and assisted by experts in relevant fields.[32] Undoubtedly, such an agency could provide a useful propaganda instrument for the circulation of government "forecasts" which incorporate particular schemes of public sector development. In this way it might provide central planners with a certain degree of leverage over developments with impact on the public sector, whether limited to that sector or initiated outside it, and thus provide some control over private corporate planning. Its persuasive force with the public would probably result from the image of representative consensus coupled with technical expertise. However, its authority might well depend on the moods and swings of public opinion interacting with its own pronouncements. And it should be noted that even this extremely moderate translation of the Commission's recommendations for indicative planning has been strongly resisted by conservative representatives of the corporate sector.[33]

To this point then, our examination of the possible directions for American planning in the near future indicates the likely emergence at best of a kind of "collusive" planning involving close cooperation between agency bureaucrats and corporation managers, with the planning needs of favored corporations quite central to the relationship, along lines already well-established in the Contract State. Moreover, this relationship, which so far has tended to be confined to corporations involved in military R & D, promises to reach into the public sector as well, particularly in areas which require the employment and development of complex technology, from urban transit to programmed education. One effect of the building of a "social-industrial" complex could be the technical overdevelopment of areas in the public sector, such as teaching, in order to suit the productive capacities and market requirements of corporations operating in these areas; so, for example, closed-circuit TV and teaching machines might be overutilized, to the detriment of the personal teacher-student relationship. But this is not necessarily the case; only a possible consequence of development in the absence of adequate publicly established standards and controls. Another problematic result would be the possible extension of corporate political-economic power down to the most intimate local level, producing a twentieth-century version of the "company town" on a magnified scale.

In the future, the possibilities for social planning in America seem to lie between two unhappy conditions: on one hand, the continuation of piecemeal attempts at central planning, stymied by fragmented administration which is itself tied to a plurality of diverging interests; on the other, the further development of collusive planning between government and business beyond effective public control, ultimately enhancing only select corporate interests. At worst, perhaps, there stands the possibility of some special combination of the two, unique to the hybrid pluralist-technocratic society which is postindustrial America in its present stage of emergence.

CHAPTER IX

Ideologies of
Government and Opposition
Today

If postindustrial society is to be a society of political-ideological consensus rather than one pervaded by social conflict, it will have to resolve the question of the legitimacy of a system of "managed democracy" from the standpoint of the public in whose name it governs, whatever its technical effectiveness. This question is relevant to the end-of-ideologists' theory of a technocratic postindustrial society, because such a society is in several respects a developmental version of a system of elitist democracy, as applied to advanced industrial society. The end-of-ideologists have attempted to join a managerial theory of democracy with the concept of an expanding welfare state, in order to make it relevant to a rapidly developing technological society which allegedly seeks to retain liberal-humanist values. Our analysis, however, indicates that incorporated into a dynamic theory of managed change for social welfare, the elite model of democracy fails to stand up to the strains of advanced development, particularly in regard to its legitimacy. We pursue this point in detail in the present chapter.

The Ideology of Consumerism:
Popular Base for Technocratic Government

Perhaps the most relevant question that can be asked of an ideology of planning in a society that remains at least formally democratic, is "planning by whom and for what purposes?" The postindustrial theory answers this question by pointing to politically neutral technocrats whose planning implements a democratically arrived at consensus. However, we have already indicated the severe limitations on the participation of various interest groups in the planning process, which may well become a virtually collusive arrangement between the corporations and the administrative agencies of the state, even if somewhat modified by the secondary participation of representatives of labor, agriculture, and the professions. As a result of the power of corporate industry to penetrate the government agency, the perspective of the agency's planners tends to meld with that of the corporate technocrats; *their* joint purposes become the essential standards for the planning process. This raises serious questions about the pace and extent to which the goals of general public sector development for "unmet human needs," as against military R & D and abstract-scientific development (as in much of the space program), will be pursued by the technocratic state, and how broad a base of popular support planning by this state will actually have in the society.

At this point the disposition of politically relevant ideology in the society becomes extremely significant. For the sake of convenience in the following discussion, we will here define an ideal-type category based on certain central tendencies in the social structure of postindustrial America since the early 1950s. This broad social category we shall refer to as the "middle masses," by which we indicate those strata whose occupations generally provide regular employment with moderate security, status, and income, and who broadly share a common life style, or array of related life styles, in the community. This section of the population is, on the one hand, neither chronically unemployed nor materially deprived, nor, on the other, employed in positions of high institutional authority, reward or prestige. This is, in fact, the preponderant "middle majority" of the population, including the upper (organized, relatively secure) working class, together with the lower midddle class — an amalgam largely of what have been the relatively comfortable blue- and white-collar working classes of the new society.[1] Though these "new masses" lack a clear-cut ideology or a comprehensive theory of the society, this does not necessarily imply that they are without some basic common set of beliefs about their positions and prospects or a common language with which to express themselves. In this respect, the language of the new middle masses is the language of what might be called "consumerism," reflecting several decades of socialization in the notion that to consume the society's product is the citizen's first duty.[2] In a word, the ideology of the middle mass is an ideology of *equal* opportunity to consume the material and social perquisites of an extremely productive, open, and still expansive society. This ideology is in turn rooted ultimately in a conception of human nature as essentially acquisitive and of the major purpose of society as being the creation of ever-increasing material wealth. These are conceptions which are shared by a vast majority and are an expression of the success of the instruments of contemporary culture — advertising and the mass media (Galbraith's "organized bamboozlement") — in developing and diffusing a common language for the mass appropriate to a highly productive society which requires expanding consumption of its product, merely in order to maintain its political and economic structures.

To the extent that the middle mass is today the major support of a culture based upon consumerism it is the potential base of political support for technocratic management of the economy. Hence the slogan of the "balanced budget" is today a thing of the past for *both* major parties; in its place stands the "new economics," involving massive fiscal and contractual intervention by government in the economy, on a deficit basis.[3] It is the cultural value of consumerism which is the thread that draws together into a common system the new unionized working class and the new corporatized middle class as well as the parties and interest organizations which represent them politically. By itself, this is not a developed ideology so much as a cultural value, a publicly proclaimed "good," though lacking a clear-cut theory or programmatic statement. This value theme is the basis of the "new consensus" on which the social technocrats optimistically premise the retention and expansion of a system of "welfare capitalism." However, the privatized "affluence" which the new economists have brought to the middle masses carries no particular commitment to the development or improvement of the civilian public sector. Certainly it hardly is a guarantee for the welfare of the poor; indeed a main theme of social criticism after the early 1960s has been the discovery of widespread poverty amidst private affluence.

Insofar as the values of consumerism bind the middle masses to the postindustrial society, they seem ready to accept its technocratic management without too much regard for the political orientation of the managers, as long as this does not infringe upon their own economic perquisites. If there is any other ideological theme which has moved them thus far, it seems to be the ideology of military preparedness for national security. This is fully consistent with an ideology of consumerism —

indeed the kernel of the ideology of the middle masses may be characterized as "comfort in security." The belief in security through military
measures has tended to dispose them toward support of military spending and military ventures officially proclaimed in the "national interest,"[4]
though there are limits to their support for such ventures, as revealed in
the case of the drawn-out Vietnam war, and particularly as the domestic social and economic costs to the middle mass have escalated.

On the other hand, they seem to lack comparably strong commitment
to social values which would lead them to accept the costs, for example,
of a thorough renewal of the urban environment; increasingly they are
outer-city or suburban dwellers, accustomed to skirting about the "other
America" of the central city in their commutation and in their concerns;
and of those still resident in the city, many seek eventually to escape its
physical decay and racial tensions. Thus, we see that the ideology of
consumerism is essentially an ideology of private comfort and convenience, tending to mute the involvement or identification of the middle
masses with public affairs and issues. To the extent that the middle
masses internalize this ideology, it tends to neutralize them with regard
to issues which have traditionally been considered the focus of ideological debate. In *this* respect it may justly be said that they are "nonideological" in their thinking, ready to accept technocratic government
so long as it "produces the goods."

However, it should be stressed here that while the success of the
technocratic society in "producing the goods," in satisfying the demands
of a population socialized to want what the economy produces, and in
erasing serious economic distinctions among the middle masses may lead
to the end of sharp ideological conflicts, it surely does not produce an
"end of ideology." Rather, as some observers have pointed out, it suggests that the materialistic ideology of the society is absorbed into the
reality of the society's life styles and social structures, *via* the economic
process itself.[5] One major result then, is the collapse of the qualities of
transcendence characteristic of the great ideological systems of the nineteenth and twentieth centuries. Under this theory, the ideology (the ideals
and ultimate values) of the integrated middle masses of the new society
becomes synonymous with their ongoing way of life (their normative
culture, its institutions, life styles, and behavioral modes), so that the
tension between values and norms, which historically has been a stimulus
to social change and reform, is removed. The utopian element in ideology
disappears; what remains is ideology operating as an affirmation of the
established values and norms, ideology as legitimation, and the disappearance of the opposition of ideologies of criticism and transcedence.
Ideology becomes little more than the explicit expression, the public face,
of the *established* values and norms, of the ongoing culture of the advanced industrial society. Culture now simply repeats and reflects the

society; though ideology does not disappear, its critical, dialectic function decays.[6]

In particular, the ideology of democracy as a ceaseless striving for the transcendent goals of social equity, justice, and freedom, and as a cultural value inspiring all citizens to participate freely in deciding the directions of societal development,[7] tends to be replaced by a concept of democracy as means, as a set of formal institutional structures — the parties and their "packaged" and advertised candidates; voting; official representation — for the achievement of specific, limited social aims, and as an organized marketplace for the choice of political leadership. Thus in both polity and economy, democracy as an ideology of social transcendence tends to be displaced by consumerism as an ideology of social integration; the transcendent ideals of classic democracy are replaced by the relatively mundane objectives of contemporary consumerism.

Ideologies of Opposition to Technocratic Government

If since the 1950s the middle mass has been the major public constituency for the technocratic management of a consumption-oriented society, what have been the sources of opposition to such a mode of government? In order to respond to this we must take note of the emergence of a number of new ideological movements during the last decade, quite contrary to the predictions of the end-of-ideology theory.

As we look back over the decade of the 1960s, reports at its outset of the death of ideology certainly appear to have been "somewhat premature." It is obvious even to the casual observer that ideological politics, almost since the publication of the end-of-ideology thesis, has become more widespread among a greater variety of groups than at the beginning of this decade. There is little sign of a reversal in the foreseeable future; current trends, if they continue, will probably make for an expansion of ideological politics, not only in the popular movements of the day, but within established political institutions as well.

Radical Rightism and Black Nationalism as Ideologies of Parochial Community

In the first place, the early assumptions of anti-ideological theorists regarding the decline of extreme right-wing ideology have been thoroughly invalidated. The "radical Right" remains today, almost two decades after the McCarthy period, as a force of considerable significance, strong enough to capture the Republican party at its 1964 convention, and persistent in its influence on the electorate even after passing that high point of strength in the party. In the future, militant rightists and rightist extremists will probably continue to exert considerable pressure on the politics of both parties, and in the political and cultural life of the lower middle class and large sections of the working class, particularly those with racist leanings or strong resentment against government spending for welfare or antipoverty programs which appear to afford them little direct benefit;[8] as a result, the radical Right will tend to act as a brake on proposed programs for expanding the civilian public sector, in both major parties. In addition, the continuing influence of a militant Right and its orientation toward the use of force to resolve domestic as well as foreign problems could remain an important factor in turning the lower strata of the middle mass toward support for military development as against public sector programs. To the extent that military programs provide a basis for local employment, local business expansion, and community growth, they bring the radical Right into the culture of consumerism and confer a degree of respectability upon it, changing its image from "red-neck" to white collar. However, the movement's membership remains essentially parochial and anticosmopolitan, taking localism — local rights, local community — as its touchstone in the struggle against central government controls and public sector programs, viewed as manifestations of "socialism."[9]

Like the radical Right, the black nationalist movement, another ideological movement which has come into prominence in the past decade, is also localist and parochial in some major respects. Actually this movement consists of many strands which are far from coordinated in policy or action. These express in some respects an ideology of resentment, in others, of desperation in face of political isolation. Though there is much criticism within the movement of bureaucratic programs run top-down without a voice for the local community, the segments which do not support violence as a matter of strategy have tended to welcome federal and foundation aid to public sector development.[10] This has been for many reasons a relatively weak movement in conventional political terms. Thus its demands for expansion of public resources for ghetto redevelopment, with no bureaucratic strings attached, have so far invoked little political force in terms of electoral constituency; in addition, these demands conflict with the conservatism of a middle mass which at least until recently has seemed satisfied with its private "affluence" or with the not too distant prospects of such, and satisfied with the management of change from above. The result is to drive the movement inwards upon itself, around the themes of political autonomy and cultural separatism.[11]

New Leftism as an Ideology of Democratic Participation

Perhaps the most significant ideological development in the past decade was the rise of the New Left, bringing with it some new concepts, and reviving a number of older, peculiarly American ideas about government and its relation to popular sovereignty. Distinctively, its members have been mainly young, white and middle- to upper-middle-class students, in good part the children of the upper strata of the middle mass and above, themselves prime candidates for accession to the technocratic elite. Yet these young people became the core of a new radicalism expressing a powerful alienation not only from their respective universities, but also from the defining institutions of contemporary economic and political life as well. If anything tends to invalidate the predictions of an "end of ideology," it has been the spectacle of these privileged prototypes of the "new men" of postindustrial society, rejecting on ideological grounds its material rewards and its opportunities for status and institutional power, and seeking to organize and educate a mass movement of protest against it.

While militant right and black power movements may be considered expressions of dislocated or displaced subcultures rooted in localism and deprivation, subcultures which will eventually shrink and become absorbed into an increasingly affluent and cosmopolitan society (a large assumption in both cases, but not totally implausible), the case is significantly different with the New Left. Unlike these other movements, the New Left has been the product of an educated middle-class student generation which is likely to grow in postindustrial society, both in numbers and in its influence on the central cultural themes and styles of that society. Like the other movements, it emphasizes the importance of "community," and views it as a social environment which is human in scale and personal in style; like them too it has opposed the idea of community to on-going structures of remote, oppressive bureaucracies. At the same time, its perspective has been cosmopolitan and international rather than localistic, expressing the opposition of young people throughout the advanced industrial societies of the world against the developing techno-organizational structure of these societies as they move into a postindustrial phase.[12]

Doctrinal rigor has had to be sacrificed by the New Left in order to allow for the broadest possible cooperation between a spectrum of groups which are separated by some degree of ideological difference. However, this has been a practical sacrifice, rather than one of principle. Similarly, the tentative, groping, provisional, incomplete statements of aims and the searching discussions about programs appropriate to aims, have hardly reflected a rejection of ideology, but the openness of a movement committed to full and free discussion of the elements which constitute an ideology; *theory, values, goals,* and *strategy.* In a sense, all of these are caught up in the phrase "participatory democracy" which has for many come to characterize the essential ideology of the New Left.[13] Internally, perhaps the most significant distinction concerning this ideology has been that which soon developed between proponents of full participation in existing institutions for purposes of structural reform and redirection, as against members of the movement who supported the creation of independent democratic institutions parallel to established bureaucratic structures, arguing that established institutions can in the last analysis not really allow for basic change. (Up to the present, the major drift since the late 1960s appears to be in the direction of injecting participationist reforms into established structures such as the political parties, rather than parallel institutional development.)

In this regard it is essential to bear in mind that the New Left's ideological positions have been strongly influenced by a kind of ideological "nativism." The movement has tended to turn away from abstract political theories of radical change, particularly from Marxist class theory based on earlier European conditions which portrayed the working class as the vanguard of change in industrial society, to confront the contemporary American political scene in its own terms. As a result during the 1960s its political strategy has involved approaches to the university community on the one hand and to black ghetto and white slum communities on the other; in each instance, communities which can be viewed as marginal to the culture of the middle mass into which most of the blue- and white-collar working class has now been assimilated. The result has been a raising of demands bearing a certain resemblance to those of the Populist revolt against the effects of emergent corporatism in early American industrial society; symbolic "initiative and recall" *via* demonstrations, demands for full political rights for all sectors of the population, demands for bureaucratic decentralization and reform, and a program of building grass-roots organizations at the local community level to encourage the use of rights and accordingly the winning of representation in the political arena.[14]

Participatory democracy, as a new value-symbol combining elements of such historic democratic values as equality, community, and the citizen's right to political participation, has functioned as a goal of organizational life in New Left organizations as well as a strategy for winning power in the larger polity. Internally, organizational emphasis has been on the development of indigenous leadership through such practices as rotation of leadership, staff working to enable expression of members rather than speaking "for" them, and reliance on substantive consensus rather than on formal parliamentary procedures, in order to encourage participation by the less experienced or articulate.

When carried to the extreme of denying the need for any organizational structure, or for leadership or coordinative functions, this has created serious organizational difficulties in the establishment and implementation of coherent organizational policy and programs, and in controlling the implicit leadership which has on occasion developed behind the scenes to provide central coordination. Thus in those cases where the lack of recognition of the need for leadership functions has meant an absence of established machinery for their control, the consequence has ironically been undemocratic leadership procedure.[15]

Perhaps the great weakness of the ideology of participatory democracy has been in the area of economic-structural theory, which has in turn been shaped by the practical exigencies of the experience of its proponents. The formative milieu of this experience was the "integration movement" for the civil and political rights of black people in America; as a result, the major preoccupation of the theory of participatory democracy has been the political system, viewed as the central locus for change, to the relative neglect of the economy and its problematic aspects.

In the latter part of the 60s, with the collapse of the civil rights movement and the expulsion of white participants by black power militants, the New Left turned its attention to the university, focussing on the theme of "student power" and demonstrating against military agencies and military-related organizations which sought to recruit or do research on campus. Thus, the major cultural and knowledge-producing institution of the postindustrial society became adopted as a focus of movement activity. This led in turn to the development of new techniques and strategies of action, with campus demonstrations and sit-ins replacing the voter registration drive, and to a divergence in theoretical perspective between the earlier conception of parallel institutions developed in the context of civil rights community projects, and the notion of participatory democracy which developed in the institutional context of the campus.

Despite the educative experience of these intimate political encounters with large-scale power structures on its own home territory, lacking an institutionalized economic base (either in corporations or in unions, for example), the New Left has largely failed to develop an adequate economic theory as an undergirding for its political program. Critical of this deficiency, Richard Flacks, a leading theorist of participatory democracy, has suggested that in the absence of effective public controls over "the allocation of resources, economic planning, and the operation of large corporations," participatory democracy will remain an ideological slogan. In his view then, the basic intellectual problem for the New Left is the delineation of practical modes of decentralized and democratized decision making in government and private organizations, linked to a system of publicly controlled national planning.[16]

As we have noted, such controls already exist within the private sector itself and increasingly in government, which has taken responsibility for regulating the level of aggregate demand for the maintenance of full

employment, and at the same time, for the curbing of inflation. As a result, the subsidization of the corporate sector with public funds has
grown tremendously — mainly through defense spending, and marginally
through urban redevelopment and investment in research, education, etc.
— to the point where state and corporate bureaucracy are today so
closely integrated as to pose serious obstacles to effective *public* control.
Flacks observes that public and private governments are today merged in
many ways, and that "this merger approximates an elitist corporatist
model (hence breaking down even the modest pluralism which once
characterized the system)."[17] His feeling is that if this trend is permitted
to go much further, it will leave no possibility for real democratic participation and control of major institutions. If the direction of social
planning is not to be decided by the political and corporate elites alone
(Galbraith's monopolization of social purpose by the "new industrial
state") the participatory democrats will have to provide a working model
for active democratic control of planning at the national level.

Supporters of participatory democracy have already devised and applied models of mobilization for the interests of the local community
through grass-roots community organizations related to significant local
institutions ranging from schools and health centers, to the Mayor's
office; moving into the sphere of economic theory, they have ventured to
suggest the possibility of democratic control over the major corporations
as well. Now, in terms of the tactics of "confrontation," the local community and its public institutions are discrete entities which are physically
present and accessible, and their decision makers can be confronted
more or less directly by the members of the community or constituents
of the given institution. At this level, a relatively simple model of "the
power structure" may suffice to guide political action, but it is a considerably more complex problem to design means by which public controls could be extended from the community to giant organizations like
the "mature" corporation, much less to the nationwide corporate sector
of the "new industrial state."

The contemporary importance to the New Left of developing appropriate theoretical models for the exercise of democratic control over the
economy, is reflected in the observation by one important movement
commentator to the effect that ideological questions — questions about
the structure and distribution of power — are especially pertinent when
societies have the capacity to solve the merely technical problems.[18]
What this points to is the continuing need for critical or radical social
theory which goes beyond constructing descriptive models of stratification or power structures and beyond the assumption that these structures can be reformed by an overlay of technocratic machinery, to

question the functional necessity and social justice of the established distributions and to pose alternative configurations.

The Ideology of Citizenship in the New Politics of Opposition

Among the various factors which bear upon it, critical social theory is significantly influenced by the nature of the opposition to a given system; though it is the product, finally, of intellectual leaders and spokesmen of the movement of opposition, these spokesmen do not work in isolation, but in relation to the outlook and concerns of that movement. The character and quality of the theory of opposition will depend on the prevailing perspective, experience, and education of the movement in interaction with that of its spokesmen, as well as on the social position and identity of the participants. (Unless the participants in the movement adopt the theory of a given intellectual spokesman and modify their own perspectives accordingly, the theory remains academic, a speculative philosophy or ethic, but unutilized, hence untestable in action. In this case other theories, or in the extreme case, no theory, may guide their political action, only a complex of attitudes toward immediate issues, personal and sentimental. This seems to be the condition of many in or around the New Left — especially the radically individualist "hippie" elements which have been recently drawn to it; here then is another source of the notion that the New Left is "nonideological.")

In the older politics of the industrial period, the opposition consisted basically of the excluded working class of the population, so that its entry into the system was ideologically identified with a major expansion of democratic participation. In the new politics of the postindustrial era, however, the working class has been integrated into a relatively comfortable middle majority which is willing to abandon the conduct of government to technocratic expertise, operating under an ideology of "elite democracy," so long as its security is maintained. The opposition, on the other hand, has been based in a scatter of minority subcultures, rather than a single major social class: the campus Left, now in apparent decline, the community-oriented Right, the ghetto blacks. The politics and ideology of contemporary opposition is now often a politics of crosscutting and contradictory subcultural protest.

What, if anything, do the rather different subcultures which have in recent years been the major sources of oppositional ideology have in common? They all have the characteristic of being removed from the culture of the mainstream, in which both material status ("consumership") and social status are taken for granted. Though there are several aspects to the problematic character of their social status, the major com-

mon aspect is that of their status as citizens. This has been clear from
the outset with regard to the radical Right. The other side of their vociferous anti-Communism, and their recurrent tirades against peoples of
other races and other countries, has been an uncertainty about their
own status as Americans, and their determination to prove themselves in
this regard. It has also expressed itself in their resentment against an
opaque government bureaucracy which decides on matters from foreign
policy to welfare and ignores the feelings of "real Americans," since it
is riddled with "sympathizers to Communism." For black Americans, of
course, the classic problem has been posed, either in terms of outright
disenfranchisement as in the South, or in terms of economic and social
discrimination which amount functionally to "second-class citizenship."
Even for middle-class blacks, this has been a persisting irritant, and the
rise of the black-power ideology finds a growing number of black intellectuals and professionals coming into the movement.[19]

For the students, the question of citizenship has been raised in several
ways: in the disparity between social and racial realities and the liberal-
democratic values to which they have been exposed, moving some to
leave the campus and become involved as citizens in the civil rights movement; in the *in loco parentis* restrictions on students, felt particularly
keenly by those returning from off-campus movement activities (e.g.
returnees to Berkeley after the summer 1964 drive for the Freedom
Democratic Party in Mississippi), but also by other students who resent
limitations on their freedoms of assembly, speech, and press, as well as
on their freedom of private personal behavior on campus and in the
dormitory. In these respects the students seek the full rights of citizens
whether they are off campus or on; the general development has been
from the former to the latter, with the Berkeley returnees demanding the
right, during the events of the fall semester of 1964, to freely organize
for off-campus civil rights actions, and not merely the right to free
advocacy of civil rights. In another respect, some students have protested the designation of the university as merely another corporate enterprise; a "knowledge industry," turning out technicians and managers
for the postindustrial society; and they have accordingly protested their
being treated like most others outside the managerial level, as members
of a "managed" class. In *this* respect, they have objected to being considered in the same way as most citizens. Recognizing this deficiency in
the current character of citizenship, some have advanced the notion of
participatory democracy, which seeks to protect the participants in *any*
institution from abitrary management from above by insuring their full
rights of "institutional citizenship."

As we have noted, the question of citizenship has been a central theme
in the politics and ideology of contemporary movements of opposition.

For the rather parochial, traditionalist radical Right, citizenship has been essentially posed in political terms, taking the form since the 1950s of a struggle against pro-Communist conspiracy and treason; and today increasingly a struggle to preserve America against cultural change and racial integration. For the black-power movement, citizenship has been viewed in social as well as political terms which appear to reflect an expansion of the traditional concept approximately along lines that T.H. Marshall has described in his work on citizenship and social development. According to Marshall, citizenship in the eighteenth century essentially involved civil liberties and property rights; in the nineteenth century, the rights of political participation were added; and during the twentieth century the concept once again expanded to include the "social rights" of basic education, welfare, and security.[20]

The appearance of the term "welfare" requires clarification. Judging by its pronouncements, the black-power movement seeks to enable black citizens to enjoy the same standards of economic security and material welfare as are widespread in the white community, but not by means of the distorted and destructive "welfare" system of dependence which has sought to socialize the black citizen to a substandard concept of wellbeing. The New Left has gone one step further to put forward the concept of what might be called institutional citizenship, based on the notion that citizenship implies the opportunity to participate in all the institutions of one's society, not merely those of the polity, in order that decision makers, regardless of their institutional location, be made accountable to their organizational constituency as they are in the polity, and that this accountability be genuine and not merely a formal ritual. As various observers have indicated, participatory democrats are quite serious about the notion of citizenship, and seek to carry it to all significant areas of social life, not merely those explicitly or officially defined as "political." Under this concept, "each man has responsibility for the action of the institutions in which he is imbedded; all authority ought to be responsible to those 'under' it, each man can and should be a center of power and initiative in society."[21]

How successful the student Left will be in pressing its efforts for participatory democracy on the campuses will depend on a complex of factors including the availability of channels to students to work in conventional political areas (e.g., the McCarthy campaign of 1968, with its appeal to campus liberals and left-liberals drew many away from the New Left program of demonstrations, and similarly it seems, for the McGovern campaign of 1972), and the competition from various community action projects based on the notion of building "parallel institutions" — community centers, freedom schools, credit unions, cooperatives, etc. However, partly due to demise of the War on Poverty from which some aid had been received for these ventures, and partly to the dearth of social and economic resources in the ghetto and slum communities where they have been instituted, these parallel institutional projects seem now to be either moribund or absorbed by the thrust of programs which have been brought under relatively close government control.[22]

For awhile what seemed to be replacing community organization as a major strategy was direct action against the perceived enemies of the community and of the movement, particularly in the form of confrontations *à la* Chicago 1968 with political leaders, agency bureaucrats, institutional leaders, and the police who seek to break up such confrontations as much as to protect their targets. However, such actions, despite their dramatic immediate impact, have required extremely high commitment and energy, especially as they have turned toward violence and the tactics of terrorism. While appealing to the most alienated and angry, particularly the "Yippies" and "Weathermen," they have seemed increasingly to alienate those segments of the movement seeking to move from immediate issues to long-range programs. These programs necessarily would have to go beyond episodic demonstrations to painstaking, drawn-out efforts at basic structural change within the settings of the society's major institutions, from universities to corporations. Unless those of its segments having long-term political perspectives can be encouraged to grow, the New Left may eventually collapse as an effective force for change, and especially if its more adventuristic sections, which have been capable of producing new "scenes" but not new structures, come to predominate.

As we have observed, the contemporary movements of opposition, though sharply divided even to the point of polarization in many of their positions, have in common the concern for their status as citizens, which their social position or cultural identity do not allow them to take for granted. The result is that in one way or another, all these movements tend to question the legitimacy of the system, since they do not feel fully integrated into it. Regardless of its material effectiveness, all tend to resent its procedures in overriding their distinctive identity, as neighborhood people, rural folk, or Southerners; as blacks; as students and young people; and in denying them, through its bureaucratic remoteness, the opportunity to shape their own environment or to influence policy, foreign or domestic, in accordance with their particular values.

Though this has been the situation over the past decade or so, the system still stands. On the one hand, these movements have been either unable or unwilling to make common cause; certainly there is little possibility for coalition between radical rightists and black-power advocates. The suggestion has been made by Carl Oglesby of the New Left that his movement and the Radical Right have some fundamental values in common on the score of their mutual interest in community, but this politically rather abstract suggestion has given no signs of bearing fruit; and whatever coalition once existed between the New Left and organizations like SNCC seems quite tenuous in this era of drift toward separatism among black militants.

In this chapter we have traced the sources of support for a technocratically governed postindustrial system in American society to a materially comfortable middle majority consisting of the relatively secure and affluent blue- and white-collar classes of contemporary society, who share life styles and attitudes best expressed in the notion of "consumerism" which has been developing in postwar American sociology since the work of David Riesman.[23] While the several sources of present and potential opposition to the system are considerably more heterogeneous in life style and socioethnic identity than the elements which support it, they can be said to share attitudes of uncertainty or resentment concerning their status as participants in the society (particularly their status as citizens), which provides ground for a common ideological classification on at least this level. Nevertheless, in itself this does not mean that they will, under presently conceivable circumstances, tend to act as a common political opposition in the manner of self-conscious members of the same social class. At the same time, it is significant that there have been marked signs of a growing "labor revolt" during the 1960s and early 1970s around automation-related issues of speedup and working conditions particularly among young workers. There is, in these developments, some suggestion of a potential future split of organized labor along generational lines, and a possible revival of intense "class politics" alongside the "status politics" movements (radical right, black power, students, and now women's movements), emergents of the past two decades. Before making any clearcut forecasts of an early revival of class politics among blue-collar workers, it should be kept in mind that the young union militants may have in store for them a long struggle against entrenched national leaderships, in office since the Thirties and Forties, who could make it extremely difficult to quickly translate their local militancy into new directions for the labor movement on a national level.[24]

Considering the existence of several sources of present and potential opposition in postindustrial America, the stability of the emergent technocratic system apparently is not so much a product of the "end" of ideological opposition as of the subcultural fragmentation which renders that opposition politically ineffective. Moreover, while the opposition and its ideologists have broken up into distinctive political-cultural camps,

the major received critical theory of the society (Marxism) which sought
to comprehend it as a whole and suggest means for its transcendence
has thus far proven incapable of organizing a coherent mass opposition.
No comprehensive substitute has been forthcoming since the new ideologists remain concerned with their own particular political and subcultural
preoccupations. Though the ideological theme of "participation," which
cuts across the subcultural differences of small town, ghetto, and campus,
is a significant symptom of widespread protest against the bureaucratization of life and the remoteness of government in the techno-
organizational society, it is by itself not yet sufficient to provide the
framework for a rounded critique of the society, or the positing of an
alternative social structure.

CHAPTER X

Emergent Issues
and
Ideology in
Postindustrial America

The theory of the end of ideology expresses a number of important convergent tendencies in advanced industrial society. First is the tendency toward the muting and elimination of those conflicts which reflected the struggles between employing and working classes of earlier industrial society, traditionally voiced in ideologies of sharp and inevitable class conflict. Second is the tendency toward the development and elaboration of a "welfare state" in which a basic minimum of social and economic perquisites is guaranteed to the various groups in the society, regardless of their particular identity, with most significance for the social security of the lower classes. And finally, as the end of ideology has evolved into a theory of postindustrial society, it has begun to articulate the tendency for the established major institutions of industry and commerce to become increasingly intertwined with and dependent upon government and the scientific-educational sector for the performance of vital functions of interinstitutional and total-societal research, planning, and coordination. Integral to the development of the "scientific," "technological," or "postindustrial" society has been the rise of administrative and knowledge elites outside the traditional business sector, as well as the rise of new professional administrators and planners within the institutions of business and industry. Leadership in the new society is increasingly a product of the interaction of decision makers in different key institutional positions, and entails a growing bid for recognition and power on the part of the new nonbusiness elites in government, the universities, and the military.

The effect of these developments has, of course, been felt not only in society but in social theory as well, and the "end of ideology" theory has closely reflected these changes in the wider society. It is important to keep in mind, in evaluating the ideological aspect of this theory of the postindustrial society, that the end-of-ideologists have already interpreted these developments as amounting to a signficant progressive trend, not only toward social amelioration through a welfare state, but also toward the more rational guidance of societal development, largely through the good offices of the emerging technocratic knowledge-elite.

This picture is in our view both overly optimistic and premature since it overlooks or minimizes not only existing countertrends to social amelioration and rationality but also the appearance within the structure of technocratically governed society of future potentialities for socially negative consequences of major proportions. To say this is not by any means to deny the contribution of the end of ideology, in its current phase as a theory of postindustrial society, to fostering awareness of emerging new forms of societal coordination and planning. It is, however, to challenge the notion that the new mechanisms of technocratic coordination now provide means whereby the "postindustrial" society will function so as to respond coherently to its evolving domestic and foreign responsibilities, in accordance with humanistic values.

Models of Integration in Postindustrial Society

Considered as a stage in the development of macrosocial theory, that variety of social theory which seeks to comprehend total societal structure and change, the end-of-ideologists' theory of postindustrial society is an important step beyond the received sociological model of modern society. In that model, developed in the course of the emergence of modern urban industrial society, the central image is of a large institutionally specialized and differentiated society (*Gessellschaft*) with a complex industrial technology increasingly controlled through bureaucratic organizations, themselves interconnected by a web of diverse legal and market relations. Typically this bureaucratic-associational society was placed in contrast with the rural "folk society," *Gemeinschaft*; a small, relatively undifferentiated society with a primitive agrarian technology, closely bound by a unitary moral code. However, the appearance of highly advanced or "post"-industrial society now requires that sociological theory move beyond the earlier *Gemeinschaft-Gessellschaft* distinction. (Similarly, the contemporary appearance of metropolitan and "megapolitan" areas of contiguous urban growth has led to the supercession, in recent posturban theory, of the earlier, simple rural-urban dichotomy based on the sharp contrast between the defined geopolitical city of early industrial society and its unurbanized countryside. In place of this dichotomy, which reflects the formerly clearcut distinction between the social ecology of industrial and preindustrial areas, "urban" sociologists must now take into consideration suburban as well as urban social structures and economies. In its posturban phase, the sociology of the urban community has become the sociology of socioeconomically, though not yet politically, integrated metropolitan regions, in a parallel to the development of the postindustrial theory of interinstitutional integration in the overall society.)[1] In particular, the displacement of spontaneous voluntaristic coordination, *via* the web of atomistic interaction in the market and the law courts, as the basic means of overall societal integration now requires the introduction of a new principle besides those represented either by the folk community or the associational society.

As we have noted, with the Second World War and the quantum leap in sociophysical scale, productive energy, and scientific knowledge in advanced industrial society, the *Gesellschaft* theory, which had been adequate to its modern phase, could no longer serve as a comprehensive image for its postmodern phase. The *Gemeinschaft-Gesellschaft* distinction, contrasting the simple communal solidarity of traditional society with the complex spontaneously coordinated network of associational interdependence in modern society, was no longer sufficient. This basic theme, around which sociological theory had organized itself during the industrial period, had become outmoded in an era in which increasingly conscious central coordination was becoming the practice for the integration of a highly differentiated institutional and social structure, for purposes ranging from economic productivity and "social welfare" to the conduct of war. Hence the introduction of the new principle of technocratic coordination, which does not merely displace the older analytic themes of tension between *Gesellschaft* and *Gemeinschaft*, urban and rural, modernity and tradition, but also challenges the notion of societal integration through pluralist consensus arrived at on the basis of bargaining and compromise between diverse groups, as the major means for determining social policy in advanced society. The principle of technocratic coordination goes beyond *Gesellschaft* to deal anew with the problem of social order or integration which had been a central problem for the classic theorists. Within the sphere of the developing large-scale organizations of earlier industrial society, this problem had been responded to by Max Weber's theory of bureaucracy, which emerged as a major solution to the question of what form organizational coordination would take in industrial society. However, bureaucratic organization provided a mode of organizational control basically suited to the vertical coordination of activities "under the roof" of a given organization; thus the problem of lateral or interorganizational coordination remained. This problem was addressed by the French sociologist Emile Durkheim, in terms of the concept of the division of labor and of functional interrelations between organizations operating through the nexus of the economic marketplace within a legal framework. While functional coordination *within* the organizations of industrial society was viewed by classic sociologists in terms of the concept of bureaucracy, coordination *between* organizations was viewed in terms of their spontaneous, unplanned mutual adjustment *via* the marketplace, conducted within the general context of the laws of contract, and supported by historically established moral and constituent obligations.[2]

In the postindustrial society, however, this haphazard, unplanned means of coordinating the interdependent activities of myriad productive organizations is clearly no longer adequate. In the new society, functional interdependence *via* the free market, associational pluralism based on multiple overlapping organizational memberships, interest bargaining, and the legal system[3] are no longer of themselves able to provide sufficiently reliable coordination among the giant highly intricate organizations of the political economy and between them and the sources of demand for their services and products. Even such relatively modern measures of coordination as industrial oligopoly, administrative pricing, vertical integration, and the like,[4] exercised by centers of power in the private economic sphere, have proven inadequate, so that the state has increasingly had to step in as a protecting and coordinating agency for the private sector. Since the Depression, there has been an enormous expansion of the role of government in that sector, ranging from the cushioning of investment risks and the subsidizing of industrial research, to the provision of policy guidelines and allocative mechanisms for the control and coordination of the overall economic framework for "private" enterprise. In addition, government intervention in the society has grown in response to other than strictly economic problems. For example, taking on the role of international leadership has demanded the centralization of diplomatic and military planning; with this, we have seen the advent of "technical decision making," and its elaboration in the form of planning and budgeting systems such as PPBS, particularly in the military sector.

The virtue of the "end of ideology," in its recent articulation as a theory of postindustrial society, resides in its contribution to clarifying these functions of emerging governmentally centralized forms of societal coordination and of the new planning and informational technologies which they involve. At the same time, however, the end-of-ideology theorists imply that the combination of technocratic mechanisms and elite consensus (the "new consensus" between the corporate, governmental, and knowledge elites), to employ these mechanisms for purposes of economic development and social control, is basically sufficient to guarantee general welfare and stability in the society on a long-term basis.

In this perspective, interlocking techno-organizational arrangements are viewed as the ultimate source of contemporary social integration, as the core of what holds the postindustrial society together. According to the end-of-ideologists' theory of postindustrial society, the various sectors of this complexly differentiated society will cohere and function smoothly for productivity, resource development, and welfare because of the new techniques of coordination wielded by expert economists, social scientists, and administrators. (Significantly this reverses the emphasis of the major contemporary attempt at a comprehensive social system theory, Parsonianism, which views the ultimate source of social integration as cultural or "moral."[5] The postindustrial theorists focus on sources of integration in the new society which are primarily structural, such as the political and economic integration of the working class, or institutional, such as the development of coordination within and between polity and economy rather than moral, ideological, or cultural. For these theorists, the basic medium of social integration in the new society is technocratic planning and the institutions which support it, rather than a widespread commitment to some central cultural system of beliefs and values, such as democracy or the Protestant ethic. In fact, to the extent that they still give it consideration, they view the culture of the new society as being still unclarified and increasingly problematic.

Problems in the Culture of Postindustrial Society

Unlike Parsons, the end-of-ideologists do not assume that society is any longer meaningfully bound together by a unifying cultural ethos such as the Protestant ethic, which figured so prominently in classic interpretations of industrial society.[6] In contrast with the earlier model of a social order united through generally shared cultural themes, the postindustrial, post-Christian culture seems to be in serious disrepair, no longer capable of providing either a coherent encompassing image of the society, or collective symbols which can meaningfully integrate its diverse occupational and ethnic subcultures. Though the "end of ideology" as a theory of development in advanced industrial society augurs an epoch of harmony and unification, we find in the postindustrial culture anything but harmony and unification. So complexly differentiated is the postindustrial society, and "so specialized, complicated or incomprehensible" are the life experiences of its various citizens, that "it is difficult to find common symbols of meaning to relate one experience to another."[7] The situation of postindustrial society, certainly in the American context, is seriously ambiguous; it is one of a rather fragmented culture no longer able to provide either comprehension of the overall society or legitimacy for its established authorities, in contrast to an increasingly integrated technocratic-institutional structure. This suggests that not only ideology, but culture as well, may be exhausted, in that it fails to provide a coherent image of the new society and its purposes which could serve as a unifying symbol to link the diverse subcultures produced by the different subgroups and institutions of the society. Apparently, the only universal symbolism which remains is that of science, but it is so abstract as to be intelligible only to a tiny, specially educated elite; so that the society runs on according to the logic of its scientifically managed institutions, cut off from the comprehension or guidance of most of its citizens.

As we have observed, the culture of scientific-technocratic society today seems no longer able to provide the necessary unification in consciousness as to what is happening to the society under the strain of advanced development. This loss of unity and coherence within the culture of technocratic society, simultaneous with the increased coherence and coordination of institutional structures, is a major point in the early analysis of postindustrial society by the end-of-ideologists. In order to clarify the situation of the culture of the developing society it is helpful to bear in mind some basic distinctions between the outlook of the managing technocratic elite and the managed middle mass in postindustrial society. (Let us assume for the moment the smooth operation of the technocratic economy, in order to focus on the "cultural problem" of this society.)

So far as the new masses — the socially integrated, relatively comfortable blue-collar or white-collar workers — are concerned, the problems of cultural coherence and fragmentation are experienced basically at an existential level rather than intellectually or theoretically. They are expressed in the strains and stresses of playing multiple, often conflicting roles in daily life, and like so much else in the routine of mass existence — the recurrent crowding, the exhausting public interaction, the "communications overload," the lack of privacy — they are ultimately accepted as intrinsic to "modern" life. At the same time, the new masses are constantly reminded by the consumerist media of the various available compensations which can help ease the social and environmental torments — the escape to the leisure-life, the home, the friends, the hobbies, and the commodities and hardware which stock home, bar and workshop, and help make life easier, cleaner, and more interesting, from the washing machine to the car to the television set, to the outfit of power tools or golf clubs or fishing gear. Not much perhaps, from the viewpoint of the Galbraithian intellectual conscious of other dimensions to life, but for the new masses these gadgets and gimmicks represent a historically unprecedented standard of life, and a very important aspect of their culture, a culture of "consumerism."

Accordingly, though the middle masses of postindustrial society may lack a clear-cut ideology or theory of the society, they are not without some common orientation toward it and toward their position and life chances in it. The end-of-ideologists themselves make this clear when they write of the growing significance of a kind of popular ideology of the "open society"[8] and of the selective adoption of middle-class life styles by the stable working class (though even the euphoria of abundant consumership has its limits, as reflected in decreasing consumer tolerance for shoddy wares, misleading advertising and pollution in recent years). If our interpretation is correct, then contrary to the end-of-ideologists, at the level of the integrated blue-collar and white-collar middle mass neither culture nor ideology is today "exhausted" but very much alive, creating devoted, even addicted, consumers and strivers within the established social framework. For the middle mass, the daily reality of consumerism and its associated social and occupational norms constitutes both an established culture and a justifying ideology.[9]

By contrast, it is at the level of the current and potential elites of the society, by virtue either of their institutional positions or of their education, that the postindustrial culture can be said to have seriously lost coherence and meaning, and thus to have become "exhausted." It is between the several elements of these elites and proto-elites, that considerable ideological division seems already to have occurred in the early phase of postindustrial society; most dramatically in the confrontation of intellectuals and students espousing radical-humanist values, versus the increasingly technocratic elites of government and economy.

As a first approximation, the gap in perspective may be understood as that between the pragmatic, "value-neutral," problem-solving approach, which by the beginning of the 1960s had become identified with the scientific technocrats, and the moralistic, value-committed, wholistic approach, which has in the past been associated with representatives of the humanist tradition, particularly with men of letters and philosophy. The dramatic rise of scientists to important advisory and administrative positions as a consequence of the Second World War, raised in the minds of some the question which of these two perspectives would in future hold the major claim on the thinking of the political elite. Of the two, which kind of "knowledge," in terms of methods, approach, subject matter, and above all, attitudes toward innovation and modernization, would shape the perspective of those in power? In response, the work of men like C.P. Snow[10] suggested the need to replace the traditional perspective of a political elite educated in the classics by an outlook more relevant to the character of the age, in which national power increasingly would depend on scientific competence translated into advanced industrial and military technology. In one respect this implied that the ruling elite might now both modernize its regime and replenish its legitimating ideology from a new stock of ideas and a new mystique, both connected with the dynamic of Science, popularly revered as a kind of secular religion. The outlook befitting an age of gunpowder and steam was clearly no longer adequate to the requirements of an age of nuclear power and electronic controls; to be persuasive, the legitimating ideology of political rule in advanced industrial society would have to be technically sophisticated and up-to-date, in touch with the "latest" in contemporary thought, whose model had overnight become that of hard Science.

By the end of the decade, the contrast between "scientific expertise" and "nonscientific" styles of inquiry and modes of decision making had been strongly vested by spokesmen of the "policy sciences" with an ideological bias in favor of "expertise." Some proponents came to distinguish these two perspectives quite categorically, as a contrast between responsible experts and "unreasonable, ideological types,"[11] or between competent technical professionals and antitechnocratic "alienated youth" or "nihilistic" intellectuals.[12] As several observers have pointed out, this has been in fact a way of legitimating the new status of the technicians of the technocratic "welfare" state, and of defending them from the critics of the actual behavior of that state at home and abroad. By the late 1960s, the development of a "value free" kind of science narrowly focussed upon the technical-administrative problems of postindustrial institutions, rather than on broader questions of the goals and purposes of these institutions, had become a hallmark of the "responsible" scientist and technical expert.[13]

Furthermore, the formal creation of an ideology of "technocratically" managed change was largely the work of members of a "third culture" connected with but distinct from the natural sciences or the humanities; specifically those social-behavioral scientists who have made it their business to interpret the impact of scientific and technological developments on contemporary society and to relate this interpretation to the concept of technocratic policy making as a social system "require-ment." In particular the theorists of the "end of ideology" have explicitly viewed themselves as playing a bridging or mediating role between the other "two cultures" in producing an image and an interpretation of a technocratically managed social system which would appeal to the diverse segments of the intellectual elite, divided not only by subject matter but also by orientation toward traditional knowledge and values as against modern and postmodern knowledge, values, and techniques.[14]

As ideologists of the technocratic management of postindustrial soci-ety and its development, the theorists of the "end of ideology" have constructed an ideology of enlightened technocracy serving the require-ments of human welfare. This ideology of the technocratic system serving humane purposes is clearly apparent in the work of the Technology Commission, which we have already discussed. Its function is to identify the legitimacy of the developing technocratic elite very closely with its material effectiveness, largely by associating the political right to rule with the technical-economic capacity to deliver the goods that constitute the basis of the "good life." At the same time, this ideology seeks to bring the diverse members of the industrial, scientific, and academic elites together with constituted political authorities in a common enterprise of social leadership.

Historically the strategy of providing a basis of cooperation between disparate social groupings or elites has often involved the designation of a common enemy, and a drawing together in mutual defense. This strategy of the end-of-ideologists, as proponents of a transition to a fully technocratic society, becomes particularly clear in the context of Daniel Bell's discussion of the relations between the contemporary uni-versity and the postindustrial society in his work *The Reforming of Gen-eral Education*.[15] Bell views the postindustrial university as a public service institution, dedicated to the nurture and grooming of human in-tellectual "capital" and its use in the service of "public needs that are defined by government agencies or foundations," needs which range from area studies programs to "secret defense research." As he indicates, the interconnections between the university and the state are close and intri-cate today, with "leading faculty" shuttling "in and out of government as policymakers and policy advisors."[16] However, all is not as well as it might be, for the university has become a target for attacks from radical Left and Right; perhaps most serious is the fact that politically moderate groups within the university itself, identifying with traditional *liberal* ideals of the university's independence from external institutional con-trols, "begin to question its involvement with the government and seek to detach themselves from such a relationship."[17] Of course, outside of the minority of radical faculty, this group would be most likely to sympathize with or provide support for radical students in their protest against these "public-service" relationships of the university.

In this light, it is interesting to consider Bell's analysis of the most important sources of conflict in the contemporary university. Viewing the university as the meeting point between contemporary knowledge and culture, Bell identifies the main source of the university's crisis as the "radical disjunction between social structure and culture" in the larger postindustrial society. The institutional structure of postindustrial society has become increasingly subject to technocratic modes of control and coordination, in the process displacing the older liberal-pluralist network of social integration. Reflecting and supporting this tendency, a technocratic perspective has developed in the university, with emphasis on scientific method and professional techniques oriented to "problem solving," and disdainful of ideology, which it "distrusts." At the same time, according to Bell, an "apocalyptic" orientation has developed, both in the university and among nonacademic intellectuals, reflecting a "current of nihilism . . . that is embattled against the technocratic society."[18]

It is this current of "nihilism," commonly associated with the proponents of the counter-culture, which Bell identifies as the major enemy of the university and of its faculty, whether they be forward-looking technocratic intellectuals or more traditional humanist liberals. Accordingly, in support of this position he cites the observation of his colleague, the well-known liberal critic and educator Lionel Trilling, to the effect that the enthusiasts of this "post-modern sensibility" have gone "beyond culture," into nihilism, into anarchy.[19] However, in focussing on "prophets of the apocalypse," such as Norman O. Brown and Susan Sontag, as the main enemies of the technocratic perspective, Bell gives short shrift to the ideas or demands of the new political radicals on campus, such as the New Left students, to whom he refers merely as "alienated youth," intimating that they have been little more than an egoistic and romantic group who talked endlessly of "participation" and "community," but lacked the practical capacities to translate these sentiments into institutional reality. In this way, the one group which was most active in directly challenging the *structure* of the university and the postindustrial society as well as their interrelations as of the late 1960s, is shunted aside as unworthy of serious consideration or support; the major concern deserving of real attention from both technocratic professionals and liberal traditionalists is the threat of the apocalyptic "counter"-*culture*, with its alleged de-emphasis of both tradition and reason in favor of immediate instinctual gratification.

This line of thought is carried to its extreme in Bell's recent essay on "The Cultural Contradictions of Capitalism."[20] Now the enemy is no longer portrayed merely as a minority counterculture led by prophets of alienation advocating a hedonistic, nihilistic "sensibility" against the larger culture; the enemy is the "post-modern" culture of postindustrial society itself. Thus, it is just at the point where the technically rational "scientifically managed" institutions of the society have achieved unprecedented "efficiency, least cost, maximization, optimization, and functional rationality" that they are said to come into direct conflict with the "anti-cognitive and anti-intellectual" cultural trends of the day.[21] Here Bell gives up discussion of the on-going and potential conflicts among the elites of the emerging technocratic society and turns his attention instead to the putative conflict between the technocratic institutional structure and the antitechnocratic counterculture, which has somehow overnight become transformed into the postmodern culture. With this shift from the earlier examination of the conflicting interests and perspectives of "scientifically rational" technocratic advisors and administrators *versus* "nonrational" pluralist politicians and interest representatives, the dimensions of rationality and nonrationality which are so central to the end-of-ideologists' earlier theorizations regarding postindustrial development, are themselves implicitly redefined. Now the deep problems of postindustrial American society are laid essentially to the disjunction between a "functionally rationalist" social structure and a hedonistic "irrationalist" culture, while the perspectives and policies of the administrative and political elites that dominate the society's major institutional structures, and their shifting conflicts and coalitions, tend to be removed from analytic attention. At the same time, the theory of the end-of-ideology makes a full reversal to suggest, not the exhaustion of movements of ideological or cultural opposition in the developing postindustrial society, but their expansion to cover the entire culture! With these abrupt shifts and reversals in its basic theoretical perspective, it is the end of ideology itself which seems to have exhausted its own usefulness to the consistent analysis of further developments in the postindustrial society. This suggests the need to look to the development of fresh theories which can help us better understand the new differentiations and conflicts in both the structure and culture of the emergent society.

"Technopolis" and Meritocracy

The end-of-ideologists' theory of the postindustrial society is one of a society in rapid and accelerating change, and increasingly subject to the planning and guidance of a scientifically competent, humanely oriented, technocratic elite. There are clear suggestions, in the concern of these theorists with future prediction for the year 2000 and beyond, that by the twenty-first century basic, far-reaching, and irreversible changes will have been wrought in the structure of advanced industrial society in the United States, Europe, and possibly Japan. However, the preoccupation of the end-of-ideologists has been with the development of a new technocratic elite, and with the increasing technocratic integration within and between major institutions of the society. Aside from some relatively short-range projections regarding changes in the structure of employment over the next decade or so, there has been little in the way of systematic discussion of the effects of technocratic development on the broad class structure of the society, much less of the kind of political and ideological cleavages which might develop by the next century under the strain of these structural changes.[22]

In this circumstance, it is worth turning to a number of suggestive speculative essays on the possible transition to a fully technocratic society (also referred to herein as Technopolis).[23] One particularly interesting future prediction is that wryly projected by the English sociologist Michael Young, in which English society by the year 2033 is divided into a distinct political-intellectual-biological elite and a dependent, genetically, and mentally inferior majority. Such a division into Alphas and Betas would be the logical outcome of technocratic employment of sophisticated methods of academic testing for the purpose of segregating different intelligence classes at an early age, and training them for their ultimate positions in the social order. While the basic aim would be a social structure designed to produce maximum organizational efficiency and economic productivity, the by-product would be a society in which intellectually less capable classes were not only certified as socially inferior but also stripped of possible leadership through the meritocratic process itself. This process co-opts those exceptional younger members of the class who may possess qualities useful to the meritocracy; thus in place of the earlier historic system of stratification by heredity, we would have a society sharply stratified by functional capacity.

Despite the sanguine promise of an "automatic Utopia" in the work of some of the prophets of Technopolis, there are certain problems relating to such configuration — problems significantly of a cultural and psychological kind; problems of the feelings of unimportance and meaninglessness which attach to the functional exclusion of the masses displaced not only from the economy but also from any significant control of the society's institutions or their development. Such problems are so serious as to suggest the need for the institutions of the society to be preemptively restructured by the society's technocratic elites in order to exert better social control over what are anticipated to be increasingly restive masses. "This could encourage tendencies during the next several decades toward a technocratic dictatorship," as Z. Brzezinski puts it.[24] Thus the long-range prophets of the future of technocratic society tend to be somewhat ambiguous about their image of it as a Utopia. As Clark Kerr, an earlier prophet, remarked: there will be a "new slavery" alongside the "new freedom," in the "fully industrialized" society of the future.[25] (Interestingly, this is the same Clark Kerr whose image of the contemporary university is that of an "Ideopolis," a complex metropolitan intellectual community, or "City of Intellect," closely tied to scientific-technical enterprises supported by business or government, and playing a key role in the training and certification of a new aristocracy of merit.[26] The role of the "multiversity" in the development and stabilization of a meritocratic Technopolis becomes quite clear in this context.)

Working on a similar theme, David Apter has sketched an absorbing profile of the dynamics of the stratification of advanced societies along meritocratic lines.[27] Like Young and Brzezinski, Apter begins from advanced industrial-democratic society, and ends with a full-fledged meritocratic society. "How," asks Apter, "does a democratic society come to rationalize this bifurcation of the community into members of the 'establishment' and the functionally superfluous, the responsible and the non-responsible, the scientifically literate and the scientifically illiterate?" Actually the way in which he poses the question suggests the answer: essentially through the coupling of status and authority ("responsibility") with scientific-technical "literacy" or expertise, so that advanced society becomes "composed of a small but powerful group of intellectually participant citizens, trained, educated, and sophisticated, while all others are reduced in stature. . . ."[28] Indeed, in just this way in the technically advanced democracies, the ideology of science and specifically of "scientific management" of the social process, seems on its way to becoming a major rationale for the drastic stratification of power and the privileges it carries.

Taken to its logical extreme, a consistently pursued meritocratic policy carries the possibility of the division of the society into a small "establishment of talent" as against "functionally superfluous" masses. Already today, there exist in American society strata of either kind: the technocratic managers of corporation and government on one hand, and on the other the millions of unemployed or underemployed, most of whose younger members come from educationally underprivileged minorities. However, Apter makes it quite clear that the transition to a full-fledged meritocratic society would be a rather complicated matter, involving not only the new official ideology of social-technocratic management, but also the counter-ideologies of several other segments of the population.

Writing in the early 1960s, when liberal social scientists perceived the greatest threat to progressive social development as coming from the old middle class and its right-wing politics, Apter showed particular concern for the reaction of those who "cannot find their places in the functionally unequal society" due to their backwater locale and mentality plus a lack of talent or training, or both.[29] These are destined to be the "disestablished" of the postindustrial meritocratic society in that the community and institutional structures they represent have been or are being displaced, either by the growth in scale of the society and the shift in locus of critical authority to the metropolitan centers and their elites, or by the development of new ideas and techniques in business, in the military, and other areas, which make the old middle classes increasingly dispensable.

The basic ideological response which Apter's old middle classes make to the meritocratic society is a turning back to the traditional themes of individuality and localism, a turning increasingly to the right, even to the "radical right," to counter the social-technocratic engineering of changes (such as integration and the "War on Poverty") which challenge their status and the *status quo* of their community life. Squeezed between the new liberal-technocratic establishment and the already marginal minorities at the bottom of the society that have desperately sought to escape from functional exclusion through political-economic integration, the old middle class would resist by attacking the meddling Washington bureaucrats together with their "egg-head" academic allies and the social programs they promote. The danger of this situation, suggests Apter, lies in the possibility that the resistance of the "disestablished" can mobilize sufficient political force to block the programs which the central government seeks to institute in order to ameliorate the hardships of the transition to a fully meritocratic society. However it should be noted that Apter is so fascinated by the prospect of a society run by centralized scientific expertise that he seems to forget that the prospects of disestablished groups would indeed be bleak if the process of "disestablishment" were actually to be carried to completion. Thus, like Brzezinski he follows the logic of the meritocratic development of society to its "inevitable" conclusion — the stark division of society into two "mutually antagonistic" groups: an "established," "responsible," technocratic elite, and a "disestablished," "nonresponsible," functionally superfluous mass. His rationale for this catastrophic splitting of the society is simply that in our society, downward mobility ("downwardness") is a measure of inability, while " 'upwardness' is a measure of ability and proficiency."[30]

In the perspective of this unabashed intellectual elitism, the functionally superfluous masses at the bottom of the meritocratic society are there not due to any social injustice or discrimination, but because they belong there, lacking the capacity to appreciate or utilize scientific-technical reason. This inadequate mass rationalizes its failure and assuages its alienation from the society through ideological myths, or "unreason." Apter characterizes the "disestablished" as being "composed of ideologues who devoutly defend unreason because they are afraid that, in the face of reason, their orientation to the world around them will fall apart and that in the process their world will disappear."[31] The technocratic elite on the other hand, representing "reason itself"(!) requires no ideology, at least not one which legitimates its special position; it has no need to rationalize its success and the power and prestige which accompany it, since its rise was based on "ability and proficiency."[32]

If the techno-meritocracy has any belief system to which it can be said to be committed, it is one of attachment to the rationality and universalism of science. However, "the ideology of science" has some very interesting status effects. "It serves to identify a group of people who are themselves important and significant because they can manipulate the science culture." In addition, "it casts out of the charmed circle (*sic*) those who are hopelessly incapable of understanding it."[33]

In this respect, the concept of a "charmed circle" of the technically competent resembles Young's portrait of "meritocracy." But unlike Young, whose work is in effect a satire on some of the unintended consequences of social-technocratic policy, Apter quite seriously portrays the perspective of the hypothetical technocratic regime under which millions of people can be made "superfluous," as essentially progresive and concerned with social "welfare" and "reform":

Social welfare, development, reform, and revolution all place new responsibilities on governments. In order to live up to these responsibilities, governments seek [technical] advice. . . . *The exercise of power is justified by the prospect of endless political reform through technical expertise.*[34]

In this way, the promise of social science becomes a general legitimating ideology for policies of development with disastrous social impact, in much the same manner that the prestige of natural science has been used to justify wasteful and dangerous policies of military development.[35] In the hands of the technocratic determinist, social science justifies the emergence of technocratic hierarchy and rationalizes the displacement of most of the formerly productive population as inevitable, in the wake of advancing scientific knowledge and the productivity of the technology based upon it. Necessity and inevitability are the hallmarks of ideological doctrine, and Apter freely admits the ideological character of a technocratically biased social science. In his view it is the ultimate ideology, the needed antidote to the ideologies of resentment and protest which characterize the "disestablished." Moreover, in this perspective social science is viewed as mediating between the technocratic elite and the masses, not only as a legitimating ideology, but also as an instrument of amelioration, useful for the design of social programs which will help ease the situation of the disestablished (without promising any essential change in their relative status, however), and thus help stabilize the techno-meritocratic society. In fact, some of the more deterministic of the technocratic intellectuals, like Zbigniew Brzezinski, are so optimistic that they imply that the technocratic society will move automatically toward a kind of technical utopia, in which living standards will rise beyond anything in human experience (e.g., average incomes of "almost $10,000 per head"), and basic social problems will no longer concern poverty, but the uses and control of mass leisure.

What we are faced with here is the notion of a highly productive, technically integrated society whose dynamics are such that, properly manipulated, it will move to transcend itself.[36] Unlike the more familiar utopias of the past, it makes no ethical appeal for social action to those alienated by the system to transform or transcend it; and unlike previous utopias, there is no mention of the need for a basic restructuring of the established institutions. By the choice of the appropriate coordinates, the achievement of utopia can be programmed into the dynamics of techno-cratic society. In this way, the utopia toward which technocratic society may be guided—Technopolis—is detached from radical political action, since the developing technocratic society is itself the revolution which culminates in Technopolis. At the helm, in place of the old-style revolu-tionary leadership, will ride the newly highly dedicated technocratic elite, culled from the various sciences and humanities and imbued with a spirit of social responsibility, particularly if the ideological efforts of their social science colleagues have any success.

Problems in the Transition to Technopolis

The preceding discussion suggests that the ideology of technocratically managed change finally leads to the belief that the transition to a fully-technocratic society (Technopolis) can be made justly and smoothly, and that its resulting benefits dictate that it *should* be made. In response to these assumptions, it is helpful to briefly review the ongoing debate regarding the applications of automation and cybernation in the Ameri-can economy by which Technopolis might ultimately be reached.

At the present early stage of transition to an automated Technopolis, there is considerable disagreement over the impact of automation on employment. Defenders of automation have claimed that the basic patterns of work are not in danger of being radically altered, since automation is just another in a continuing historical chain of technological changes and represents a logical evolution of industrial techniques, rather than a drastic break with the past. Related arguments have been that automation increases productivity, thereby raising living standards and stimulating demand, which in turn creates employment. Other arguments have been that the pace of automation has been and will probably remain a slow one, owing to the long-range planning, the huge investment, and the large numbers of trained personnel it requires, so that any resulting unemployment is manageable through appropriate government-sponsored retraining programs. Thus, to the extent that exponents of privately instituted automation acknowledge that it displaces workers, they claim that the pace of automation is such that the numbers are not substantial, that the overall contribution to productivity produces compensating effects, and that government can step in to fill whatever employment gaps may remain.[37]

Alongside these rationales for privately controlled automation, the evidence seems to be growing that automation's effects may be far more serious, and more difficult to manage, than these optimistic estimates have indicated. Government studies have reported that though advancing technology has given rise to new industries and new jobs it has also resulted in considerable displacement of employees; there is little comfort to the displacees unable to quickly find or adjust to other employment, in the fact that new work opportunities may "eventually" be created. Thus though total employment increased and *average* unemployment rates fell from over 6 percent in 1961 to under 4 percent in the late years of the decade,[38] important pockets of "hard-core" unemployment have been growing since the mid-1950s. For example, while the overall unemployment rate rose to about 5 percent as of early 1970, among blue-collar factory workers it was already near 6 percent, and almost 8 percent for nonfarm laborers.[39] Taking race directly into account, nonwhite unemployment rates have run approximately double the rates for whites, at least since the mid-1950s.[40] Over this period the laborer and the unskilled production worker have been hardest hit by the introduction of automation and other technological advances in recent years. A major change in the composition of the labor force has been occurring, with the number of white-collar workers by the mid-Fifties exceeding for the first time the number of blue-collar workers, and the gap has been growing ever since.[41]

To this point, then, the impact of automation and other manual labor-saving improvements in the production technology of the society has been making itself felt. What is yet to be experienced on so significant a scale is cybernation, centering around the employment of computers for handling information and making various kinds of logical decisions.[42] This, of course, can have a major effect on the patterns of employment in the world of the office worker, whether the setting is that of a bank, an insurance company, a real-estate firm, or a major corporation; so long as routine (and increasingly, not-quite-so-routine) operations of data collection, tabulation, and processing are entailed, the door is open for the introduction of the computer. As a number of analysts have indicated, the result of large-scale cybernation, added to the effects of automation, might well be technological disemployment for major sections of the middle mass, including not only the semi-skilled factory and office workers but also the junior and middle segments of management itself.[43]

Though it is difficult to say precisely what effect this would have on class structure, it would certainly tend to create anew sharp class differences, rather than continuing the trends toward a finely graded overlapping class structure which have contributed to the de-ideologizing of class differences.[44] Instead of this kind of continuous stratification, broad gaps in the occupational structure could conceivably develop, as many jobs in middle management, as well as routine or low-skilled office work, were displaced by cybernation, and as many factory jobs continued to be displaced by automation. The new structure would be composed essentially of managers and executives responsible for formulating and administering major organizational policies; scientifically trained technical and social service professionals and experts responsible for program innovation and development in their respective areas; skilled technicians operating, monitoring, and servicing increasingly automated institutional and production complexes; and skilled and semiskilled workers in service occupations outside the sphere of the new automated technology. These groups would differ among themselves not only in income and life style, but also in authority and work patterns. Yet, while the differences between these occupational groups might become significant, due to the decimation of intermediate classes by widespread automation, they would be small compared to the widening gap between the employed population considered as a whole, and the growing numbers of unemployed in the society. In effect, the middle masses of the present day occupational structure would have been seriously reduced in number, especially in the areas of routine lower-level blue- or white-collar occupations, and the unemployed underclass would be swollen by their addition; in brief, the trend under extensive automation-cybernation would be to convert the contemporary working class to an increasingly unemployed class. Some reversal of this tendency may occur as a result of the growth of service occupations, especially public service occupations connected with government, education, and health, but this would be heavily dependent on politically sensitive policies for expansion of the public sector and cannot be relied on as a "guaranteed" or "automatic" development.

In the current period, while automation has still remained relatively limited,[45] two basic schools of thought have developed. One, the "aggregate-demand" approach, stresses the capabilities of government intervention for the purposes of job creation. Assuring sufficient aggregate demand through a variety of fiscal measures is appealed to as a powerful instrument to maintain employment. In this view, the stimulation of aggregate demand by government action can provide enough new employment opportunities to make any displacement resulting from automation of work procedures only temporary. However, there are any number of analysts who are not so confident about the effects of automation being "temporary." These observers, generally connected with the "structuralist" approach, view job dislocation as often being permanent, since those being displaced frequently have little education or skill with which to make the transition to new occupations. In addition, they regard the effects of automation as being the displacement not simply of individual workers, but of whole classes of jobs, particularly those which are mechanically repetitive or involve only routine decision by the worker. They see the basic structure of occupations being profoundly altered through the elimination of jobs in manufacturing, and through the spread of automation to occupations which process paper as well as those which manufacture products: to the corporate office with its routine clerical employees, and even to the level of middle management, which finds itself increasingly unable to compete with the speed and dependability of information-processing systems. Some foresee in this a radically new occupational structure like that described earlier, involving drastic reduction in the size of the routine blue- and white-collar working class, and the emergence of a "new working class" consisting of the bulk of the scientific, technical, and professionally trained work force.[46]

Under these circumstances, the more moderate structuralists, such as the 1964 Ad Hoc Committee on the "Triple Revolution" (in cybernation, warfare, and civil rights), have laid stress on the need for programs of job retraining or on the creation of public service positions requiring little retraining, especially aimed at low-skilled workers. They have also proposed some form of income maintenance (basically a "negative income tax") for those workers who would not be significantly affected by these other programs.[47] Together these measures might possibly ease the transition to a basically automated economy, and serve to ameliorate its material effects. However, from the viewpoint of the more radical structuralists (as in the case of a minority of the Triple Revolution Committee), serious questions exist as to the relevance of job-creating or job-retraining programs in a society which they view as rapidly moving from a condition of scarcity, (wherein the grounds for individual income have traditionally been the job) to a condition of abundance (in which traditional notions of job, "work," and their relation to the right to economic income are increasingly being challenged). It has been their judgment that the period of transition to an automated society is already well under way and will be much less gradual than that envisioned by the moderates, so that this urgently poses the problem of massive disemployment and therefore a basic redefinition of the grounds for income distribution.[48] For these "radical structuralists," public works programs to stimulate employment have meaning only in the context of a world of industrial production which is rapidly being left behind; they do nothing to cope with the problems of work, income, and leisure which an automated postindustrial society brings in its train. From their perspective, the capability now exists for a small part of the labor force, using automated technology, to produce the economic needs of the whole society. In order to meet the possibilities of large-scale disemployment which this raises, they proposed a guaranteed income as a matter of right to every citizen in the new society-of- abundance, envisioning that as a basic new mode of income distribution.[49] Though the moderate majority of the Triple Revolution Committee also urged commitment to a guaranteed income, this was apparently intended more as a supplementary mode of income distribution aimed at those without work, than a basic mode of distribution for the overall society.

In a sense, the government's reply to the Triple Revolution Committee's manifesto was embodied in the 1966 Report of the National Commission on Technology, Automation, and Economic Progress, which we have discussed in an earlier chapter as a kind of benchmark of the social-technocratic position toward the problems of employment and income in a period of increasing automation (see chapter 7). In effect, this report combined the aggregate-demand approach, which relies on government stimulation of overall demand through spending and tax policies, with the recommendations of the moderate structuralists for job retraining, creation of public service jobs for those workers not reachable by retraining, and income maintenance for the rest. However, unlike the Ad Hoc Committee's proposals, there was no mention of the need for political action by the union movement, or for political action by any other movement working with or on behalf of the growing numbers of technologically disemployed. The solution, with little surprise, was a technocratic one formulated by a government-appointed elite commission, to be researched and administered by government agencies. In the absence of significant political support, however, the government has thus far done very little to implement the recommendations of the Commission, and in recent years unemployment has actually been permitted to rise in order to hold down inflation.

In closing this chapter, it is worth mentioning one of the reviews of the Technology Commission report which we have discussed above. This was a review by the economist Robert Lekachman which, though admiring of the liberal and humane thrust of the Commission's recommendations, was highly critical of its implicit underlying approach.[50] Essentially, observes Lekachman, the Commission's long-term philosophy for bringing about needed change consists in the development of better knowledge by public authorities, particularly the federal government, which it assumes will act as the patron of social improvement. The Commission's substantive suggestions consist largely of recommendations for research into community needs; establishing a system of social cost accounting; and establishing a commission on national goals. These recommendations suggest that we have the technology to do anything we collectively decide upon doing; all that lacks is the knowledge about how it should be applied to improve the society. This, as Lekachman puts it, amounts to "a recipe for cool research rather than hot politics, orderly university training rather than untidy street demonstrations, and the forging of a consensus out of rational thought rather than out of conflicts of ideologies and interest...."[51] As he sees it, however, this is unrealistic, because technical insight does not presuppose social reform. Even when the technical knowledge or administrative means already exist, as in the case, for example, of established systems of public health or social insurance, there is no assurance that their services will be extended to all who need them. There must first be a *political* commitment to social change, before the felt need for reforms is translated into the appropriate *technical* measures to implement them. The application of scientific and administrative techniques for human welfare waits upon the gathering of sufficient political pressure to see that they are so applied. As Lekachman put it, even today in late twentieth-century America,

> Significant alteration in the way we conduct our lives seems mainly to come about through social and political conflict, extra-legal action, riots in the streets, and the death of martyrs.[52]

CHAPTER XI

Review and Conclusions

Traditionally, ideology has played a key role in the interpretation of society and social goals in times of conflict, crisis, and change. Moreover, those who view ideology in this way, as a dynamic aspect of the culture, rather than simply as a political weapon or tool, tend to recognize its capacity to "grasp, formulate, and communicate social realities that elude the tempered language of science."[1] Thus ideology is not merely emotional, irrational, distorting rhetoric (though it can be this too), but a vital agent in the formulation of schematic images of the social order and its problems, and of alternative configuration whereby the rich but blocked potentialities of the system can be set free.[2] In the past, ideology has reflected present crises and projected future prospects, while the body of the culture stood as the fixed ground of established social understandings, against which contending ideologies traced the figures of conflict and change. This historical function of ideology, however, is essentially ignored by the end-of-ideologists. They stress that today ideology is no longer viable as a means of social analysis or interpretation; the gross simplifications and the extreme and violent actions engaged in by the ideologues of recent times have lost the trust and respect of people for ideological thought, and this is particularly true of the intellectual strata of society. The implication is that today only "social science" theory is capable of making the required analysis of what has occurred and of synthesizing the elements of the emerging new society in the form of a new model of social reality; in short, it is social theory which must take the place of ideology as the dynamic element of cultural re-interpretation. Today, according to the end-of-ideologists, social theory must play the role of interpreting the pattern of the present and of suggesting paths to the future. However, left in their hands, it will be a social theory which incorporates the technical methods and outlook of the new technocratic meritocracy of which they are leading members, and which they view as destined and qualified to guide the future development of the postindustrial society.

We have traced the work of the end-of-ideologists from their explication of the contemporary inadequacy of traditional pluralist modes of decision, to their own response with an ideological theory of centralized technocratic control and coordination. As a theory, we have examined its revision of earlier pluralist models of the society, in which it has steadily given greater significance to the role of the state, particularly the central executive, in the political-economic coordination of the society, and to the importance of an emerging scientific-professional class to the functions of conscious rational development and planning which it associates with the state. However, since the enterprise of planning does not necessarily define the purposes which it implements, we have noted that the functional rationality of the planners, which the end-of-ideologists view as the basis of a more rational society, can also serve narrowly economic, destructive, and irrational ends. To the extent that the end-of-ideology's portrait of technocratic planning ignores this distinction between functional rationality and the substantive irrationality of many of the ends which it serves today, it produces an ideology of rationalistic legitimation for these ends (e.g., the computerized Vietnam "pacification" program, and its use in supporting claims that the sympathies of the Vietnamese peasantry were being won through American expertise in community organization and rural development; or, even better, the computerized strategic-bombing program, supposedly effective not only in hitting military targets, but also in distinguishing them from civilian areas).[3]

The image of the rise of a rationalist "technocracy" in a "postindustrial" society tends to draw attention away from the persisting power of private interests, particularly those of corporate management, and the growing power of nominally public state-managerial interests, in the making of political-administrative policies which have profound effect upon societal development. Today, it is true that as a result of government efforts to develop a technical-administrative framework for relating to the claims of different institutions and agencies with interests in military technological development, government agencies are no longer so highly accessible to the influence of the enterprises of the Contract State whose emergence and expansion they had themselves originally helped subsidize. Yet despite the imposition of sophisticated budgetary and managerial controls, the substantive policies of agencies like the "new" technocratically managed Pentagon hardly seem to reflect a higher rationality today than when they were internally more divided and not subject to such explicit central control. Furthermore, the general growth in economic power and political influence of the still privately managed major corporate units of the economy has continued in various ways, and the prospect that these institutions will next move into the field of public sector development, leaves considerable uncertainty as to whether public or private interests will thereby be served, as well as the future relations of public civilian agencies of government with private corporate interests.

The continuing growth and concentration of private loci of power pursuing their own interests in the society has yielded them an unparalleled position in which they have become essential to achieving basic interests of the overall society. In this way, the line between private interests and public interest has been seriously blurred. At the same time, we observe that the social technocrats of the state have themselves developed a special interest in their role as authoritative professional reformers, so that aside from the influence of external private power blocs in qualifying or countering the public interest with their own policy interests, the technocratic agents of the central state itself tend to establish a vested interest in their own role in the planning and execution of programs of social reform such as the "war on poverty." Despite an ideology of professional universalism and rationalism, this can mean in practice the substitution of the perspectives and values of often middle-class-oriented social planners for that of the client community; such is the particularism of benevolent paternalism, which seeks to re-create the community in its own image.

Consistent with the paternalism of the social technocrats regarding their role in the social planning process has been their attitude toward the making of policy in the putative "postindustrial democracy." In their view, policy is properly made by the establishment of consensus between elite leaders of the major interests in the society, a practice which in fact tends to slight the interests of those who are relatively unorganized and unestablished, and which also discourages general participation beyond that of the respective interest leaders. Because of their concern to win the support of major power blocs for their planning objectives, the social technocrats have on various occasions exhibited considerable reluctance to attack the myths ("free enterprise," "the nonpolitical corporation," etc.) which veil the important role of these interests, and particularly of the dominant members of the corporate sector, in the planning which does go on in the economy. Instead they have turned their attention to reforms which would further centralize *governmental* structure, integrating the local level and tying it more closely to the federal level of government. Thus their strategy has been to seek first to strengthen and streamline government so as to extend its power over particularistic private interests "outside" the state; however, this strategy overlooks the new interpenetration of state and corporate sector, in which the state today is as much an arm of the industrial sector as the other way around. And even if government controls can provide the state with the deciding role in this relationship, there remains the problem of the remoteness of this "new industrial state" as a whole from popular participation, comprehension, or control.

Today, the base of support for the technocratic coordination and interlinking of state and corporate industry consists of the relatively comfortable "middle mass" of the society, socialized to a culture of consumerism, which together with an essentially military concept of national security has constituted the major theme of its rather depoliticized ideology in the postwar era. Standing in opposition to the new technocratic state for the present and near future, are those in the society who feel their full status as citizens and their rights and capacities to participate in the making of social policy unrealized or threatened in some way, so that their allegiance to the theme of technocratic government is impaired. Unlike the historic ideological opposition of the working class, however, this is an opposition based upon distinct subcultures in the society, with little prospect of real unification between the separatist "black power" advocates and their white middle-class student allies in the "new Left," and none between radical Right and these other two. While the appeal of the radical Left has seemed for the most part limited to the campus, and of the black militants to the ghetto, the ideology of the radical Right, which is in many respects the most primitive and "fundamentalist" of the three, has at points appeared to have the greatest potential for spreading beyond its immediate parochial base to national political importance, as resentment against technocratic decision making and its practitioners grows under the expanding impact of technocratically planned automation and cybernation.

The practice of "planning for" the incompetent masses, taken to its extreme, and made a principle for the overall system rather than merely its poverty segment, is a distinctive characteristic of what some have called "the meritocracy."[4] This meritocracy is thus far only an incipient managerial-professional "establishment" produced by the zealous application of policies of selection-by-talent which "disestablish" or render "functionally superfluous" most others in the society. Yet the on-going process of expanding automation and cybernation, carried far enough, would indeed tend to produce a meritocratic stratification of the population into a technocratic elite, a lower technician class, and a residual service stratum, with the rest of the society's employment seriously jeopardized.[5] In the absence of appropriate ameliorative programs on the part of government, the issue of automation and its effects on the "middle mass" could thus become one of greater scope and immediacy than have been either the Vietnam War or the threat of ghetto revolt.

We have considered in the foregoing chapters some of the possible effects which the posing of such an issue might have on the strata which currently support the technocratic government of the new industrial state. If such a government failed over the long term to take appropriate action with regard to automation, there could be foreseen serious erosion of support for the established centrist parties and a drift of lower-middle and working-class strata either toward the Right or the Left. Such a political shift of the middle masses from the centrist parties, entailing the possible polarization of these masses, would probably not be quick in coming. It would most likely first be preceded by the breakup of a working consensus between liberal and conservative elements within the major parties. However, under protracted circumstances in which the demands of the middle mass could not be accommodated through established party representation, the result could be a political paralysis which might open the way to a resolution by force and the installation of a dictatorial regime.

It is interesting that even Brzezinski, who foresees the development of a "technetronic" society not unlike the technomeritocracy we have discussed, sees the possibility of dictatorship as an aspect of this configuration. In his view, however, dictatorial controls would anticipate rather than follow crises, and would constitute a major means of stabilizing the new society against the emotional outburst of its frustrated, unemployed, and purposeless masses.[6] Interestingly, such an interpretation foresees the need for dictatorship even if material amelioration can be provided for the disemployed masses of the society; as Brzezinski reasons, the discontent of the "disestablished" masses of an affluent technopolis would be based not primarily on economic want, but on the psychocultural disorientation of their political nonparticipation and economic dependency in a fully technocratic society. Surely a complex technocratic dictatorship is not entirely to be excluded, if adequate provisions are not made to satisfy strivings for meaningful social-political participation by the new masses of Technopolis, and particularly if its affluence is not as great or as evenly distributed as Brzezinski assumes. Thus we have the historically unique possibility of a choice between a new kind of "value-neutral," politically flexible "techno-totalitarianism" (cloaking itself in the mantle of a meritocracy of technical knowledge that best understands the public interest), which may yet be distinctive to the postindustrial society, and the more familiar political brands of dictatorship formerly associated with the industrial era.

Under such circumstances, the hazardous direction in which technological development is carrying us, and the question of which direction we *want* to go, require a more coherent perspective than that which is offered today by the major existing movements of protest against these developments: the New Left, with a viewpoint which has not matured or integrated itself sufficiently to be more than a kind of proto-ideology; the black power movement, whose perspective is shaped by the parochial ghetto context; and the Radical Right, who seek the preservation of an archaic, repressive traditionalist community. The parochialism of these latter two movements, and the theoretical vagueness of the New Left, leave the social theorist with an important task of analysis and criticism, if for no more than "academic" purposes of understanding.

To the extent, however, that social science has itself become a vehicle for meritocratic, technocratic ideology, the task of theoretical self-criticism becomes a vital one, in order to restore social theory to a position of some kind of independence. This must be understood as part of the larger enterprise of overcoming particularism in social theory as well as analyzing and criticizing it in both prevailing and emergent political ideologies.[7] Thus, the self-identification of social-technocratic intellectuals with the central state cannot *per se* be viewed as a step beyond particularism so long as the state remains the closely coupled bride of powerful economic-political interests in the society. Under these circumstances, social science as an ideology of the superior rationality of central coordination becomes in fact a mask for the powers who retain the planning-oriented technocrats for their own purposes. Moreover, even if corporatist interest relations could be brought under the hegemony of the state, the particularism of the paternalistic social planner, with his often narrow social-intellectual perspective, would remain as a problem.

The social theorist as a systematically critical intellectual will take seriously and examine carefully the ideologies of the day for their central conceptions as responses to ongoing structural and cultural development, and for their impact on the political scene, particularly on the making of social policy, which in turn affects structural developments in the society. He will recognize that he cannot afford simply to ignore these movements and their beliefs, or to decry them as extremist. For in seeking to identify the ideas and values over which men in the emerging postindustrial society come into conflict, or toward which they are for the first time beginning to grope, ideology can serve the theorist as a rich source of data on this society.

Despite the technocratic ideological theory which proclaims the "end of ideology," it is quite clear that ideology has not ended, but only changed form over the past generation, reflecting the emergence both of new political problems and of issues submerged or ignored for decades and now surfacing in the movements directed not only toward racial or ethnic-group rights, but also toward the rights of women, homosexuals, the blind, the welfare-dependent, and other groups sharing common identities and problems which have failed to fit the assumptions of the earlier New Deal consensus or of the ideology of "the affluent society" which followed it. Moreover, the new ideologies of protest, discontent, and resentment now afoot among relative minorities may spread through the bulk of the population in response to the disruptive impact of automation on established occupational, cultural, and political rights and positions.

Today, a new cultural synthesis is being sought in which the human need for meaning and relevance based on the experience of social participation and democratic control can find institutional recognition, and in which the new technological character of society as a system of productive abundance can find realization, through the re-evaluation of such basic institutions as work and its relation to the individual's special identity as well as his material sustenance. This will involve among other things a reconsideration of the conceptions of work and leisure in relation to both the community and the individual; of what comprises meaningful work and socially useful production; and of what constitutes a socially justifying basis for personal income, consumption, and leisure. And these redefinitions will inevitably involve once again the basic questions of community and purpose which have been so neglected in the ascendance of theories focussed upon "system," "decision making," and now "system guidance."[8] Unless these basic redefinitions, involving the socioeconomic relation of man to man, of man to the physical environment and to his own nature, and of man to the technology which mediates his relations to all of these, can be achieved and implemented, the society will be unable to complete on the sociocultural level the "silent revolution" which responsible observers describe as being already well under way in the technology. As Richard Titmuss puts it, failing a major transformation of values, only an "impoverishment of social living" can be the result of this second, "postindustrial" revolution.[9] There seems little doubt that for better or worse, ideology will play an important role in the struggle for value transformation.

Notes

Introduction

1. Cf. Christopher Lasch, *The Agony of the American Left* (New York: Random House, 1969).
2. Cf. C. Wright Mills, *The Power Elite* (New York: Oxford University Press, 1959).

Chapter I

1. Apparently the social debut of this line of thinking came at a conference on "The Future of Freedom" held in Milan, Italy in September 1955, under the auspices of the Congress for Cultural Freedom. See Edward Shils, "The End of Ideology?" *Encounter* 5 (November 1955): 52-58. See also Seymour Martin Lipset, *Political Man* (Garden City, N.Y.: Doubleday, 1963), pp. 439-40; and Daniel Bell, *The End of Ideology* (New York: Crowell-Collier, 1961), p. 440, n 168, for background references. For further background, see Lipset, "The Changing Class Structure and Contemporary European Politics," *Daedalus* 93 (Winter 1964): 271-303.
2. See, in particular, the essay on "The End of Ideology in the West," in Bell, *End of Ideology*, pp. 393-402, and "The End of Ideology?" in Lipset, *Political Man*, pp. 439-56. See also Raymond Aron, *The Opium of the Intellectuals* (New York: Doubleday, 1957), which originally appeared in French in 1955. Both

Lipset and Bell refer to aspects of the work of the American sociologist Edward Shils; Bell to Shils's essay "Ideology and Civility," in the *Sewanee Review*, Summer 1958, and Lipset to his article "The End of Ideology?" See also Shils's "The Calling of Sociology," Epilogue to *Theories of Society*, ed. Talcott Parsons, Shils, Kaspar Naegele, and Jesse Pitts (New York: Free Press, 1961), pp. 1405-50, for discussion of the rise of a "sociological outlook" and its potential for facilitating social consensus, apparently of seminal importance to the "end-of-ideology" position. For the essential end-of-ideology statements of Bell, Lipset, Aron and Shils, together with a number of provocative critiques, see Chaim I. Waxman, ed., *The End of Ideology Debate* (New York: Simon and Schuster, 1968).

3. Lipset, *Political Man*, pp. 440-41.
4. *Ibid.*, p. 444.
5. Bell, *End of Ideology*, p. 397.
6. For an early source of this theme, cf. Peter Drucker, *The New Society* (New York: Harper, 1949).
7. Cf. Lipset, *Political Man*, ch. 2: "Economic Development and Democracy," pp. 27-63.
8. On the theme of "citizenship," see *ibid.*, pp. 73-75, 82. See also T.H. Marshall, *Class, Citizenship, and Social Development* (Garden City: Doubleday, 1965), esp. the essay "Citizenship and Social Class," pp. 71-134. On the theme of the welfare state, see Lipset, *Political Man*, p. 443; cf. Bell, *End of Ideology*, p. 311. Cf. the essays on the welfare state in Marshall, *Class, Citizenship, and Social Development*, pp. 257-323.
9. Lipset, *Political Man*, pp. 442-43. For a sharply critical comment on this claim, see Stephen W. Rousseas and James Farganis, "American Politics and the End of Ideology," in Waxman, ed., *End of Ideology Debate*, pp. 206-28.
10. See for example, Clark Kerr, John T. Dunlop, Frederick Harbison, Charles A. Meyers, *Industrialism and Industrial Man* (New York: Oxford University Press, 1960), esp. pp. 17, 287-88.
11. Lipset, *Political Man*, p. 453.
12. *Ibid.*, p. 452.
13. Bell, *End of Ideology*, p. 312.
14. At this point in his work, Bell identified the older radical critics with the politically "weary," though highly sophisticated, intellectuals associated with such periodicals as *Dissent*, who were then shifting from traditional political critiques to the examination of the cultural problems of America as a mass society. (*Ibid.*, p. 313.)
15. *Ibid.*, p. 310; cf. Lipset, *Political Man*, pp. 10-11.
16. Bell, *End of Ideology*, p. 312.
17. *Ibid.*, p. 311; cf. Lipset, *Political Man*, pp. 367-71.
18. Bell, *End of Ideology*, p. 311. See also Daniel Bell, ed., *The Radical Right* (Garden City, N. Y.: Doubleday, 1964), esp. the articles by Lipset (pp. 307-71), and Richard Hofstadter (pp. 75-95), which contain seminal discussions of the concepts of "status anxiety" and "status politics."
19. Bell, *End of Ideology*, p. 313; cf. Lipset, *Political Man*, pp. 298-99.
20. Bell, *End of Ideology*, p. 400.
21. See Daniel Bell and Henry Aiken, "Ideology—A Debate," in Edgar Litt, ed., *The Political Imagination*, p. 154, reprinted from *Commentary*, October 1964.
22. Bell, *End of Ideology*, p. 397.
23. *Ibid.*, p. 16; cf. p. 400, where Bell comments that the analytic perspective embodied in the end-of-ideology theory "closes the book . . . on an era . . . of easy 'left' formulae for social change." See also Lipset, *Political Man*, p. 445.
24. Cf. Arthur Schlesinger, Jr., *The Vital Center* (Boston: Houghton Mifflin, 1949). This book was one of the first of the postwar period to express the mixture of social pessimism, reaction against earlier involvements with the radical Left, and ideological anti-Communism which came to characterize the new

liberalism of the Cold War era. See on this James P. Young, *The Politics of Affluence, Ideology in the United States Since World War II* (San Francisco: Chandler, 1968), pp. 29-33. On the related "cultural politics" of the liberalism of the Cold War era, (and, in particular, the role of organizations like the Congress for Cultural Freedom), interwoven with a pointed critique of the end-of-ideology position, see Lasch, *Agony of the American Left*, pp. 63-114, 171-19.

25. Seymour Martin Lipset, "The Changing Class Structure & Contemporary European Politics," p. 296.

26. *Ibid.*

27. Bell, *End of Ideology*, pp. 43-45, 311, 397. Cf. William Delany, "The Role of Ideology: A Summation," in Waxman, ed., *End of Ideology Debate*, pp. 291-314. As Delany observes, the ideological position of the end-of-ideologists is "a synthesis of Marxism and liberal styles of belief and value around a central core of managerialism.... From managerialism they draw a preference for administrative over political means, for gradual, manipulated social change over rapid change based upon political movements ... and, finally, a great respect for technical-professional expertise." Also see Paul Jacobs and Saul Landau, *The New Radicals* (New York: Random House, 1966), pp. 257-66, on the theme of managerial or "corporate" liberalism.

28. Writing in the *End of Ideology*, Bell succinctly described postwar American society as characterized by a "general acceptance of corporate capitalism, modified by union power, and checked by governmental control. . . ." (*Ibid.*, p. 109.) Under later attack by Henry Aiken for his implicit acceptance of the institutional *status quo*, Bell replied by identifying himself as a "democratic socialist" interested in basic social and economic change. (See Litt, *The Political Imagination*, p. 156.) Aiken responded by questioning the seriousness of Bell's reply, noting that in the body of his work Bell had "opted emphatically and without qualification for 'the mixed economy'—which, of course, no socialist could accept save as a temporary stop-gap." (Litt, *Political Imagination*, p. 161). Though Lipset has from the outset been somewhat more explicit in stating his own political identification with the "democratic left" (*Political Man*, p. xxv), like Bell the economic underpinnings of his position leave something to be desired; neither gives any concentrated attention to the question of whether the modifications of contemporary Western capitalist systems *via* welfare programs and policies of government intervention have actually resulted in basic institutional changes, as against modified but still essentially capitalist economies. See in this regard the essay by Shigeto Tsuru, "Has Capitalism Changed?" in Tsuru, ed., *Has Capitalism Changed?* (Tokyo: Iwanami Shoten, 1961), pp. 1-68.

29. On modern revisionist socialism, see C.A.R. Crosland, *The Future of Socialism* (New York: Macmillan, 1957), for observations on the political adjustment of the socialist movement to a managerially reformed corporate capitalism similar to that incorporated into the "end-of-ideology" thesis. Cf. Henry Aiken, "Ideology—A Debate," p. 154.

30. Bell, *End of Ideology*, pp. 44, 90.

31. *Ibid.*, p. 44.

32. *Ibid.*, p. 70.

33. Cf. Karl Mannheim, *Ideology and Utopia* (New York: Harcourt, Brace, 1936), pp. 55-59.

34. Cf. Chalmers Johnson, *Revolutionary Change* (Boston: Little, Brown, 1966), p. 87.

35. Bell, *End of Ideology*, pp. 393-95, *passim*.

36. *Ibid.*, p. 394.

37. Considerable controversy has followed the exposition of the end-of-ideology thesis, not the least with regard to its precise meaning and the degree to which it serves as a vehicle for an ideological position in its own right. For good examples of this criticism of the thesis, see Waxman, ed., *End of Ideology Debate*,

especially the essay by Robert A. Haber ("The End of 'The End of Ideology,'"
pp. 373-82). In the wake of such discussion several friendly reviewers of the
thesis have tended to interpret it as *not* literally meaning the "end" or "exhaustion" of political ideology in advanced society, but rather its *general* "decline"
or "reduction." See M. Rejai, W.L. Mason, and D.C. Beller, "Political Ideology:
Empirical Relevance of the Hypothesis of Decline," *Ethics* 78 (July 1968):
309. This is consistent with the position taken in the present work, with two
important qualifications: first, the conflict of *particularistic* ideologies representing discrete interests in the society seems to continue without interruption, and
may even be encouraged by the new role of the state as economic patron to
politically organized claimants. Second, the observation by Rejai, *et al.*, that the
thesis indicates the "increasing irrelevance of 'total' or 'extremist' ideologies," is
misleading in equating "total" with "extremist." For the thesis does not simply
dispense with total ideology, but actually tends to endorse a moderate yet comprehensive social-democratic ideology which is a blend of "conservative socialism" (Lipset) and "welfare capitalism" (Bell). In short, the thesis is not pointed
at *all* total ideologies, but only at those which its authors identify as "radical"
or "extremist."

Because of the complexity of recent ideological developments in the United
States as the leading "postindustrial" society, another qualification is appropriate; namely, that the decline of total ideologies and ideological conflicts which
the end-of-ideologists described at the close of the 1950s was a decline of *traditional* class ideologies and conflicts associated with an earlier stage of industrial
developments; as the society moves into a "postindustrial" phase, with a new
occupational and social structure, new ideologies and conflicts may well emerge,
as already seems the case. Cf. Lasch, *Agony of the American Left*, p. 174; and
cf. Morris Janowitz and David R. Segal, "Social Cleavage and Party Affiliation:
Germany, Great Britain, and the United States," in Calvin J. Larson & Philo
C. Wasburn, *Power, Participation, and Ideology: Readings in the Sociology of
American Political Life* (New York: David McKay, 1969), pp. 458-78.

38. See Bertram M. Gross, ed., *Social Intelligence for America's Future: Explorations in Societal Problems* (Boston: Allyn & Bacon, 1969), esp. preface, pp.
v-xi.
39. *Ibid.*, p. viii.
40. Cf. Mannheim, *Ideology and Utopia*, pp. 192-211. See also Aiken, "The Revolt
Against Ideology," in Litt, *The Political Imagination*, pp. 147-49.
41. Gross, ed., *Social Intelligence*, p. viii. If all of this sounds familiarly like the
position of the end-of-ideologists, the connection is not hard to find, and may
be traced to a circle of influential liberal academics actively in contact with governmental and academic agencies and commissions interested in closing the gap
in "social intelligence" identified during the Johnson administration's attempted
War on Poverty. Prominently included in this circle was Daniel Bell himself,
who is identified in several connections as active in the "current expansion of
social indicator activity," in the essay "Developing Social Intelligence" by Gross
and Springer. (*Ibid.*, pp. 3-44.) Bertram Gross has himself been active in
broaching the need for an annual "social report," preparing "a special issue of
THE ANNALS as a trial-run Social Report." (*Ibid.*, p. x) Ultimately two large
issues of *THE ANNALS*, published in May and September of 1967, were used
in putting together the document finally issued in the closing hours of the Johnson administration, titled *Toward a Social Report* and released by Wilbur
Cohen, the outgoing Secretary of Health, Education and Welfare. Thus, it is
interesting to note that the perspectives and activities of Gross and Bell have
overlapped and combined in fostering the Social Indicators Movement.

Significantly, in listing the background historical factors to the development
of the Social Indicators Movement, Gross and Springer reproduce some of the
major themes in the end-of-ideology position. They include "the increasing
maturation of the social sciences, ... the entry into public policy positions of a

broadening array of intellectuals, professionals, modern-style managers, technologists, scientists, [and] the acceptance of the new economics by both conservatives and liberals," all items familiar to those who have followed the development of the end-of-ideology position. In addition, they make explicit a factor only hinted at in various ways by the end-of-ideologists, as prerequisite to the realization of technocratic development efforts; namely, the emergence of a new breed of corporation executives with "fact-based styles of management and broader social perspectives." (*Ibid.*, p. 17.)

42. See Zbigniew Brzezinski, "America in the Technetronic Age, New Questions of Our Time," *Encounter*, January 1968, pp. 16-23, for a discussion based on premises much like those of Bell and Lipset, of the need for developing "pre-crisis management institutions" as a regular means of social control in the post-industrial era. (*Ibid.*, p. 21.)

43. Cf. Aiken, "Ideology—A Debate," pp. 150-51.

44. Cf. R. Joseph Monsen, Jr. and Mark W. Cannon, *The Makers of Public Policy: American Power Groups and Their Ideologies* (New York: McGraw-Hill, 1965), pp. 19-21.

45. On the ideology of traditional aristocratic elites, cf. William Kornhauser, *The Politics of Mass Society* (Glencoe: Free Press, 1959), pp. 26-29.

46. Cf. Karl Mannheim, *Ideology and Utopia*, pp. 55-75.

47. Cf. Kornhauser, *Politics of Mass Society*, pp. 30-35.

48. Cf. Clifford Geertz, "Ideology as a Cultural System," in David Apter, *Ideology and Discontent* (London: Collier-Macmillan Ltd., 1964), pp. 44-77.

49. Samuel M. Beer and Adam B. Ulam, *Patterns of Government: The Major Political Systems of Europe* (New York: Random House, 1967), pp. 32-68, and pp. 155-57 on "Common Purpose and Interests" in relation to "political culture," p. 41. See also Lucian Pye and Sidney Verba, *Political Culture and Political Development* (Princeton, N.J.: Princeton University Press, 1965).

50. Analytically it is possible to differentiate between the political culture of the governing elite and the political culture of the governed mass. It should first be acknowledged that much of the political culture of the mass in a stable society incorporates and translates into simpler language and more immediate symbolism for the masses of people in the society, the justifications of the elite for its political position, and can be viewed as a kind of functional "subculture" of the larger political culture. However, to the extent which nonelite groups or strata succeed in articulating the *conflict* of their aims and interests with those of the elite, or with those of *other* nonelite groups, they produce a political "counterculture" expressing their unique political identity and objectives through their own symbols and slogans (e.g., the clenched fist or *v*-sign, as against the salute). When this counterculture becomes articulated in the form of distinctive assumptions and ideals about the society and some kind of strategy for achieving these goals, we may speak of the group's "political ideology."

51. It is in this context that the continuing interest of the end-of-ideologists in the relationship between stability, legitimacy, and political conflict should be understood and appraised. (See, for example, Lipset, *Political Man*, ch. 3: "Social Conflict, Legitimacy, and Democracy," pp. 64-86.)

52. Though religious ideologies have persisted as important elements of ideological belief for various groups in industrial society, they have tended to become increasingly secularized with the maturation of that society. Cf. Will Herberg, *Protestant—Catholic—Jew* (Garden City, N.Y.: Doubleday, 1956), esp. pp. 82-89.

53. Cf. Kenneth Boulding, *The Meaning of the Twentieth Century* (New York: Harper & Row, 1964), pp. 159-62.

54. See C. Wright Mills, *The Power Elite*, pp. 269-97; cf. Bell, *End of Ideology*, p. 55. Also see Marc Pilisuk and Thomas Hayden, "Is There a Military-Industrial Complex Which Prevents Peace?: Consensus and Countervailing Power in Pluralistic Systems," in Robert Perucci and Marc Pilisuk, eds., *The*

Triple Revolution: Social Problems in Depth (Boston: Little, Brown, 1968), pp. 77-110.

55. "Alienation is not nihilism but a positive role, a detachment, which guards one against being submerged in any cause, or accepting any particular embodiment of community as final." (Bell, *End of Ideology*, pp. 16-17.)

56. Daniel Bell, "Notes on the Post-Industrial Society (I)," *The Public Interest*, Winter 1967, pp. 32-33. Cf. Seymour Lipset, "The Changing Class Structure of Contemporary European Politics," esp. pp. 277-78, on the related theme of societal modernization through the action of managerial elites.

57. Cf. Daniel Bell, "Notes on the Post-Industrial Society (II)," *The Public Interest*, Spring 1967, pp. 107-8.

58. See Robert E. Lane, *Political Ideology* (New York: Free Fress, 1962), pp. 10-16. Cf. C. Wright Mills, *The Marxists* (New York: Dell, 1962), pp. 12-13; Talcott Parsons, "An Approach to the Sociology of Knowledge," *Transactions of the Fourth World Congress of Sociology* (Louvain, Belgium: International Sociological Associations, 1961), pp. 25-49; Gibson Winter, "The Conception of Ideology in the Theory of Action," *Journal of Religion* 39 (January 1959): 43-49; and William Delany, "The Role of Ideology: A Summation," in Chaim I. Waxman, ed., *End of Ideology Debate*, pp. 291-314.

Chapter II

1. See Arthur F. Bentley, *The Process of Government* (Chicago: University of Chicago Press, 1908); and E. Pendleton Herring, *Group Representation Before Congress* (Baltimore: Johns Hopkins Press, 1929) for early pre-New Deal statements of pluralist theory. For work in the 1940s and early 1950s which consolidated and formalized this theoretical position, see E. Pendleton Herring, *The Politics of Democracy* (New York: W.W. Norton, 1940); V.O. Key, *Politics, Parties and Pressure Groups* (New York: Knopf, 1942); Wilfred Binkley and Malcom Moos, *A Grammar of American Politics* (New York: Knopf, 1950); David Truman, *The Governmental Process* (New York: Knopf, 1951); and Earl Latham, *The Group Basis of Politics* (Ithaca: Cornell University Press, 1952). See also Robert A. Dahl, *et al.*, *Social Science Research on Business: Product and Potential* (New York: Columbia University Press, 1959), pp. 1-44, esp. pp. 18-20, for comments and bibliography on the development of the pluralist position to the late 1950s.

2. On the role of the electoral system in the provision of institutionalized channels for expressing conflict and measuring consensus between various interests in society, see Lipset, *Political Man*, pp. 230-78. On the process of political interest bargaining, see Robert A. Dahl and Charles E. Lindblom, *Politics, Economics, and Welfare* (New York: Harper and Row, 1953), pp. 325-34. See also David Truman, "Federalism and the Party System," in Arthur W. Macmahon, ed., *Federalism Mature and Emergent* (New York: Columbia University Press, 1955), pp. 115-36, for a pluralist interpretation of the American party system.

3. Earl Latham, "The Group Basis of Politics: Notes for a Theory," *American Political Science Review*, June 1952, p. 390.

4. Essentially the role of the democratic politician is to help "maintain a working balance" among competing interest groups. By acting as a political middleman or "broker," he serves to facilitate both compromise between conflicting groups and coalition between groups with common interests. Of course the overall pattern of coalition and compromise cannot be determined by any single political actor in pluralist theory. It is the organs of the state as a whole, and particularly the legislature, through which the "broker" role functions on a large scale, connecting interest groups with official political representation; hence the pluralist

image of the democratic state as a "broker state." (Cf. Key, *Politics, Parties and Pressure Groups*, p. 24.)

5. Latham, "Group Basis of Politics," pp. 390-92, *passim.*
6. Oliver Garceau, "Interest Group Theory in Political Research," *ANNALS of the American Academy of Social and Political Science*, September 1958, p. 106. Cf. Joseph LaPalombara, "The Utility and Limitations of Interest Group Theory in Non-American Field Situations," *Journal of Politics* 22 (February 1960): 29-49.
7. Ralph Miliband, *The State in Capitalist Society* (London: Wiedenfeld & Nicolson, 1969), p. 8.
8. *Ibid.*, p. 9.
9. Garceau, "Interest Group Theory," p. 109.
10. Dahl, *et al.*, *Social Science Research on Business*, p. 36.
11. Ravid Riesman, with Nathan Glazer and Reuel Denney, *The Lonely Crowd* (New Haven: Yale University Press, 1951), pp. 242-54.
12. Miliband, *State in Capitalist Society*, p. 4.
13. Cf. Robert A. Dahl, "A Critique of the Ruling Elite Model," *American Political Science Review*, June 1958; and *Who Governs* (New Haven: Yale University Press, 1961); Dahl and Lindblom, *Politics, Economics, and Welfare*; David Truman, "The American System in Crisis," *Political Science Quarterly*, December 1959, pp. 481-97. Cf. V.O. Key, *Public Opinion and American Democracy* (New York: Knopf, 1961). For a cogent critical analysis of modern elite-pluralist theory, see Peter Bachrach, *The Theory of Democratic Elitism* (Boston: Little, Brown, 1967); and Henry Kariel, *The Decline of American Pluralism* (Stanford, California, 1961), esp. pp. 180-83. See also Dahl and Lindblom, *Politics, Economics, and Welfare*, pp. 255-57 on the inequality of elites and nonelites in modern bureaucratic organizations, including those with explicit interest-representation functions such as parties and trade unions. As they put it, the modern organizational leader's hand "is the hand that runs the adding machine," so that he is in a position "to count his own preferences, not as equal, but as worth ten or a hundred or a thousand times more than the preferences of everyone else in the organization." (*Ibid.*, p. 256.)
14. Miliband, *State in Capitalist Society*, p. 4.
15. Lipset, *Political Man*, pp. 183-229, esp. pp. 189, 221.
16. David Riesman and Nathan Glazer, "Criteria for Political Apathy," in Alvin W. Gouldner, ed., *Studies in Leadership* (New York: Harper & Bros., 1950), p. 519, cited in Lipset, *Political Man*, p. 186.
17. Francis G. Wilson, "The Inactive Electorate and Social Revolution," *Southwestern Social Science Quarterly* 16 (1936): 76, cited in Lipset, *Political Man*, p. 227.
18. *Ibid.*, pp. 227-29.
19. David Riesman, "Private People and Public Policy," *Bulletin of the Atomic Scientists* 15 (1959): 205, cited in Lipset, *Political Man*, p. 228.
20. Mills, *Power Elite*, esp. pp. 242-324. Cf. Irving Louis Horowitz, ed., *The New Sociology* (New York: Oxford University Press, 1964), for further work among sociologists and social psychologists during the 1960s along the lines pursued by Mills.
21. Theodore Lowi, *The End of Liberalism: Ideology, Policy, and the Crisis of Public Authority* (New York: W.W. Norton, 1969), ch. 3: "The New Public Philosophy: Interest-Group Liberalism," pp. 55-97.
22. On the question of relations between the state and the business class, Mills pictured the top political and military leaders of the state as being closely linked with a corporate institutional elite which represented the contemporary form of the upper class of wealth in advanced industrial society. However, he did not go so far as to unambiguously identify the business class as the dominant partner in the power-elite triangle. This apparent ambiguity was most likely a product of his emphasis on the shift from class bases of power to institutional bases of

power in a highly institutionalized society, though it tended to suggest some unclarity over the precise role of the upper class of wealth in the political system. Mills, *Power Elite*. Cf. T. B. Bottomore, *Elites and Society* (Baltimore: Penguin Books, 1968), "From the Ruling Class to the Power Elite," pp. 24-47; and Arnold M. Rose, *The Power Structure, Political Process in American Society* (New York: Oxford University Press, 1967), esp. pp. 1-39.

23. Bell, *End of Ideology*, "Is There A Ruling Class in America? The Power Elite Reconsidered," pp. 47-74, esp. 68-70.

24. *Ibid.*, cf. pp. 88-89.

25. *Ibid.*, p. 68.

26. *Ibid.*, p. 109, where Bell describes modern America as a "business society" within which there is a "general acceptance of corporate capitalism, modified by union power, and checked by government control. . . ."

27. *Ibid.*, pp. 88-89, cf. pp. 120-21.

28. Riesman, *Lonely Crowd*, pp. 242-54. Cf. William Kornhauser, " 'Power Elite' or 'Veto Groups'?" in Seymour Martin Lipset and Leo Lowenthal, eds., *Culture and Social Character* (Glencoe: Free Press, 1961), pp. 252-67.

29. Bell, *End of Ideology*, "America as a Mass Society: A Critique," pp. 21-38; "The Refractions of the American Past: On the Question of National Character," pp. 95-102; and "The Mood of Three Generations," pp. 299-314.

30. *Ibid.*, pp. 32-35.

31. *Ibid.*, p. 32. While this may be true from the viewpoint of the subjective experience of these individuals, it does not respond to the structural critique levelled by Mills regarding the antidemocratic effects of bureaucratization on organizational life. On the distinction between the existential and structural analyses of mass society, and their respective roots in aristocratic and democratic perspectives, see Kornhauser, *Politics of Mass Society*, pp. 1-25.

32. *Ibid.*, pp. 70-73, 90-91.

33. See Jacques Ellul, "Western Man in 1970," in Bertrand de Jouvenel, ed., *Futuribles, Studies in Conjecture* (Geneva: Librairie Droz, 1963), 1: 37-41.

34. On the role of the New Deal in shaping the dominant themes of our contemporary political culture, cf. Young, *The Politics of Affluence*, pp. 46, 203-4. On the "New Capitalism" see Bell, "The Breakup of Family Capitalism," in *End of Ideology*, pp. 39-45.

35. Bell, "Notes on Post-Industrial Society (I)."

36. *Ibid.*, p. 33.

37. Bell, *End of Ideology*, p. 14.

38. *Ibid.*, pp. 53-55.

39. Cf. Robert Heilbroner, "Counter-Revolutionary America," *Commentary* 43 (April 1967): 31-38.

40. Cf. the excellent discussion in Robert Presthus, *Men At The Top: A Study in Community Power* (New York: Oxford University Press, 1964) of the revision of American pluralism from a concept centered on the importance of "individual participation in the policy-forming process through primary voluntary groups" to one focussed on the participation of elite leaders of modern bureaucratic organizations. (*Ibid.*, pp. 17-20.) In this regard, he quotes V.O. Key, to the effect that "the critical element for the health of a democratic order consists in the beliefs, standards, and competence of those who constitute the influentials, the opinion-leaders, and the political activists." (*Public Opinion and American Democracy* (New York: Knopf, 1961), p. 558. Presthus describes the shift to policy making by elite interest leaders as "elitism"; however, we find it useful to distinguish this type of elitism from the more monolithic type of a single unified elite which is often used by pluralists as a counterconcept to democratic pluralism; hence for purposes of clarity we will refer to Presthus's "elitism" as "elite pluralism."

41. Cf. Bottomore, *Elites and Society*, pp. 26, 30, for a pertinent discussion of protracted resistance to change in nineteenth century English social and political institutions. Current allegations regarding the rapid political ascendancy of a

"technocratic elite" should be viewed critically, particularly since this "elite," which so far for the most part functions in the service of established executive groups in contemporary government and industry, cannot yet be regarded as even a class *with an independent base of power* in the same sense as the emerging industrial bourgeoisie of the nineteenth century. Cf. Loren Baritz, *The Servants of Power: A History of the Use of Social Scientists in American Industry* (Middletown, Conn.: Wesleyan University Press, 1960).

42. Bell, "Notes on Post-Industrial Society (II)," p. 105.
43. Bell, "Notes on Post-Industrial Society (I)," p. 30.
44. It has recently been observed that it would be more appropriate to refer to the new stage of societal development as "super-industrial society," representing not a basically new social organization but a late phase of overdeveloped corporate industrialism. (See Michael W. Miles, *The Radical Probe: The Logic of Student Rebellion* [New York: Atheneum, 1971], and the review by Christopher Lasch in "Can the Left Rise Again?" *New York Review of Books*, October 21, 1971.) For clarity of reference, however, we have retained the "postindustrial" terminology, with these qualifications in mind.

Chapter III

1. Lipset, "Changing Class Structure & Contemporary European Politics," pp. 271-72.
2. Bell, "Post-Industrial Society (I)," p. 28.
3. Richard J. Barber, *The American Corporation: Its Power, Its Money, Its Politics* (New York: Dutton, 1970), p. 7.
4. *Ibid.*, p. 74.
5. *Ibid.* On figures for 1920, see Colin Clark, *The Conditions of Economic Progress* (London: Macmillan, 1940), p. 346; for 1970 see U.S. Dept. of Labor, Bureau of Labor Statistics, *Employment and Earnings* 17, no. 6 (December 1970): 35. The "primary" sector of production includes agriculture, forestry, and fishing industries; the "secondary" sector includes manufacturing, mining, and construction industries; the "tertiary" sector includes domestic, personal, and professional services, trade, transportation, and communication industries, and government. (Cf. Seymour Lipset and Reinhard Bendix, *Social Mobility in Industrial Society* [Berkeley and Los Angeles: University of California, 1966], pp. 83-84.) Rounding decimals, the figures for 1920 and 1970 were as follows, as percent of total employment:

Sector	1920	1970
Primary	28	4
Secondary	33	35
Tertiary	39	61

6. Bell, "Post-Industrial Society (I)," p. 28, and U.S. Department of Labor, *Employment and Earnings*, pp. 34-35. Comparable figures for women are that about 61 percent of the female labor force of 30 million held white-collar jobs as of 1970, with about two-thirds, or 12 million, of these white collar jobs in clerical or sales positions. Nevertheless, this left close to 6 million women in professional, technical, or managerial positions, so that over 30 percent of the total professional-technical-managerial labor force consisted of women, a sizable proportion which should not be overlooked by identifying women with "minor clerical or sales jobs" as Bell appears to do when he narrows his focus to the males in these positions. (Bell, "Post-Industrial Society (I)," p. 28.) As Victor Fuchs notes, because service occupations do not demand special physical strength, "women can compete on more nearly equal terms with men. . . . The

ultimate effects of these simple changes could be very far-reaching ... the advent of a service economy should make for greater equality between the sexes." "The New Society (I): The First Service Economy," *The Public Interest* (Winter 1966): 7-17. Accordingly, we might expect that women will become a growing component of the "technocratic class" based on these upper white-collar occupations with perhaps some interesting political and cultural results.

7. Bell, "Post-Industrial Society (I)," p. 30.
8. Robert Heilbroner, *The Limits of American Capitalism* (New York: Harper & Row, 1966), pp. 50-54.
9. Bell, "Post-Industrial Society (I)," p. 30.
10. Bell, "Post-Industrial Society (I)," pp. 28-35.
11. *Ibid.*, p. 30.
12. *Ibid.*, pp. 28-30, *passim.*
13. Young, *The Politics of Affluence*, pp. 63-73.
14. Bell, "Post-Industrial Society (II)," p. 105.
15. *Ibid.*, p. 108.
16. *Ibid.*
17. On this, see Robert J. Art, *The TFX Decision—McNamara and the Military* (Boston: Little, Brown, 1968); cf. Andrew Shonfield, *Modern Capitalism* (London: Oxford University Press, 1965), pp. 341-42, esp. p. 342, n 29.
18 Samuel Huntington, *The Common Defense* (New York: Columbia University Press, 1961), pp. 125-32.
19. *Ibid.*, pp. 241-43. Until the early 1960s, public opinion tended to defer to administration policy regarding national security, the only exception being the matter of foreign aid. This was particularly true when the administration took a strong policy stand, but even when it did not, public opinion was at least permissive with regard to added spending for stronger defense. In the early 1960s, the major exceptions were confined to the area of policies related to nuclear war and defense, as evidenced in strong public opposition to the underground shelter program and support for a nuclear test ban. Public opposition to defense policy did not tend to become more generalized until the military reverses of the Vietnam War and the mobilization of public sentiment by anti-war organizations and political leaders in the late 1960s. The recent intensive campaign against the ABM system in the Congress may indicate a turning point, reflecting a change in the public's earlier permissive attitudes toward administration formulation of military policy. *Ibid.*, p. 251.
20. See Stephen M. David, "Leadership of the Poor in Poverty Programs," in Robert H. Connery, ed., *Urban Riots, Violence and Social Change* (New York: Vintage Books, 1969), pp. 90-104, for a thorough discussion of the successive revisions of the 1964 Economic Opportunity Act, which over a four-year period finally resulted in the substantial vesting of "control of community-action programs largely with local political leaders" (*ibid.*, p. 102), through such measures as elimination of the "maximum feasible participation clause," and through requiring that the community action agencies be public rather than private nonprofit organizations (as almost 80 percent were at the inception of the programs). In this way, the Congress, which initially supported the general War on Poverty program, came to remove control of the program's community-action agencies from the hands of immediate local representatives and to vest it in representatives designated by local political officials. (*Ibid.*, p. 99.) Cf. David Stoloff, "The Short Unhappy History of Community Action Programs," in Marvin E. Gettleman and David Mermelstein, eds., *The Great Society Reader: The Failure of American Liberalism* (New York: Random House, 1967), pp. 231-39; and Alfred J. Kahn, *Studies in Social Policy and Planning* (New York: Russell Sage, 1969), pp. 28-29, 44-53.
21. As James L. Sundquist writes in an article titled "The End of the Experiment?" the various "social and economic innovations" of the Kennedy-Johnson period were left unfinished shortly after their legislative acceptance by Congress,

owing to the sharp competition for money and leadership by the Vietnam War. The "more costly measures, such as large-scale public employment programs, income maintenance plans, and fundamental reform of the public welfare system, were referred to study commissions or simply deferred." James L. Sundquist, ed., *On Fighting Poverty* (New York: Basic Books, 1969), pp. 235-36. Commenting on the Congressional reaction to the growing "welfare rights" movement and the antipoverty programs of the 1960s, Alfred Kahn observes that "a bipartisan coalition in Congress concluded that it had been misguided by the premises of 1962; social services as designed at that time had not cut relief rolls. . . ." Thus, despite the considerable mobilization by proponents of public welfare and governmental antipoverty efforts, as well as strong opposition by Congressional liberals, Congress passed at the end of 1967 a series of amendments that seemed to ignore much of the country's overall social welfare thrust of the early sixties. They were quite inconsistent with simultaneous developments in antipoverty, aid to the city, and educational programs (Kahn, *Studies in Social Policy and Planning*, p. 121). There is an interesting resemblance here to the earlier experience of the New Deal, when social programs of a moderately egalitarian nature were stalemated within a few years by a growing opposition organized politically around a bipartisan conservative coalition in Congress. (Cf. William Leuchtenberg, *Franklin D. Roosevelt and the New Deal* [New York: Harper & Row, 1963], pp. 252-74.)

22. John K. Galbraith, *The New Industrial State* (Boston: Houghton Mifflin, 1967).
23. *Ibid.*, pp. 150-51, 153.
24. *Ibid.*, p. 70.
25. Contrary to Galbraith's emphasis on the decision-making autonomy of the corporate technostructure, see Adolph A. Berle, "Economic Power and the Free Society," in Andrew Hacker, ed., *The Corporation Takeover* (Garden City, New York: Doubleday, 1963), who writes: "For practical purposes, therefore, the control or power element in most large corporations rests in its group of directors and it is autonomous—or autonomous if taken together with a control bloc" (p. 93). (For Berle's views on the "soulful" corporation and its directors, see *The Twentieth Century Capitalist Revolution* [New York: Harcourt Brace, 1954].)
26. Galbraith, *New Industrial State*, p. 24.
27. *Ibid.*, p. 28.
28. *Ibid.*, pp. 296-317.
29. Many corporate consultants to government bureaus remain on corporation salary, specifically exempted from conflict-of-interest charges through laws hastily pushed through Congress during the Korean War. See Grant McConnell, *Private Power and American Democracy* (New York: Knopf, 1966), pp. 262-64.
30. Galbraith, *New Industrial State*, pp. 339-40.
31. *Ibid.*, p. 296.
32. *Ibid.*, pp. 327-30.
33. On this point, cf. Berle, "Economic Power," pp. 92-93, and Gabriel Kolko, *Wealth and Power in America* (New York: Praeger, 1962), pp. 61-62.
34. Galbraith, *New Industrial State*, pp. 282-95.
35. *Ibid.*, p. 290. Cf. however, Shonfield, *Modern Capitalism*, pp. 64-65, 124, for the view that the "Keynesian revolution" was the consequence of a change in political attitudes rather than academic insights regarding the utility of governmental intervention in the economy.
36. Galbraith, *New Industrial State*, p. 292.
37. *Ibid.*, pp. 389-99.
38. *Ibid.*, pp. 293-94.
39. Cf. Don K. Price, *The Scientific Estate* (Cambridge, Mass.: Harvard University Press, 1965); Donald W. Cox, *America's New Policy Makers: The Scientists'*

Rise to Power (Philadelphia and New York: Chilton, 1964); and Ralph E. Lapp, *The New Priesthood: The Scientific Elite and the Uses of Power* (New York: Harper & Row, 1965).

40. Cf. Alvin Boskoff, "Postponement of Social Decision in Transitional Society," *Social Forces*, March 1953, pp. 229-34, in which Boskoff employs Mannheim's distinction between the nonrationality of politics and the rationality of administration in explaining the social indecision of pluralist society.

41. Galbraith, *New Industrial State*, pp. 343-62.

42. Daniel Bell, *The Reforming of General Education* (New York: Columbia University Press, 1966), pp. 307-11.

43. On the development of politically based cleavages among scientists in the postwar period, cf. H. L. Nieburg, *In The Name of Science* (Chicago: Quadrangle Books, 1966), pp. 117-83, esp. pp. 158-83, ch. IX: "The Emergence of Pluralism." Cf. Warner R. Schilling, "The H-Bomb Decision: How to Decide Without Actually Choosing," *Political Science Quarterly*, March 1961 (in Nelson, *The Politics of Science* (New York: Oxford University Press, 1968), pp. 308-28; esp. pp. 313, 317, 321), on the background to President Truman's decision in 1950 to proceed with development of the H-bomb, provided by the debate between different groups of scientific advisors, and the manner in which this debate combined "political and military as well as technical considerations." (*Ibid.*, p. 313.) Cf. also Enid Curtis Bok Schoettle, "The Establishment of NASA," in Sanford A. Lakoff, ed., *Knowledge and Power* (New York: Free Press, 1966), pp. 162-270; esp. pp. 165-73, 212-20, 240-46, on the tension between the various civilian and military-scientific visions of a space program.

44. Daniel Greenberg, "The Myth of the Scientific Elite," *The Public Interest*, Fall 1965, p. 53.

45. *Ibid.*, p. 62.

Chapter IV

1. Nieburg, *In The Name of Science*, ch. 10, "The Contract State," pp. 184-99. In the present chapter we are indebted to this excellent work which has recently begun to receive the wide recognition it deserves for its thorough investigation of the military-industrial "R & D" complex and its development. See also John K. Galbraith, *New Industrial State*, chs. 26, 27, "The Industrial System and The State, I, II," esp. pp. 296-302, 309-14.

2. Examples are the establishment of Navy Yards after WWI, the Naval Research Lab and the Army Electronics Lab between WWI and WWII, the expansion of the Jet Propulsion Lab (JPL) of Cal Tech during WWII, and the establishment and growth of the Army's Redstone Arsenal after WWII. (Cf. Nieburg, *In the Name of Science*, pp. 218-19, 230-35.)

3. Cf. Robert Borosage, "The Making of the National Security State," in Leonard S. Rodberg and Derek Shearer, eds., *The Pentagon Watchers* (Garden City, N.Y.: Doubleday, 1970), pp. 3-63. As Borosage indicates, the contracting authority of the services "was delineated in the Armed Services Procurement Act of 1947." Though the act stipulated that military contracts with industrial suppliers or university researchers should proceed on the basis of advertising and bidding, "any one of sixteen exceptions" could allow for a negotiated contract instead; the effect was to release the services from competitive bidding requirements, whenever it was deemed in the "defense interest"; and this was more often than not, i.e., in about two-thirds of the dollar value of postwar contracts. (*Ibid.*, pp. 24-25.)

4. While the cost plus fixed-fee contract was a more liberal arrangement than the fixed-price contract requirements established after WWI, it seemed at the time less open to abuse than the practice during that war of determining profit as a percentage of total cost, which was often conducive to cost inflation. In the

course of World War II the cost-plus contract became the major instrument for military procurement of aircraft, ordnance equipment, and ammunition; over one-third of all procurement was arranged through cost-plus contracts, totalling over $50 billion. Despite the fact that Senator Truman's WWII defense-spending committee uncovered widespread profiteering under these contracting arrangements, the cost-plus contract became a basic instrument for government procurement during the ensuing Cold War. (*Ibid.*, pp. 201-2.) Cf. House Committee on Government Operations, *Systems Development and Management*, Hearings, 87th Cong. 2nd sess., 1962, esp. Part 3, pp. 231-32, and House Committee on Government Operations, *Comptroller General Reports to Congress on Audits of Defense Contracts*, Hearings, 89th Cong., 1st sess., 1965, pp. 170-71.

5. Nieburg, *In the Name of Science*, p. 190.
6. House Committee on Government Operations, *Eleventh Report, Organization and Management of Missile Programs*, House Report No. 1121, 86th Cong., 1st sess., 1959, pp. 129-30.
7. Nieburg, *In the Name of Science*, pp. 190-91.
8. *Ibid.*, p. 220. Contracting out government work was construed by the Eisenhower administration as a means of preventing "unfair competition" by government in-house facilities *vis à vis* private contractors. Cf. *Bureau of Budget Bulletin 60-2*, September 21, 1959, which emphasized maximizing R & D performance by private contractors. This approach was adhered to in spite of admonitions from the president's own Science Advisory Committee, which cautioned against pursuit of such a policy, noting that "government laboratories are vital national assets whose activities will need to keep pace" with expanding R & D programs and that "undue reliance on outside laboratories . . . could greatly impair the morale and vitality of needed government laboratories." (U.S., President, Science Advisory Committee, Report, *Strengthening American Science* [Washington: Government Printing Office, 1959], p. 425.)
9. See Nieburg, *In the Name of Science*, pp. 269-77, 284-85. Cf. House Committee on Government Operations, *Comptroller General Reports*, 89th Cong., 1st sess., 1965, Appendices 2A-E, pp. 735-835. See also House Armed Services Committee, *Overpricing of Government Contracts*, Hearings, 87th Cong., 1st sess., 1961, pp. 14-16.
10. *Ibid.*, p. 278. The idea that defense contracting has meant "super-profits" for favored contractors has been challenged in an article by George E. Berkley, a political scientist. (See "The Myth of War Profiteering," *The New Republic*, December 20, 1969, pp. 15-18). Berkley notes that while defense contractors have often derived much of their annual revenue from war contracts, their highest profits have come from nondefense sales. He refers to a study made in 1969 by the Logistics Management Institute, which showed that "the average profit margin for all U.S. sales industry was 8.7 percent of sales, but that the average profit margin on defense work was only 4.2 percent of sales." (Apparently these figures apply to 1968 though Berkley does not make this explicitly clear.) In fact, he notes that the actual nondefense to defense profits ratio may be higher than this two-to-one rate, since "low-profit defense work" was included in the overall industrial average profit. (*Ibid.*, p. 16.) He does note, however, that the data for this study came from the contractors themselves and "was attacked in some quarters" on that account, but he reassures the reader that for the sake of stock market appearances and the politics of corporate mergers, defense contractors had probably tended to overstate rather than understate profits. (*Ibid.*, pp. 17-18.) One critic of the study cited by Berkley notes that the Logistics Management Institute (a "think tank" working under contract to the Pentagon) used "unverified, unaudited data obtained on a voluntary basis from a sample of defense contractors" and that nearly half of this sample (42 percent) returned no data on their profit situation. See Richard F. Kaufman, "The Military-Industrial Complex," in Jerome H. Skolnick and Eliott Currie, eds., *Crisis in American Institutions* (Boston: Little, Brown,

1970), p. 185. Furthermore, since the Institute's study was made for the Pentagon rather than the stock market, it seems plausible that those suffering *lowest* profits under the Defense Department's "cost-effectiveness" contract reforms of recent years, would be most motivated to respond; at the least we must agree with Kaufman that "there is no way of knowing whether the contractors who refused to participate ... included the ones making the highest profits." *Ibid.* Kaufman also cites a General Accounting Office study which compared average profits negotiated in defense contracts during the last half of 1966 with those for the period 1959 through 1963, finding an increase of 26 percent; moreover, he notes that these profit rates, calculated as a percentage of costs, tend to understate the "true profit level." He cites in this regard a 1962 tax case in which North American Aviation claimed profits of 8 percent as a percentage of costs, whereas "the tax court found that the company had realized profits of 612 percent and 803 percent on its investment in two succeeding years." (*Ibid.*) He further cites a study by Murray Weidenbaum which measured profit rate as a percentage of investment and found that from 1962 to 1965 "a sample of *large* defense contractors earned 17.5 percent net profit ... while companies of similar size doing business in the commercial market earned 10.6 percent." (*Ibid.*, our emphasis.) This finding of higher defense profits, based on investment, is confirmed by David E. Sims, "Spoon-Feeding the Military—How New Weapons Come to Be," Rodberg and Shearer, eds., *Pentagon Watchers*, pp. 225-65. Sims observes that "if profits are measured as a percentage of sales, then they have been low ... but ... a more accurate measure of profit is the return on net investment." The profit margin as a percent of sales for 1962-65 was only 2.6 percent for a sample of defense firms as against 4.6 percent for industrial firms (close to the two-to-one ratio cited by Berkley), but profits calculated as a return on net investment were 17.5 percent as against 10.6 percent for the defense *versus* industrial sample, as reported by Wiedenbaum. (Figures presented to the Subcommittee on Antitrust and Monopoly, Summer 1968, and quoted in *ibid.*, p. 229). This apparent discrepancy is explained by the fact that the Defense Department has made a "policy of providing government-owned property and federal working capital to defense contractors," and that this has particularly been true in the case of larger contractors. (*Ibid.*)

11. Borosage, "National Security State," p. 26. These interlocking relationships between military, political, and industrial interests first crystallized during World War II, through the medium of *ad hoc* governmental and quasi-governmental agencies set up to promote continuing contact between leaders in these several institutional sectors. Both military and political leaders established regular communication with industrial leaders through industrial and technical advisory committees and boards. Secretary Forrestal (then Secretary of the Navy, later to become the first Secretary of Defense), brought together defense contractors to found the National Security Industrial Association in 1944. By 1948 there were over a dozen industrial advisory committees to the government's R & D Board; by 1949 the government's Munitions Board was receiving assistance from almost a score of advisory committees, made up of approximately 400 top industrial executives. As Borosage notes, "These advisory committees greatly influenced the contracting process." (*Ibid.*, p. 29.) He goes on to quote the Steelman report on advisory committees issued in 1947, which observed that advisory committees "are influential in awarding contracts commonly negotiated without competitive bidding." This would tend to favor the largest enterprises or universities seeking contracts, since such institutions often have associations with the "outstanding scientists of the country," who along with their officers, "often ... sit upon the program-planning and evaluating committees," (Quoted in *Ibid.*)

12. Don K. Price, *The Scientific Estate* (Cambridge, Mass.: Harvard University Press, The Belknap Press, 1967), p. 11.

13. Nieburg, *In the Name of Science*, pp. 254-55. Some idea of the scale of excessive pricing and profit in the R & D sector is provided by a 1961 GAO

sample of about 5 percent of contract awards, by dollar value, which revealed overcharges of $60 million, or over $1 billion projected to 100 percent; by 1964, the size of ascertainable overpricing in a 5 percent sample had multiplied almost tenfold to about half a billion dollars, or $10 billion projected to 100 percent. (*Ibid.*, p. 269.)

14. The danger of untoward influence has been compounded by the fact that the industrial contractor often employs as contract negotiators corporate officials who can significantly affect the contract officer's career; many negotiators are ex-military or government agency officials who retain friendly ties with members of congressional committees responsible for overseeing agency operations. Charles E. Jacob, *Policy and Bureaucracy* (Princeton, N. J.: Van Nostrand, 1966), pp. 178-79.

15. House Committee on Government Operations, *Comptroller General Reports to Congress on Audits of Defense Contracts*, 89th Cong., 1st sess., 1965, p. 46.

16. Cf. Sims, "Spoon-feeding the Military," p. 228.

17. Nieburg, *In the Name of Science*, pp. 190-95. See also Richard J. Barber, "The New Partnership: Big Government and Big Business," in Robert Perucci and Marc Pilisuk, eds., *The Triple Revolution*, pp. 224-26; and John K. Galbraith, "The Big Defense Firms are Really Public Firms," *New York Times*, Section 6, November 16, 1969, pp. 164, 167.

18. Nieburg, *In the Name of Science*, p. 196; cf. Barber, "The New Partnership," pp. 218-24; Jacob, *Policy and Bureaucracy*, p. 117.

19. See Galbraith, *New Industrial State*, pp. 8-10 and Robert L. Heilbroner, *The Limits of American Capitalism* (New York: Harper & Row, 1967), pp. 8-14.

20. House Committee on Government Operations, *Systems Development and Management*, Hearings, 87th Cong., 2d sess., 1962, pp. 1103-1228.

21. For a detailed discussion, see Nieburg, *In the Name of Science*, ch. 13, "The New Braintrusters," pp. 244-67.

22. *Ibid.*, p. 190.

23. Cf. Jacob, *Policy and Bureaucracy*, pp. 77-81, 182-86; Heilbroner, *Limits of American Capitalism*, pp. 49-58; and Price, *Scientific Estate*, pp. 227-42.

24. Cf. Jacob, *Policy and Bureaucracy*, p. 185.

25. *Ibid.*, p. 178.

26. *Ibid.*, p. 77.

27. *Ibid.*

28. Hans Morgenthau, *The Purpose of American Politics* (New York: Vintage Books, 1960), p. 277.

29. Cf. Sanford Lakoff, ed., *Knowledge and Power, Essays on Science and Government* (New York: Free Press, 1966), pp. 242, 253; and Nieburg, *In the Name of Science*, pp. 46-49.

30. As Borosage points out, the military budget has been shielded from congressional control by virtue of a number of factors, including the secrecy and complexity of the national security establishment and the dependency of many congressmen and their home districts on the largess of the military complex. ("National Security State," pp. 50-53.) Add to this the climate of postwar public opinion stirred by "war-scares" emanating from the Congress, the executive, and the military establishment, with its numerous public information facilities. (*Ibid.*, pp. 45-51.) As a result, the public tended without much question to support requests for military expenditures during the first two postwar decades, until the "credibility gaps" of the late 1960s, which were largely related to the visible failure of administration promises regarding the course of the war in Vietnam. See appendix following chapter 6 for a discussion of the different levels of federal expenditure for military and civilian programs during this period.

31. Alain C. Enthoven and K. Wayne Smith, *How Much is Enough? Shaping the Defense Program*, 1961-1969 (New York: Harper & Row, 1971).

32. Nieburg, *In the Name of Science* pp. 20-21. As Nieburg indicates, "The key symbol of the change was the formal cancellation in December of the Air Force Dynasoar program." (*Ibid.*, p. 53.) In place of the cancelled Dynasoar

program, the Air Force soon put forward a proposal for a manned orbiting laboratory (MOL) which it had nurtured for almost five years as a project of the first importance.

33. Among their tactics for evading McNamara's new budgetary controls, the Air Force and its supporters sought to assign MOL to NASA "where Congress could find it uninhibited by McNamara's scrutiny." (*Ibid.*, p. 59.) In the case of the Supersonic Transport, Nieburg indicates that government support for development of a commercial SST came as a "substitute means for maintaining the financial health . . . of the private carriers," in view of the displacement of supersonic bombers such as the B-70 by the shift to strategic missiles. (*Ibid.*, p. 325.)

34. In an article on the "end of ideology," Stephen Rousseas and James Farganis have observed how committed the late President Kennedy was to the Bell-Lipset thesis. To this effect, they cite his address before the Economic Conference in Washington in May 1962: "The fact of the matter is that most of the problems, or at least many of them that we now face, are technical problems, are administrative problems. They are very sophisticated judgements which do not lend themselves to the great sort of 'passionate movements' which have stirred this country so often in the past. Now they deal with questions which are beyond the comprehension of most men." And a month later, at his 1962 commencement address at Yale, he observed: "What is at stake in our economic decisions today is not some grand warfare of rival ideologies which will sweep the country with passion but the practical management of a modern economy . . . ." Cited in "American Politics and the End of Ideology," in Irving Louis Horowitz, *The New Sociology* (New York: Oxford University Press, 1946), p. 284.

35. This report, written under the name of David Bell, Kennedy's Budget Director, and including McNamara himself as one of the committee's participants, expressed concern that government management capabilities had been reduced because of Defense Department's overdependence on interested contractors for technical advice relevant to weapons, development policy, and for management functions more appropriately performed by government agencies. See Nieburg, *In the Name of Science*, p. 334-50.

36. *Ibid.*, p. 364.

37. *Ibid.*, pp. 369-73. Cf. House Committee on Armed Services, *The Aerospace Corporation*, 89th Cong., 1st sess., 1965, pp. 149-50; House Committee on Government Operations, *Comptroller General Reports*, Hearings, 89th Cong., 1st sess., 1965, pp.170-71, 640-41.

38. House Committee on Government Operations, *Comptroller General Reports*, p. 452.

39. Increasing centralization of control over military budget has not necessarily meant the elimination of programs involving massive waste of resources. Thus the C-5A, with cost overruns of over $2 billion, was authorized by Secretary McNamara and endorsed by his successor Clark Clifford, despite "internal Defense Department studies questioning the cost-effectiveness of the huge military transport plane." Cf. Tom Klein, "The Capacity to Intervene," in Rodberg and Shearer, eds., *The Pentagon Watchers*, pp. 195-98, 207-8. It appears that the Pentagon's political commitment, established under McNamara, to a capability for rapid deployment of armed forces anywhere in the world, consonant with a global "interventionist" policy, clearly outweighed the technical questions of cost-effectiveness. (With respect to its use as an instrument of executive "interventionist" policy, Senator Fulbright noted "the C-5A does not itself represent a commitment to anybody, but it represents a significant new facility for the making of commitments in the hands of the executive." Quoted in Klein, "Capacity," p. 207).

40. See Mills, *The Power Elite*, esp. pp. 269-97. Cf. Bell, *End of Ideology, pp.* 55-56.

Chapter V

1. Cf. Harold D. Lasswell, *National Security and Individual Freedom* (New York: McGraw-Hill, 1950); Arthur A. Ekirch, Jr., "Toward the Garrison State," in *The Civilian and the Military* (New York: Oxford University Press, 1956); and Louis Smith, "The Garrison State, Offspring of the Cold War," *The Nation* 177 (December 5, 1953): 461.
2. Seymour Melman, *Pentagon Capitalism* (New York: McGraw-Hill, 1970), p. 1.
3. *Ibid.*, p. 2.
4. *Ibid.*, p. 1.
5. *Ibid.*, p. 2.
6. *Ibid.*, p. 1.
7. *Ibid.*, p. 4.
8. *Ibid.*, p. 2. On the parasitic nature of military production, which uses manpower and materials without producing "goods or services that can be used for further production or for the present level of living," see Seymour Melman, "American Needs and Limits on Resources: The Priorities Problem," in Perucci and Pilisuk, *The Triple Revolution*, pp. 211-17. See also Melman, *Pentagon Capitalism*, p. 3, for "inventories of depletion" in social and technological areas. For figures which graphically translate military production into equivalent improvements in living standards, see Melman, *Our Depleted Society* (New York: Holt, Rinehart and Winston, 1965). Melman estimates that an additional $76 billion expenditure in the civilian public sector would be required to bring basic social facilities and services up to a minimal standard of adequacy. ("American Needs," pp. 211-12.)
9. *Ibid.*, p. 9.
10. *Ibid.*, p. 13. Cf. Galbraith, *New Industrial State*, esp. pp. 296-317, and Weidenbaum, Remarks before American Economic Association, December 1967, quoted in Melman, *Pentagon Capitalism*, p. 13.
11. Melman, *Pentagon Capitalism*, p. 12.
12. *Ibid.*, p. 13.
13. *Ibid.*, pp. 10-11.
14. *Ibid.*, p. 7.
15. *Ibid.*, p. 28.
16. *Ibid.*, p. 11.
17. For discussions emphasizing the likelihood of continuing heavy concentration of defense contracting within a limited number of large firms in about half a dozen industries, located predominantly within about a dozen states, see Charles J. Hitch, "The Defense Sector: Its Impact on American Business" in Herbert I. Schiller and Joseph D. Phillips, eds., *Super-State: Readings in the Military-Industrial Complex* (Urbana, Ill.: University of Illinois Press, 1970), pp. 131-55, and Murray Weidenbam, "Defense Expenditures and the Domestic Economy," in Edwin Mansfield, ed., *Defense, Science, and Public Policy* (New York: W.W. Norton & Co., 1968), pp. 13-32. For discussions of the conglomerate movement of the 1960s and its effects on furthering corporate concentration, see Richard Barber, *The American Corporation*, esp. pp. 26-52; cf. Paul Sweezy and Harry Magdoff, "The Merger Movement: A Study in Power," in David Mermelstein, ed., *Economics: Mainstream Readings and Radical Critiques* (New York: Random House, 1970), pp. 77-90; and David Horowitz and Reese Erlich, "Litton Industries: Big Brother as a Holding Company," also in Mermelstein, *Economics*, pp. 91-104. As Barber points out, the merger movement of the 1960s differed from earlier such movements in that it most often led to the consolidation of firms in different industries rather than in the same or allied industries. The result was increased managerial-financial concentration simultaneous with entreprenurial diversification of older established

industries moving into new high-growth product or service lines, ranging from plastics, computers, and communications to life insurance, real estate, and education-information. Cf. Barber, *The American Corporation*, 35-43, 48-52, 162-64.

18. Eli Ginzberg, Dale L. Hiestand and Beatrice G. Reubens, *The Pluralist Economy* (New York: McGraw-Hill, 1965).

19. *Ibid.*, pp. 57-81, 88.

20. Melman, *Pentagon Capitalism*, pp. 23-24, 53-54, 68-69. According to Melman, in the context of the "state management" structure the Pentagon's readiness to pay for contractors' cost-overruns has amounted to the granting of investment capital by a central industrial management office to divisions of its firm; through capital subsidies of this kind the state management has assured the maintenance and growth of its own industrial base. Despite declared intentions to reduce defense costs through the utilization of elaborate systems of "program budgeting" and "cost-effectiveness," the cost of the TFX plane was $12.7 million per plane by December 1969, or about 3.25 times the initial cost estimate of $3.9 million. This was almost the same ratio of average costs to initial estimates which had prevailed in the pre-McNamara period (3.2) (*Ibid.*)

21. There exists today a whole segment of the defense industry consisting of firms predominantly committed to military production, with dependence upon government contracts and capital grants so great that they constitute what might be referred to as "disposable" enterprises, whose output and very existence are essentially determined by the Pentagon in accordance with its program aims. Such firms can either be set working at full productive capacity or effectively shut down, largely on the decision of Pentagon officials. See Melman, *Pentagon Capitalism*, pp. 47, 77-78, for lists of firms with heavy contract or fixed-capital dependence on the Pentagon during the 1960s. Melman refers to heavily-dependent firms such as Lockheed, General Dynamics, and McDonnell-Douglas, as Pentagon "sub-managements" or "sub-firms." (*Ibid.*, pp. 48, 78.) See also Alvin Toffler, *Future Shock* (New York: Bantam Books, 1970), pp. 132-33, for a discussion of the creation of "disposable divisions" within major firms to handle contracted projects of a limited life span. Toffler's discussion fixes on Lockheed's creation of a special project organization for the building of the C-5A; our application of the concept would extend it to cover Lockheed itself and similar firms, which can be viewed as "disposable" enterprise-units of the "state management."

22. Cf. Charles A. Reich, "The New Property," *Public Interest* 3 (Spring 1966): 57-89, esp. 58-66.

23. Bell, "Post-Industrial Society (I)," pp. 27-28; cf. Victor Fuchs, "The First Service Economy," *The Public Interest* 2 (Winter 1966): 7-17.

24. Barber, *The American Corporation*, p. 74.

25. *Ibid.*, p. 79.

26. Bell, "Post-Industrial Society (I)," p. 27.

27. *Ibid.*, pp. 74-75; cf. Ginzberg, et al., *The Pluralist Economy*, p. 85.

28. While the goods-producing industries have raised their output dramatically, particularly since the 1950s, owing to mechanization and automation they have increased relatively little, or even reduced, their labor forces. At the same time there has since the 1950s been increasing demand for private services connected with rising income, and for public services, particularly as a result of expanding suburban developments requiring new school systems, police, fire, etc., as well as the mounting inner-city concentration of public service-dependent populations. In addition, the expansion of higher education has made available a larger pool of persons with the requisite skills for the service occupations. Together, factors such as these have made for the growth of the service sector, which is based upon occupational structures that are not so readily automatable (though computerization now threatens a whole range of service occupations in the corporate office). Garth L. Mangum, *The Manpower Revolution: Its Policy Consequences* (New York: Doubleday, 1966), pp. 239-41, 250-52.

29. Barber, *The American Corporation*, p. 80; cf. Ginzberg, et al., *op. cit.*, p. 115.
30. Barber, *The American Corporation*, pp. 79-80. Though we are disinclined to share Barber's optimism regarding the social problem-solving capabilities of corporate business (whether on a profit or "nonprofit" basis), we are indebted in this chapter to his extensive coverage of the emerging possibilities for government-corporate cooperation in the public sector, regarded as a market for joint "interest investment."
31. Fuchs, "The First Service Economy," pp. 7-17. The nation's nonprofit research institutions (which for the end-of-ideologists come close to symbolizing the postindustrial era) have indeed deeply affected the procedures as well as the products of the more traditional profit-oriented industrial sector. Their sharpest impact on both scores so far has been on the newer goods-producing industries such as aerospace, electronics, and computers, but the new management procedures and tools first developed at "think-tanks" like RAND—from systems engineering to computer simulation and Program Evaluation Review techniques—have become part of standard practice throughout the "mature" corporate sector.
32. Barber, *The American Corporation*, p. 119.
33. *Ibid.*, p. 126.
34. *Ibid.*, p. 133.
35. *Ibid.*
36. *Ibid.*, p. 135. Cf. John J. Corson, *Business in the Humane Society* (New York: McGraw-Hill, 1971), p. 132, table 6.5.
37. Barber, *The American Corporation*, pp. 134, 136.
38. *Ibid.*, pp. 135, 137, 139. In 1969, federal support for industrial R & D amounted to $9.1 billion, as against $8.2 billion expended by private industrial sources. (*Ibid.*, p. 135.)
39. *Ibid.*, pp. 137-38.
40. Cf. *ibid.*, pp. 130-42.
41. *Ibid.*, p. 187.
42. *Ibid.*
43. *Ibid.*, pp. 188-89.
44. *Ibid.*, p. 189.
45. As Richard Barnet points out, with the exception of the Pentagon, all government agencies bring their budget requests to the Bureau of the Budget as submittal data to be balanced and resolved in terms of the larger picture of national resources and needs, and the final budget recommendations are then made to the president by the Bureau's director. In the case of the Pentagon, however, the secretary of defense visits with the Budget director only as a negotiating step, and then brings his recommendations for the defense budget directly to the president, rather than leaving the final recommendations to the Budget Bureau. It is the president who makes the final decision, "on the basis of his best political judgement." Prior to that final political judgment, "there is no context in which to balance domestic needs and military requirements." (Richard Barnet, *The Economy of Death* [New York: Atheneum, 1969] p. 136.)
46. Government's role as an expanding consumer of both goods and services in the nondefense sector seems clear, if we take the trends of the 1960s as a basis; government spending in the area of education and manpower training went from $1.3 billion in 1960, at the conclusion of the Eisenhower administration, to $2 billion at the beginning of the Johnson administration, to $7 billion by the conclusion of the latter, for an overall increase of over five times. In the area of health (services and research) the comparable figures are $0.75 billion, $1.7 billion, and $9.7 billion, an overall increase of over twelve times. (*The Budget in Brief*, Bureau of the Budget, 1970, p. 67-68: "Budget Outlays by Subfunction, 1959-1970".)

    Recognizing the sales prospects in the education market, some larger electronics firms, for example, have already entered the field, usually by first acquiring a textbook or educationally related publishing house. Firms which have shown interest in the possibilities of developing educational hardware and systems for "programmed learning," include IBM, General Learning (a joint venture of GE and Time magazine), Litton, TRW (formerly basically aerospace production or management firms), and a number of smaller "systems-electronics" companies (Barber, *The American Corporation*, p. 210). Note, moreover, that these are private, profit-oriented firms, rather than nonprofits.

47. Barber, *The American Corporation*, pp. 207-8.
48. *Ibid.*, p. 78.
49. *Ibid.*, p. 206.
50. *Ibid.*, p. 221.
51. *Ibid.*, p. 219.
52. *Ibid.*
53. *Ibid.*, p. 220.
54. *Ibid.*, p. 220. Our emphasis.
55. *Ibid.*, p. 78.
56. *Ibid.*, pp. 201-14.
57. *Ibid.*, pp. 203-5.
58. *Ibid.*, p. 207.
59. Cf. *ibid*, pp. 76-82, to the effect that nonprofits today "dominate" in the areas of health and education and hold a very important and growing position in research services.
60. Joseph Bensman and Arthur J. Vidich, *The New American Society: The Revolution of the Middle Class* (Chicago: Quadrangle Books, 1971).
61. *Ibid.*, p. 177.
62. *Ibid.*, p. 182.
63. *Ibid.*
64. See Galbraith, *New Industrial State*, pp. 341-42 on the space program as a feasible substitute for defense programs.
65. Bensman and Vidich, *New American Society*, p. 182.
66. Robert Allen, *Black Awakening in Capitalist America: An Analytic History*, (Garden City, N.Y.: Doubleday, 1969), p. 64.
67. *Ibid.*
68. *Ibid.*, pp. 178-80. Cf. Earl Ofari, *The Myth of Black Capitalism* (New York: Monthly Review, 1970), pp. 67-85, ch. 3: "Whose Capitalism?" Ofari, who is like Allen a young black author, views the "black capitalism" currently supported by sophisticated corporate and government leaders as an instrument for the technological-administrative exploitation of the black community, through the agency of a black middle-managerial class now being created in both the private and public sectors. Cf. Anne Kelley's review of Robert Allen's *Black Awakening*, in the *Black Scholar*, October 1971, pp. 50-56; see also Lelia Evans, "Neo-Colonialism and Development of the Black Ghetto: Model Cities," *Black Lines* (Fall 1970); and Ralph H. Metcalf, "Chicago Model Cities and Neocolonialism," *Black Scholar*, April 1970.
69. Allen, *Black Awakening*, p. 178n. Allen believes that the League's recent adoption of black nationalist rhetoric, and the dropping of its integrationist stance, has actually encouraged the support of the foundations, who realistically recognize the decline of the older integrationist leadership and the usefulness of relating to leaders that can command loyalty to programs which are community-centered. Cf. the comments of Whitney Young in a speech to the 1968 convention of CORE, announcing that the Urban League now "believes strongly in that interpretation of black power that emphasizes self-determination, pride, self-respect and participation and control of one's destiny and community affairs." Quoted in *Ibid.*
70. *Ibid.*, p. 181.
71. *Ibid.*
72. *Ibid.*, p. 180.
73. Cf. Bruce L. R. Smith, "The Future of the Not-for-Profit Corporations," *The Public Interest* 8 (Summer 1967): 127-42.

Appendix

1. James L. Clayton, ed., *The Economic Impact of the Cold War: Sources and Readings* (New York: Harcourt, Brace, & World, 1970), p. 29, table 2.
2. Melman, *Pentagon Capitalism*, p. 2.
3. Clayton, *Economic Impact*, p. 29; and *Budget of the United States Government*, 1969-72.
4. Lyle Fitch, "Eight Goals for an Urbanizing America," in George S. Masannat, ed., *Basic Issues in American Public Policy* (Boston: Holbrook Press, 1970), p. 310.
5. Harold L. Wilensky and Charles N. Lebeaux, *Industrial Society and Social Welfare* (New York: Free Press, 1965), pp. v-lii: introduction, "The Problems and Prospects of the Welfare State."
6. *Budget*, U.S., 1955, 1972.
7. *Congressional Quarterly*, January 29, 1971, pp. 209, 211.
8. Cf. Melman, "American Needs," p. 211.
9. *The Budget for Fiscal Year 1970, Special Analysis Q:* "Federal Research, Development, and Related Programs," tables Q-1 and Q-3, pp. 240-41.
10. *Budget in Brief, U.S.*, 1970, "Budget Outlays by Subfunction," 1959-1970.
11. Melman, "American Needs," p. 211.
12. Charles Schulze, *et al., Setting National Priorities: The 1972 Budget* (Washington: The Brookings Institution, 1971), tables 1-3, p. 13.
13. Murray L. Weidenbaum, *The Modern Public Sector: New Ways of Doing the Government's Business* (New York: Basic Books, 1969), pp. 172-77.
14. Senator William Proxmire, "Blank Check for the Military," *Congressional Record*, 91st Cong., 1st sess., March 10, 1969, 115, S2521.
15. James Tobin has estimated that after government transfer payments, the gap remaining between the incomes of the poor and the poverty line of the mid-1960s was about $11 billion as of 1966. See Tobin, "Raising the Incomes of the Poor," in Kermit Gordon, *Agenda for the Nation* (Washington: The Brookings Institution, 1968), p. 104.
16. Proxmire, "Blank Check," p. S2519.
17. Kenneth Boulding, "The War Industry and its Effects," in Schiller and Phillips, eds., *Super State*, p. 156.
18. *Ibid.*, p. 158.

Chapter VI

1. Cf. Philip Hauser, "The Chaotic Society: Product of the Social Morphological Revolution," *American Sociological Review* 34 (February 1969): 1-19; and Daniel Bell, "Unstable America: Transitory and Permanent Factors in a National Crisis," *Encounter*, June 1980, pp. 11-26.
2. Cf. John F. Kain, "The Distribution and Movement of Jobs and Industry," in James Q. Wilson, ed., *The Metropolitan Enigma: Inquiries into the Nature and Dimensions of America's "Urban Crisis"* (Garden City, N.Y.: Doubleday, 1970, pp. 1-43.
3. See Walter Heller, *New Dimensions of Political Economy* (Cambridge, Mass: Harvard University Press, 1966); Herbert Stein, *The Fiscal Revolution in America* (Chicago: University of Chicago Press, 1969); Arthur M. Okun, *The Political Economy of Prosperity* (Washington, D.C.: The Brookings Institution, 1970).
4. Otto Eckstein, "The Economics of the 1960's—A Backward Look," *The Public Interest* 19 (Spring 1970): 86. Cf. Report of the National Commission on Technology, Automation, and Economic Progress, *Technology and the American Economy* (Washington, D.C.: U.S. Government Printing Office,

1966), 1:100. "The growth rate of output, which had been as high as 5.2 percent a year between 1947 and 1953, slowed to 2.4 percent between 1953 and 1960.... An increase in unemployment was the immediate result." The authors go on to note that under the prevailing rate of productivity increase, "an addition to the GNP growth rate of only 0.4 percent a year would have prevented unemployment from rising."

5. Mangum, *Manpower Revolution*, p. 122.
6. Eckstein, "Economics of the 1960's," p. 86.
7. *Ibid.*, p. 87.
8. *Ibid.*, p. 88.
9. *Ibid.*
10. As Eckstein notes, the first preoccupation of Kennedy and his advisors was actually with obtaining tax reduction as an economic stimulus, rather than a tax reform considerably less acceptable to major interests in the private sector and hence a possible "millstone around fiscal policy." *Ibid.*, p. 87.
11. Cf. Heilbroner, *Limits of American Capitalism*, p. 83.
12. Cf. David Bazelon, "Big Business and the Democrats," *Commentary*, May 1965, pp. 38-46.
13. Cf. H. Brand, "U.S. Economic Policy; From FDR to LBJ," *Dissent* 11 (1964): 121-27.
14. Eckstein, "Economics of the 1960's," p. 90.
15. *Ibid.*
16. Cf. Dick Netzer, "The Visible Tax System," in Sar Levitan, ed., *Blue-Collar Workers* (New York: McGraw-Hill, 1971), pp. 280-81.
17. In part this was an appeal to liberals that they need no longer fear big business, and that they gave up trying to dismantle it through anti-trust. At this point as one critic put it, for Galbraith "the answer to bigness is not the destruction of large concentrations of economic power, but rather the creation of new concentrations to act as counterweights to them." Young, *Politics of Affluence*, p. 52. Cf. John K. Galbraith, *American Capitalism: The Concept of Countervailing Power* (Boston: Houghton-Mifflin, 1956), pp. 111, 151.
18. Young, *Politics of Affluence*, p. 78.
19. Cf. Bell, *End of Ideology*, pp. 89-94, for an early perception of this process.
20. The call for more public sector investment was a theme Galbraith had struck earlier in *The Affluent Society*, where he argued that American affluence was in fact a "privatized" affluence enjoyed by consumers as individuals or families, while public services and the urban environment suffered from serious neglect. Cf. John K. Galbraith, *The Affluent Society* (New York: New American Library, 1958), esp. pp. 198-211.
21. Cf. Michael Harrington, *The Other America* (New York: Macmillan, 1962); Louis A. Ferman, Joyce L. Kornbluh, and Alan Haber, eds., *Poverty in America*, rev. ed. (Ann Arbor: University of Michigan Press, 1968); Ben B. Seligman, *Poverty As A Public Issue* (New York: Free Press, 1965); Herman P. Miller, *Rich Man, Poor Man* (New York: Thomas Y. Crowell Co., 1964).
22. National Commission on Technology, Automation, and Economic Progress, *Technology and the American Economy* (Washington, D.C.: Government Printing Office, 1966), Vol. 1.
23. *Ibid.*, p. xii.
24. *Ibid.*, p. xiv.
25. *Ibid.*, p. xiii.
26. *Ibid.*, p. 17.
27. *Ibid.*, p. 22.
28. *Ibid.*, p. 29.
29. *Ibid.*, p. 30, table 5.
30. *Ibid.*, p. 31.
31. *Ibid.*
32. *Ibid.*, p. 33.
33. *Ibid.*, p. 35.

34. *Ibid.*, p. 37.
35. There are differences in specifics regarding the Commission's public works programs which are worth noting; New Deal programs were aimed at providing employment throughout the economy during a period of generally high unemployment, whereas the Commission's proposals are tailored to the circumstances of heavy long-term unemployment concentrated at certain points in the social structure (e.g. minorities, youth, farmers) during a period of generally low unemployment. (Cf. Paul K. Conkin, *The New Deal* [New York: Thomas Y. Crowell, 1967], p. 35.) However, these proposals do incorporate the New Deal's concept of using the government as an "employer of last resort" when the private labor market fails; the difference being that the public service programs would be aimed at "structural" unemployment, rather than general unemployment (toward which the government's aggregate demand-management activities would be directed). In addition, the Technology Commission's recommendations lie in the area of public services where nonprofessionals and paraprofessionals can be fairly quickly absorbed, whereas the New Deal programs emphasized public construction, which involves a somewhat longer delay in putting employees to work, and therefore a relative delay in economic impact (*Ibid.*)
36. Technology Commission, *Technology and the American Economy*, pp. 40, 41.
37. *Ibid.*, p. 77.
38. *Ibid.*
39. *Ibid.*
40. *Ibid.*, pp. 77-88.
41. *Ibid.*, pp. 95-98.
42. Bell, "Post-Industrial Society (I)," pp. 28-30.
43. Using the symbol of "technetronic society" in a manner very like that of the "postindustrial" rubric, Z. Brzezinski points out: "In the technetronic society, scientific and technological knowledge, in addition to enhancing productive capabilities, quickly spills over to affect directly almost all aspects of life. . . . The growing capacity for calculating instantly most complex interactions . . . increases the potential scope of self-conscious direction, and thereby also the pressures to direct, to choose, and to change." Brzezinski, "America in the Technetronic Age," *Encounter*, January 1968, p. 18.
44. Technology Commission, *Technology and the American Economy*, pp. 99, 100.
45. *Ibid.*, p. 100.
46. Bell, "Post-Industrial Society (I)," pp. 32-35, and "(II)," pp. 107-8.
47. Daniel Bell, "Government by Commission," *The Public Interest* 3 (Spring 1966): 7.
48. *Ibid.*, our emphasis.
49. Technology Commission, *Technology and the American Economy*, p. 6.
50. *Ibid.*
51. *Ibid.*, p. 7.
52. *Ibid.*, our emphasis.
53. Cf. *Baltimore Sun*, June 18, 1971, which reports that only after a previous veto of a public service employment bill in 1970, followed by rising unemployment to over 6 percent by May 1971, was the Nixon administration "willing to accept compromise legislation aimed at creating 150,000 public service jobs" (not, however, in a long term program, but only in a "transitional two-year program"). In addition, contrary to the Technology Commission's recommendations (*Technology and the American Economy,* pp. 36-37), the administration proposed the deletion of the Senate provision making nonprofit organizations (in particular, state and local antipoverty agencies) eligible for federal support in providing jobs. Furthermore, the bill finally signed by the president would provide public service jobs "only when the unemployment rate is at 4.5% or more nationwide" or in high unemployment areas "where unemployment reaches 6% or more." (*Baltimore Sun,*

July 9, 1971). Cf. the goals of the Technology Commission (*Technology and the American Economy*, p. 35), which sought permanent reduction of unemployment to the minimum level determined by unavoidable labor turnover, possibly even below 3 percent.

54. Cf. Solomon Barkin, "The Decline of the Labor Movement," in Andrew Hacker, *The Corporation Take-Over*, pp. 216-38.

55. Bell, "Government by Commission," p. 6.

56. Cf. *Baltimore Sun*, June 30, 1971, which reports that President Nixon vetoed a public works and regional development bill because "construction jobs have 'notoriously long lead times'" and that "spending under the public works bill would not be at full flow for a least 18 months," by which time its effects could be inflationary.

57. For a clearly presented analysis of the shrinkage of blue-collar employment in organized industries, and the difficulties involved in organizing white-collar and service workers, cf. Barkin, "Labor Movement," pp. 217-19, 224-35. Barkin believes employers of white-collar and service personnel may preemptively move to cybernate their operations in anticipation of the possibility of growing unionization among their employees. He asks, "How many service organizations will accept the complications of union negotiations, strikes, personnel services, and higher wages in preference to investing in cybernation?" *Ibid.*, p. 195. Donald Michael, "Cybernation: The Silent Conquest," in Hacker, *Corporation Take-Over*, pp. 183-215.

58. As Daniel Moynihan points out regarding the PPBS system which was introduced throughout the agencies of the federal government in the mid-1960s after its earlier application in the Defense Department, "By the end of the decade it had all but disappeared as an element in decision-making, at least at the higher level of government." In his opinion, "the McNamara colonization of the domestic departments of the federal government with the system of benefit-cost analysis developed in the Pentagon failed," largely owing to "lack of talent,... resistance of the program bureaucracies, and ... insensitivity of PPBS analysis to the actual complexities of social interventions...." Daniel Moynihan, "Policy vs. Program in the '70's," *The Public Interest* 20 (Summer 1970): 91-92.

59. Cf. Daniel Bell, "Unstable America," *Encounter*, June 1970, pp. 11-26. "In the areas of education, welfare, social planning, there has been little knowledge that one can draw upon for policy purposes.... The failure of liberalism, then is in part *a failure of knowledge*." *Ibid.*, p. 25 (emphasis in original).

60. The power and tenacity of the system of interest group liberalism is evidenced in the fact that even ideologically militant organizations for change in the black community such as SNCC and CORE have come to interpret "black power" essentially in terms of admittance to the established interest-system and the bargaining conducted between those interests; i.e., as "getting a piece of the action" rather than a commitment to revolutionary programs. Cf. Robert Allen, *Black Awakening in Capitalist America*, esp. pp. 108-61.

61. Dahl and Lindblom, *Politics, Economics and Welfare*.

62. *Ibid.*, pp. 3,5.

63. *Ibid.*, pp. 16, 18.

64. *Ibid.*, p. 8.

65. *Ibid.*, p. 19.

66. *Ibid.*, pp. 171-226.

67. *Ibid.*, pp. 227-71.

68. *Ibid.*, pp. 272-323.

69. *Ibid.*, pp. 324-65.

70. *Ibid.*, p. 82.

71. *Ibid.*, pp. 85-88.

72. *Ibid.*, pp. 6-18, esp. the diagrams on pp. 10-17, *passim*, illustrating the wide variety of organizational structures and modes of action open to modern policy makers, including "choices available between government ownership

and private enterprise," "choices available between direct and indirect controls" for employment and spending, etc.

73. "The advantages of hierarchical organizations in business, military life, government, and elsewhere seem so obvious and their conflict with equal control so blatant that liberal democratic theory and social practice tend to be unreconciled.... Two questions arise, then. First ... what are the gains and what are the costs of hierarchy? Second, under what conditions do the gains outweigh the costs? ... The second question is a complex one and is in fact one way of posing the subject of most of this book." Dahl and Lindblom, *Politics, Economics, and Welfare*, p. 233.

74. Cf. *ibid.*, pp. 20-25, 57-168. See also Alfred J. Kahn, *Theory and Practice of Social Planning* (New York: Russell Sage Foundation, 1969), esp. pp. 1-28. Kahn tends to emphasize the processes involved in "calculation," or as he more broadly calls it, "policy formulation," in steps from goal statement to specific program delineation and feedback, though he recognizes the importance of social controls in his discussion of program budgeting and of programming problems in the delivery of social services (*ibid.*, pp. 240-304), and in the need to take account of political variables in planning (*ibid.*, pp. 16, 339).

75. In order to carry their strategy for administrative planning beyond the point of a mere intellectual exercise, the end-of-ideologists must see to the development of institutional arrangements which will provide the supporting context, the technical facilities, and the structural linkages for translating projected rational policy into real social action. Cf. Daniel Bell, "The Idea of a Social Report," *The Public Interest* 15 (Spring 1969): 72-84. Here Bell recommends that the government publish regularly a Social Report which will evaluate the effectiveness of government programs with respect to societal changes as measured by specific social indicators. Rather than lodge responsibility for such a report in a single cabinet agency, it should be written by some independent agency, with good access to government data, and with professional staff who are not government officials, but preferably independent academics. He suggests enlarging the Council of Economic Advisers "into a Council of Economic and Social Advisers", with the responsibility of a combined report. (*Ibid.*, p. 84.) However, prerequisite to such an undertaking is the proper orientation of social science itself, or at least of "the sociological profession," which will include "the strengthening of the commitment of the sociological profession to ... the expansion of macrosociological interests, the refining of conceptual categories, the testing of the quantitative data, and the training of students in social analysis...." (*Ibid.*)

76. Cf. Marshall, *Class, Citizenship and Social Development,* pp. 78-90, 105-26.

77. Cf. Raymond A. Bauer, ed., *Social Indicators* (Cambridge, Mass.: The MIT Press, 1966), especially the essays by Bauer, Albert D. Biderman, and Bertram M. Gross.

78. Bell, "Post-Industrial Society (II)," pp. 114-18; Gross, "The State of the Nation: Social Systems in Accounting," in Bauer, *Social Indicators*, pp. 154-271; and Amitai Etzioni, *The Active Society: A Theory of Societal and Political Processes* (New York: Free Press, 1968).

79. Gross, "State of the Nation," p. 208.

80. *Ibid.*, pp. 208-10.

81. *Ibid.*, p. 209.

82. *Ibid.*

83. *Ibid.*, p. 210. Commenting on the work of men like Bertram Gross and Raymond Bauer on the development of feedback systems for monitoring the results of societal action, Eleanor B. Sheldon and Howard E. Freeman observe that in practice proponents of "the feedback system approach" find it very difficult to show just how a social system model and relevant measures of programmatic efforts are to be developed in relation to available social indicators. In the setting of priorities among national goals "indicators must

be regarded as inputs into a complex political mosaic" and can be politically employed by proponents as well as critics of any given policy; of themselves, "they do not make social policy development any more objective;" indeed their definition itself "reflects socio-political values" and their meaning depends on the measurement context in which they are placed by interested interpreters. In the area of program evaluation research, Sheldon and Freeman are highly skeptical of the attempt to substitute the use of social indicators for experimentally designed evaluation, largely because of the great difficulties in controlling for a myriad of contaminating variables, which tends to impede the unambiguous analysis of program effectiveness.

In addition, these authors are dubious about the usefulness of economic analogies in proposals for a system of social accounts. They emphasize that outside of economics, social theory does not yet adequately specify social system variables and their interrelations; and in the absence of adequate theory, "one can hardly suggest that there exists . . . a set of measures that parallel the economic variables." Finally, unless feedback is relatively prompt (less than a year), complex social programs will not be amenable to sensitive manipulation of appropriate variables for the achievement of stated goals. Thus while they recognize the usefulness of social indicators for improving descriptive and analytic activities in social science, they caution against the tendency to "oversell" such indicators associated with the current social-indicator "movement". Cf. Eleanor Bernert Sheldon and Howard E. Freeman, "Notes on Social Indicators: Promises and Potential," in Carol H. Weiss, *Evaluating Action Programs: Readings in Social Action and Education* (Boston: Allyn & Bacon, 1972), pp. 166-73.

84. *Ibid.*
85. Amitai Etzioni, "Guiding Social Change," in Phillip Ehrensaft and Amitai Etzioni, eds., *Anatomies of America: Sociological Perspectives* (New York: Macmillan, 1969), p. 407.
86. Amitai Etzioni, "A Theory of Societal Guidance," in Sarajane Heidt and Amitai Etzioni, eds., *Societal Guidance: A New Approach to Social Problems,* (New York: Thomas Y. Crowell Co., 1969), p. 21; Etzioni, "Guiding Social Change," p. 407.
87. Etzioni, "Guiding Social Change," p. 402.
88. Norbert Wiener, *The Human Use of Human Beings: Cybernetics and Society* (Garden City, N.Y.: Doubleday, 1954), pp. 178-82.
89. Etzioni, "Theory of Societal Guidance", p. 26.
90. Etzioni, *Active Society,* pp. 288-90.
91. *Ibid.*, p. 273.
92. *Ibid.*, pp. 264-65.
93. Etzioni, "Guiding Social Change," p. 409.
94. Etzioni, *Active Society,* pp. 282-305.
95. *Ibid.*, pp. 488, 520.
96. *Ibid.*, p. 490.
97. *Ibid.*
98. *Ibid.*, pp. 520, 534.
99. *Ibid.*, p. 530.
100. *Ibid.*, p. 520.
101. *Ibid.*, p. 530.
102. Gross, "State of the Nation," p. 154.
103. Technology Commission, *Technology and the American Economy,* p. 107.
104. Shortly after the establishment of wage-price controls by the Nixon administration, Secretary of Commerce Maurice Stans met with "11 of the nation's top industrialists," to obtain the views of business on steps to be taken after the expiration of the 90-day freeze. Though he declined to specify their recommendations, Stans reported "there was a general conclusion . . . that the process of controlling inflation after November 12 cannot be accomplished on a voluntary basis" and that "some type of control system will be necessary." The report goes on to note that "The 11 industrialists who met with Mr.

Stans" were all chairmen of the boards of their firms, and included Roche of GM, Borch of GE, Gott of U.S. Steel, Harper of Alcoa, and Batten of J. C. Penney. Further, "Mr. Batten is chairman of the Business Council, the elite group of the nation's 100 leading industrialists that has close ties to the government and particularly to the Nixon administration," *Baltimore Sun,* August 25, 1971.
105. Cf. Allen, *Black Awakening,* pp. 162-206.

Chapter VII

1. Cf. Michael Brown, *The Politics and Anti-Politics of the Young* (Beverly Hills: Glencoe Press, Macmillan Co., 1969); see also Robert T. Golembiewski, Charles S. Bullock III, and Harrell R. Rodgers, Jr. *The New Politics: Polarization or Utopia* (New York: McGraw-Hill, 1970).
2. Cf. Bell, "Post-Industrial Society (I)," p. 35; Gross, *Social Intelligence for America's Future,* pp. vi-viii; see also Peter F. Drucker, "Notes on the New Politics," *The Public Interest* 4 (Summer 1966): 13-30, and esp. p. 25, where he speaks of the "educated professional middle class" as the "new majority" which will be the indispensable element in any successful national political coalition, as against the older majority base composed of labor and the ethnic blocs.
3. Kevin Phillips, *The Emergent Republican Majority* (New Rochelle, N.Y.: Arlington House, 1969), cf. Everett Ladd, Jr., Charles Hadley, and Lauriston King, "A New Political Realignment?" *The Public Interest* 23 (Spring 1971): 46-63, for a critical review of Phillip's argument that changing voter loyalties constitute a significant long-term trend against the Democratic party. At the same time, however, they recognize the political importance of the developing "new ethnocultural frontier", in the shift of ethnic-political conflict from Catholic *versus* Protestant since the 1930s to the current confrontation of blacks *versus* whites. (*Ibid.,* pp. 55-59.)
4. Cf. Alain Touraine, *The Post-Industrial Society, Tomorrow's Social History: Classes, Conflicts and Culture in the Programmed Society,* trans. by Leonard F.X. Mayhew (New York: Random House, 1971).
5. Cf. James L. McCamy, "The New American Government of Science and Technology," in Paul J. Piccard, *Science and Policy Issues, Lectures in Government and Science* (Itasca, Ill.: F.E. Peacock, 1969) pp. 37-50.
6. Drucker, "Notes on the New Politics," p. 20.
7. *Ibid.,* pp. 20-21.
8. Cf. G. William Domhoff, *Who Rules America?* (Englewood Cliffs, N.J.: Prentice-Hall, 1967), esp. pp. 38-114; and Richard J. Barber, "The New Partnership: Big Government and Big Business," in Perrucci and Pilisuk, eds., *Triple Revolution,* pp. 218-29. With reference to the Johnson administration, Barber observed that "In the process of forming a New Partnership with big business, the harsh fact is that the present Administration has surrendered much of its ability to select the means that will protect the public from concentrated economic power. In effect, through adherence to the consensus philosophy it has become less a partner than a captive of big business." (*Ibid.,* p. 229.)
9. Cf. Harold Seidman, *Politics, Position, and Power: The Dynamics of Federal Organization* (New York: Oxford University Press, 1970), esp. pp. 203-4, 250-52, 256-68. Seidman views COMSAT (The Communications Satellite Corporation) in the category of "twilight zone" organizations, neither clearly public or private in their management or responsibility, though the composition of its management seems to favor its private investors. Particularly interesting is Seidman's observation that "COMSAT was used as the model for the National Housing Partnerships authorized by the Housing and Urban Development Act of 1968" (*ibid.,* p. 250), and that the latter act converted

the Federal National Mortgage Association from a "Government Corporation to a Government-sponsored private corporation" of whose fifteen directors only five are publicly appointed. As Seidman notes, the implications of the Housing and Urban Development Act are highly serious because they suggest that the distinctions between public and private spheres can be arbitrarily set aside, even though this may invite "private usurpation of governmental power." (*Ibid.*, pp. 254-55.) Under this principle, he observes, formerly public agencies such as TVA and FHA could be declared non-governmental institutions, public expenditures could be excluded from the budget, and civil service regulations, conflict-of-interest laws, and other laws controlling the activity of public officials could be circumvented.

10. Sanford A. Lakoff, "Scientific Society: Notes Toward a Paradigm," in Piccard, *Science and Policy Issues*, p. 61.
11. Theodore Lowi, *The End of Liberalism: Ideology, Policy and the Crisis of Authority* (New York: W. W. Norton, 1969).
12. Lakoff, "Scientific Society," pp. 57-61. Cf. Drucker, "Notes on the New Politics," pp. 14-15.
13. John McDermott, "Knowledge is Power," *The Nation*, April 14, 1969.
14. Lakoff, "Scientific Society," p. 65.
15. *Ibid.*, pp. 65-66.
16. Cf. Aaron Wildavsky, "Rescuing Policy Analysis from PPBS," in Robert H. Haveman and Julius Margolis, eds., *Public Expenditures and Policy Analysis* (Chicago: Markham, 1970), pp. 461-81.
17. Cf. Lakoff, "Scientific Society," p. 67.
18. Cf. Lowi, *End of Liberalism*, pp. 58-67: "Liberalism-Conservatism: The Empty Debate."
19. *Ibid.*, p. 61.
20. *Ibid.*, p. 63.
21. *Ibid.*, p. 67.
22. *Ibid.*, p. 65.
23. *Ibid.*, p. 63. As Lowi observes, the policies articulated by the social security system "are 'liberal' only because they are governmental; they are conservative in their impact on social structure and opportunity." He views old age insurance, unemployment compensation, etc., as instruments of overall governmental fiscal policy, which help to maintain aggregate demand in countercyclical fashion, through the business cycle, but have no effect toward changing basic class structure. Cf. Harold L. Wilensky and Charles N. Lebeaux, *Industrial Society and Social Welfare* (New York: Free Press, 1965), pp. v-lii, 148-67. Taking account of the rapid rise in expenditures for the various social insurances in the decade from the mid-1950s to the mid-1960s, the authors note that both in its absolute level and in its rate of growth, social insurance (which was least egalitarian) "dwarfed the other public programs."
24. Possibly the most important rationalization of interest group liberalism under the Johnson administration was the doctrine of "creative federalism," under which a significant parcelling of powers between the federal government and other structures of power, both governmental and private, would occur. Lowi, *End of Liberalism*, pp. 82-83. Cf. Max Ways, "Creative Federalism and the Great Society," *Fortune*, January 1966, p. 122. The Nixon administration proposals for revenue sharing in the form of "no strings attached" grants from the federal government to the states are perfectly consistent with this doctrine.
25. Lowi, *End of Liberalism*, pp. 55-67. Cf. Robert Alford, *Party and Society* (Chicago: Rand-McNally, 1963), pp. 11-12.
26. Arthur Schlesinger, Jr., *Kennedy or Nixon — Does it make Any Difference?* (New York: Macmillan, 1960), p. 43.
27. Cf. Lowi, *End of Liberalism*, pp. 106-7; Conkin, *The New Deal*, pp. 41-43.
28. The NRA was created in a moment of crisis, under a threat of a general strike for legislation to establish a thirty-hour week and thereby create over

five million new jobs in the depths of the Depression, in late 1932. For a view of NRA as the conception of sophisticated business leaders seeking to create employment without major reduction of the work week, and to allow for national industrial planning "with a minimum of challenge to the institutions of a profit economy," see William Leuchtenberg, *Franklin D. Roosevelt and the New Deal* (New York: Harper & Row, 1963), pp. 56-57.

29. *Ibid.*, pp. 56-57, 64-66, Cf. Conkin, *The New Deal*, p. 24.
30. Cf. Leuchtenberg, *Roosevelt and the New Deal*, p. 69, who notes that the codes created a "series of private economic governments" through their delegation of pricing and production powers to trade associations. Rather than expanding output and aiding recovery, "The large corporations which dominated the code authorities used their powers to stifle competition, cut back production, and reaped profits from price-raising. . . ." In consequence, "the private interests of business corporations overwhelmed the public interest." (Leuchtenberg, *Roosevelt and the New Deal*, p. 70.)
31. Conkin, *The New Deal*, p. 37.
32. Lowi, *End of Liberalism*, p. 107.
33. Perhaps the clearest symbol of the vesting of public power in the interest groups comprising the local farm bureaus (the base of the pyramid at whose pinnacle stands the American Farm Bureau Federation) has been the dual status of the county agents in this system. As McConnell notes, "Most agents were publicly paid organizers and functionaries of the Farm Bureaus; at the same time they were the Department of Agriculture's only field service across the nation." The basic anomaly was that Farm Bureaus as "constituent units" of the Agriculture Department's programs, were public agencies, at the same time that the state and national federations to which they belonged were private associations. (McConnell, *Private Power*, pp. 232-33.)
34. Owing to the Agriculture Department's emphasis on the "principle of leadership," the wealthier, more influential farmers were organized into the Bureau committees which then proceeded to determine among other things the price support allotments for the parity program. (McConnell, *Private Power*, pp. 231-33; cf. Conkin, *The New Deal*, p. 42.)
35. Lowi, *End of Liberalism*, p. 110.
36. *Ibid.*, p. 102; cf. pp. 103-12.
37. *Ibid.*, p. 115.
38. Quoted in *ibid.*, p. 118.
39. *Ibid.*; cf. Grant McConnell, *Private Power*, p. 276.
40. Lowi, *End of Liberalism*, p. 118; cf. Seidman, *Politics, Position, and Power,* p. 243. Seidman notes that the BAC cut its official connection with the Commerce Department and changed its name to Business Council, rather than comply with regulations aimed at preventing conflicts of interest, under the Kennedy administration. (*Ibid.*, pp. 242-43).
41. Barber, *The American Corporation*, pp. 199-200; McConnell, *Private Power*, p. 276 also lists 60 *active* members; Bernard D. Nossiter, *The Mythmakers: An Essay on Power and Wealth* (Boston: Houghton Mifflin, 1964), p. 3, refers to a total "self-perpetuating" membership of "about 160"; all agree that the membership is drawn from top business leaders in their respective fields.
42. Thus the War Resources Administration, based on an Industrial Mobilization Plan which drew upon the experience of the First World War, set up a central board whose members were top executives of U. S. Steel, AT & T, GM, and Sears Roebuck, plus the presidents of MIT and the Brookings Institution. Through this format, labor's role tended to diminish over the course of the war, while that of industrial leaders grew. McConnell, *Private Power*, pp. 60-61, 256-57.
43. *Ibid.*, p. 260. Cf. Seidman, *Politics, Position and Power*, p. 92, on expanding influence of industry advisory committees under the Eisenhower administration. Cf. Samuel Beer, "Group Representation in Britain and the United States," The

ANNALS, AAPSS, September 1958, pp. 130-40, on the expanding role of industry advisory committees in relation to the New Deal and the defense effort of World War II. See also Kaufman, "Military Complex," p. 188, who reports on the current special relationship between business advisory groups and the Defense Department.

44. Cf. McConnell, *Private Power*, pp. 260-63 on the WOC's, otherwise known as "dollar-a-year men."

45. *Ibid.*, pp. 264-66.

46. *Interim Report of the Antitrust Subcommittee of the Committee of the Judiciary on WOC's and Government Advisory Groups,* U.S. House of Representatives, 84th Cong., 1st sess., 1956, pp. 7-8, quoted in McConnell, *Private Power,* p. 268.

47. *Interim Report,* pp. 10-11.

48. *Ibid.,* p. 99.

49. McConnell, *Private Power,* pp. 264-69.

50. *Ibid.,* p. 269.

51. *Ibid.,* pp. 268-71.

52. *Ibid.,* pp. 270-72.

53. G. William Domhoff, *The Higher Circles: The Governing Class in America* (New York: Random House, 1970), p. 190. These influential business members of the Council played an important part in endorsing the Roosevelt administration's proposals for a federal social security program, and helped counter criticisms of the program made by conservative business groups like NAM and the Chamber of Commerce. *Ibid.,* pp. 211-14.

54. McConnell, *Private Power,* pp. 276-77.

55. *Ibid.,* p. 276.

56. These special functions, coupled with its inaccessibility to public view, naturally raised the question whether the Council was a public or a private body. The issue was at least formally resolved when in 1962, President Kennedy issued an executive order spelling out regulations for the establishment and conduct of advisory committees which specified that all committee meetings be held subject to official approval and in the presence of government officials, with minutes taken, and with government formulating the agenda. Refusing to comply with these regulations, the BAC cut its official connection to the Commerce Department, and changed its name to the Business Council. (Cf. Seidman, *Politics, Position, and Power,* pp. 242-43.) Substantively, however, this seems to have changed little, since "the same group of top business leaders continued to have the services of the same staff, which they continued to pay, and to have much the same access to the same governmental officials." (Cf. McConnell, *Private Power,* pp. 277-78.)

57. See Lowi, "American Business, Public Policy, Case-Studies, and Political Theory," *World Politics* 16 (July 1964): 677-715, for an interesting discussion of distinctions between these policy modes which seems applicable up to about the Second World War. However, the recurring enlargement (under the pressure of national crises since the 1930s) of the target unit for governmental action from the single enterprise (formerly typical of distributive policy) or the class of enterprises (formerly typical of regulatory policy) to the national economy has somewhat blurred the distinction between distributive and regulatory policy, and at the same time has produced subcategories *within* each policy mode, based on the scope of the target unit.

58. Cf. Domhoff, *The Higher Circles,* pp. 207-18.

59. Cf. McConnell, *Private Power,* pp. 272-76. The leading domestic policy organizations today, besides such corporate-financed foundations as Ford, Carnegie and Rockefeller, would probably include the Committee for Economic Development (CED), which has effectively served since the 1930s as the research and education arm of the Business Council; The National Planning Association (NPA), with ties to the Council of Economic Advisors; The National Indus-

trial Conference Board, closely connected with the National Association of Manufacturers; and the prestigious Brookings Institution; among those organizations specializing in foreign affairs, there is notably the Council on Foreign Relations (CFR), articulating with the National Security Council in the Executive Branch; again the CED, in its foreign-policy capacity; the RAND Corporation; the Stanford Research Institute; and related "think tanks" operating in the area of military and foreign policy. On these policy-related organizations, see Domhoff, *The Higher Circles*, pp. 112-34, 186-94 and "How the Power Elite Set National Goals," in Robert Perucci and Marc Pilisuk, eds., *The Triple Revolution Emerging* (Boston: Little, Brown, 1971). On the CED, see Karl Schriftgeisser, *Business Comes of Age* (New York: Harper & Row, 1960), and *Business and Public Policy* (Englewood Cliffs: Prentice-Hall, 1967). On the NPA, see David Eakins, "The Development of Corporate Liberal Policy Research in the United States" (Ph.D. dissertation, University of Wisconsin, 1966). On the CFR, see, *The Council on Foreign Relations, A Record of Twenty-Five Years* (New York: CFR, 1947); Joseph Kraft, "School for Statesmen," *Harper's Magazine*, July 1958; and Lester Milbrath, "Interest Groups and Foreign Policy," in James N. Rosenau, ed., *Domestic Sources of Foreign Policy* (New York: Free Press, 1967).

60. Cf. Domhoff, *Who Rules America?*, pp. 28-30.
61. Cf. Barrington Moore, Jr., "Thoughts on Violence and Democracy," in Robert H. Connery, ed., *Urban Riots: Violence and Social Change* (New York: Random House, 1968), pp. 3-14.
62. Cf. Lowi's analysis, which views redistributive policy as the province of "peak associations" and counter-elite bodies which produce clearly differentiated, internally consistent ideological positions with regard to redistributive issues. The Business Council is more than simply a "peak association" of some given industry (e.g. the Petroleum Council), since it brings together representatives from a spectrum of leading organizations covering American industry and commerce as a whole; in this respect, it is something of a "peak association" of peak associations; and will usually tend to put forward several policy lines, which may or may not be resolved through a compromise formulation, (Cf. Lowi, "American Business, Public Policy, etc.")
63. On the integrative, coordinative role of the National Security Council and the Office of Science and Technology in their respective areas, see Jacob, *Policy and Bureaucracy*, pp. 66-68, 169-70, 183-87.
64. Technology Commission, *Technology and the American Economy*, p. 106.
65. Daniel P. Moynihan, "The Professionalization of Reform," *The Public Interest*, Fall 1965, pp. 6-16.
66. *Ibid.*, pp. 8, 9.   ⁻
67. *Ibid.*, p. 12.
68. *Ibid.*, pp. 15-16.
69. *Ibid.*, p. 14.
70. On the continuity between the "welfare-state" aspects of Progressivism and the New Deal, cf. Sidney Fine, "The General-Welfare State in the Twentieth Century," in Charles I. Schottland, ed., *The Welfare State* (New York: Harper & Row, 1967), pp. 46-49; on the significance of the Progressive era as the historical context for the emergence of the concept and practice of interest group negotiation, particularly between capital and labor, cf. Domhoff, *The Higher Circles*, pp. 158-78. On the New Deal as a "broker state" serving as a mediator between different interests, cf. Leuchtenberg, *Roosevelt and the New Deal*, pp. 84-89; on the clash between the interest-oriented "broker state" aspect of the New Deal, and its reform-oriented "welfare-state" aspect, cf. *ibid.*, pp. 90-94.
71. Bell, "Unstable America,"pp. 24-25.
72. Cf. Arnold S. Kaufman, "Strategies for New Politics," *Dissent*, January-February 1969, pp. 12-19; where Kaufman argues from a populist-liberal

point of view for working for changes within the Democratic party as a possible vehicle for participatory democracy.

73. Cf. Julius Duscha, "Stop! In The Public Interest!," *New York Times Magazine,* March 21, 1971, pp. 4-18 *passim.* Eileen Shanahan, "Nader Asserts Monopolies Mulct the Public of Billions," *New York Times,* June 6, 1971, pp. 1, 55.
74. Leuchtenberg, *Roosevelt and the New Deal,* pp. 84-94.

Chapter VIII

1. Technology Commission, *Technology and the American Economy,* pp. 101-2.
2. Peter Bachrach, "Corporate Authority and Democratic Theory," in David Spitz, ed., *Political Theory and Social Change* (New York: Atherton Press, 1967), p. 259.
3. McConnell, *Private Power,* p. 287.
4. *Ibid.,* p. 288.
5. *Ibid.,* pp. 288-90.
6. *Ibid.,* p. 288.
7. Technology Commission, *Technology and the American Economy,* p. 108.
8. Andrew Shonfield, *Modern Capitalism: The Changing Balance of Public and Private Power* (London: Oxford University Press, 1965), p. 145. Cf. John Hackett and Anne-Marie Hackett, *Economic Planning in France* (Cambridge, Mass.: Harvard University Press, 1963); Neil W. Chamberlain, *Private and Public Planning* (New York: McGraw-Hill, 1965); and Gerald Serkin, *The Visible Hand: The Fundamentals of Economic Planning* (New York: McGraw-Hill, 1968), pp. 165-69.
9. Shonfield, *Modern Capitalism,* 168.
10. *Ibid.,* pp. 129-30.
11. *Ibid.,* p. 148.
12. *Ibid.,* pp. 139-40.
13. *Ibid.,* p. 139.
14. *Ibid.,* pp. 160-61.
15. *Ibid.,* p. 82.
16. Cf. Michael Shanks, *The Stagnant Society* (London: Penguin Books, 1961); and S.M. Lipset, "Changing Class Structure and Contemporary European Politics," p. 276; here Lipset attributes to union resistance part of the responsibility for the British failure to modernize.
17. Shonfield, *Modern Capitalism,* p. 351.
18. *Ibid.,* pp. 350-53.
19. Harrington, "The Social-Industrial Complex," *Harper's,* November 1967, pp. 55-60.
20. *Ibid.*
21. *Ibid.*
22. Cf. *New York Times,* January 23, 1966.
23. Harrington, "Social-Industrial Complex," p. 60.
24. Technology Commission, *Technology and the American Economy,* p. 107. Cf. Michael Harrington, *The Accidental Century* (Baltimore, Maryland: Penguin Books, 1966), pp. 88-89; and Heilbroner, *Limits of American Capitalism,* pp. 92-93.
25. Technology Commission, *Technology and the American Economy,* p. 108.
26. *Ibid.,* p. 75.
27. Shonfield, *Modern Capitalism,* p. 128. As Shonfield puts it here: "In some ways, the development of French planning in the 1950's can be viewed as an act of voluntary collusion between senior civil servants and the senior managers of big business. The politicians and the representatives of organized labour were both largely passed by. The conspiracy in the public interest

between big business and big officialdom worked, largely because both sides found it convenient. . . ."

28. Nieburg, *In the Name of Science*, p. 194.

29. *Ibid.*, p. 194-95.

30. *Ibid.*, p. 195.

31. As we have noted, Michael Harrington explicitly rejects the recently created image of corporate enterprise faithfully executing the social goals of the community. In his view, business methods are inapplicable to these programs, since they emphasize economic return rather than "uneconomic" values such as racial and class integration, beauty or privacy. As he puts it: "America might unwittingly hire business to build a new urban civilization on the basis of the very money-making priorities which brought the old civilization to crisis. The contractor might not simply execute the contract. He might draw it up as well." (Harrington, "The Social-Industrial Complex," p. 56.) In the case of the newly developing electronic-teaching industry, for example, companies might "design machines and programs for private use and then, as a careless, money-making afterthought, unload them on school systems as well." (*Ibid.*, p. 57.) Even the *Wall Street Journal*, he notes, has reported developments which tend to substantiate these fears: "New schools to a considerable extent have to be built around the electronic gear that will cram them." (Cited in *ibid.*)

32. Technology Commission, *Technology and the American Economy*, p. 106.

33. Cf. comment by Mr. Sporn, *ibid.*, p. 107.

Chapter IX

1. See Harold L. Wilensky, "Mass Society and Mass Culture," *American Sociological Review* 29 (April 1964): 173-96. Wilensky uses the term "middle mass" there to mean the aggregate of the upper-working class and the lower-middle class. Similarly, in our usage, "middle mass" includes the upper blue-collar, skilled manual working class and the lower white-collar, sales, clerical, and lower professional-service class. Cf. Charles H. Anderson, *Toward A New Sociology, A Critical View* (Homewood, Ill.: Dorsey Press, 1971), pp. 105-7. See also Wilensky, "Class, Class Consciousness, and American Workers," in William Haber, ed., *Labor in a Changing America* (New York: Basic Books, 1966), p. 13; cf. Richard Hamilton, "The Marginal Middle Class: A Reconsideration," *American Journal of Sociology*, April 1966.

2. Cf. Norton E. Long, "Citizenship or Consumership in Metropolitan Areas," in Scott Greer, *et al.*, eds., *The New Urbanization* (New York: St. Martin's Press, 1968). As Long observes: "The current trend to reduce citizenship, at least at the local level, to a sort of free-floating consumership, attests the serious decline of the appreciation of political values." (*Ibid.*, p. 368.) In an important sense, the upper-middle class has been a style leader for the consumerist culture, which apparently combines an attempt to emulate earlier upper-class life styles such as suburbanism and the consumption of leisure in cultural pursuits, with the mass provision of consumer goods and services in a spreading "department store" culture. (Cf. Bensman and Vidich, *New American Society*, pp. 148-49; and David Riesman, *The Lonely Crowd*, rev. ed. [New Haven: Yale University Press, 1964], pp. 19, 148-74.)

3. Walter Heller, *New Dimensions of Political Economy* (Cambridge, Mass.: Harvard University Press, 1966); Herbert Stein, *The Fiscal Revolution in America* (Chicago: University of Chicago Press, 1969); Arthur M. Okun, *The Political Economy of Prosperity* (Washington, D.C.: The Brookings Institution, 1970).

4. Cf. Melman, *Pentagon Capitalism*, pp. 211-13, and Marcus Raskin, Comments quoted in Erwin Knoll and Judith N. McFadden, eds., *American Militarism, 1970* (New York: Viking Press, 1969), Chapter 1: "The National Security Establishment," p. 24. Also see Marc Pilisuk and Tom Hayden, "Is There a Military-Industrial Complex That Prevents Peace?," in Perrucci and Pilisuk, eds., *The Triple Revolution Emerging*, pp. 82-89 for a comparative image of the groups which have benefitted in the postwar period from military expenditures, indicating broad convergence in the area which we have termed the "middle mass."

5. Cf. Herbert Marcuse, *One-Dimensional Man* (Boston: Beacon Press, 1964), pp. 11-12.

6. *Ibid.*, pp. 58-62.

7. Cf. Hans Morgenthau, *The Purpose of American Politics* (New York: Random House, 1964), pp. 3-37.

8. This by no means assumes that either the white lower middle or upper working class is racist *per se*; rather it seems clear that much recent resentment in these groups has been based on the increased competition for jobs as the economy contracted in the late 1960s. It is entirely possible that the experience of growing unemployment for white workers was exacerbated by what they perceived as the greater relative gain of blacks in income and employment, and by the antipoverty programs which were given such public prominence after the mid-Sixties. See Leonard S. Silk, "Is There a Lower-Middle-Class 'Problem'?," in Sar Levitan, ed., *Blue-Collar Workers* (New York: McGraw-Hill, 1971), pp. 7-19, esp. p. 13. Cf. Richard Hamilton, "Black Demands, White Reactions, and Liberal Alarms," in Levitan, *Blue-Collar Workers*, pp. 130-53, confirming the central importance of the tightening job market to increasing black-white tensions in the late 1960's, and for data indicating that in 1968, with the exception of the South, segregationist attitudes and support for the Wallace candidacy were relatively low (under 15 percent) throughout the country with little variation by occupational class.

9. Cf. Bell, ed., *The Radical Right*, esp. pp. 1-104; 307-71.

10. Cf. Robert Allen, *Black Awakening in Capitalist America*, Chaps. IV and V, pp. 108-206, for the interesting review and discussion of the role of organizations like CORE which have adopted both the black power rhetoric and the function of middlemen for funneling programs and capital from corporate foundations and public agencies into black communities, while at the same time eschewing aggressive violence.

11. Stokely Carmichael and Charles V. Hamilton, *Black Power, The Politics of Liberation in America* (New York: Random House, 1967); Lewis M. Killian, *The Impossible Revolution? Black Power and the American Dream* (New York: Random House, 1968), esp. pp. 125-76; Floyd B. Barbour, ed. *The Black Power Revolt* (Boston: Porter Sargent, 1968), pp. 149-203; Allen, *Black Awakening*, pp. 132-44.

12. Jacobs and Landau, *The New Radicals*, esp. pp. 3-14, 149-71; Mitchell Cohen and Dennis Hale, *The New Student Left* (Boston: Beacon Press, 1966), esp. pp. 1-49, 270-88; and Jack Newfield, *A Prophetic Minority* (New York: Signet Books, 1967); Massimo Teodori, ed., *The New Left: A Documentary History* (Indianapolis: Bobbs-Merrill, 1969).

13. Cf. Richard Flacks, "The Uses of Participatory Democracy," *Dissent* 13 (November-December 1966): 701-8; and Staughton Lynd, "The New Radicals," *Dissent* 12 (Summer 1965). See also Teodori, *The New Left*, pp. 34-54, 163-239.

14. Cf. Young, *The Politics of Affluence*, pp. 41-49.

15. Cf. Richard Rothstein, "Representative Democracy in SDS," New University Conference Position Paper, n.d.

16. Flacks, "Uses of Participatory Democracy," pp. 707-8.

17. *Ibid.*, p. 707.

18. *Ibid.*, p. 708.
19. Barbour, ed., *The Black Power Revolt*, esp. pp. 207-44.
20. S. M. Lipset, "Introduction," in T. H. Marshall, *Class, Citizenship, and Social Development* (New York: Doubleday, 1965), p. x.
21. Flacks, "Uses of Participatory Democracy," p. 701.
22. Cf. the Model Cities programs under which Community Action Programs have tended to be subsumed, in the process reducing or constraining the citizen participation aspect emphasized in the early CAP's. See Roland L. Warren, "The Model Cities Program, An Assessment," in National Conference on Social Welfare, *The Social Welfare Forum* (New York: Columbia University Press, 1971); and Warren, "Model Cities First Round: Politics, Planning, and Participation," *Journal of the American Institute of Planners* 35 (1969).
23. Cf. Riesman, *The Lonely Crowd.*
24. Cf. Stanley Weir, "U.S.A.: The Labor Revolt," in Maurice Zeitlin, ed., *American Society, Inc.* (Chicago: Markham, 1970), pp. 465-501; and William Faunce, "Automation and the Automobile Worker," *Social Problems* 6 (Summer 1958): 68-71. See also Agis Salpukas, "Young Workers Disrupt Key G.M. Plant," *New York Times*, January 23, 1972, pp. 1, 41, who reported that production on the Chevrolet Vega assembly line ("the world's fastest") at General Motors' Lordstown, Ohio plant had been disrupted mainly by young workers protesting speedup and stringent work discipline which forced them to "work too hard and too fast to be able to turn out quality automobiles." According to this report, the "outcome of the labor dispute . . . could have wide repercussions for United States industry," seeking to meet growing foreign competition through increased productivity. Moreover, the dispute "comes at a time when the Nixon Administration is stressing rising productivity as the way to stop inflation and the influx of foreign goods." (This dispute was settled after a brief strike lasting three weeks, after which many local grievances remained to be resolved. Though the Lordstown local of the United Auto Workers Union was provided the services of experienced negotiators by the UAW International they got little financial support, since the UAW treasury had not yet recovered from the expenses of the strike against GM in 1970. Cf. "Vega strike ends, but the issue still boils," *Business Week*, April 1, 1972, pp. 22-3. For background, see "Spreading Lordstown syndrome: assembly-line worker discontent," *Business Week*, March 4, 1972, pp. 69-70 and B. J. Widick, "The Men Won't Toe the Vega Line," *The Nation*, March 27, 1972, pp. 403-4).

Chapter X

1. Scott Greer, *The Emerging City* (Glencoe, Ill.: Free Press, 1964). Greer's work is particularly useful to understanding the effects of increasing scale, energy, and income in the postwar era, in exploding the traditional urban structure of the city, and unseating received urban-sociological theory.
2. Cf. Talcott Parsons, *Sociological Theory and Modern Society* (New York: Free Press, 1967), pp. 18-19.
3. On the web of pluralist membership and its significance for political, associational, and cultural participation, see Lipset, *Political Man*, pp. 211-26; Bell, *End of Ideology*, pp. 108-9; and Clark Kerr, et al., *Industrialism and Industrial Man* (Cambridge, Mass: Harvard University Press, 1960), pp. 288-97. On interest bargaining, see Dahl and Lindblom, *Politics, Economics, and Welfare*, pp. 324-65; Lipset, *Political Man*, pp. 297-99; and Bell, *End of Ideology*, pp. 120-22. On the relevance of the legal system to interorganizational coor-

dination in pluralist society, see Talcott Parsons, *Sociological Theory*, pp. 3-34, esp. p. 18.

4. Cf. Charles H. Hession, S. M. Miller, and Curwen Stoddart, *The Dynamics of the American Economy* (New York: Alfred A. Knopf, 1965), pp. 162-70, 183-86; and Galbraith, *New Industrial State*, pp. 26-31.

5. Talcott Parsons, *The Social System* (Glencoe, Ill.: Free Press, 1951), pp. 50-51, 96-101. Cf. Susan Keller, *Beyond the Ruling Class* (New York: Random House, 1963), p. 91.

6. Cf. Talcott Parsons, *Sociological Theory*, ch. 12: "Christianity and Modern Industrial Society," pp. 385-421.

7. Daniel Bell, "The Disjunction of Culture and Social Structure: Some Notes on the Meaning of Social Reality," *Daedalus* 94 (Winter 1965): 216.

8. Cf. Lipset, "Changing Class Structure and Contemporary European Politics," p. 276: cf. T. B. Bottomore, *Classes in Modern Society* (New York: Random House, 1966), pp. 84-87.

9. Cf. Herbert Marcuse, *One-Dimensional Man* (Boston: Beacon Press, 1964), pp. 11-12, 58-62.

10. C. P. Snow, *The Two Cultures and the Scientific Revolution* (Cambridge: Cambridge University Press, 1959).

11. Irving Kristol, "Letter from New York: Teaching In, Speaking Out: The Controversy Over Viet Nam," *Encounter*, August 1965, pp. 65-70.

12. Daniel Bell, *The Reforming of General Education* (Garden City, New York: Doubleday, 1968), pp. 314-15.

13. Noam Chomsky, *American Power and the New Mandarins: Historical and Political Essays* (New York: Random House, 1969), pp. 345-46.

14. Bell, *End of Ideology*, pp. 15-16.

15. Bell, *Reforming of General Education*.

16. *Ibid.*, p. 313.

17. *Ibid.*

18. *Ibid.*, pp. 314, 315.

19. *Ibid.*, pp. 316, 317.

20. Daniel Bell, "The Cultural Contradictions of Capitalism," *The Public Interest* 21 (Fall 1970): 16-43.

21. *Ibid.*, p. 43.

22. See, for example, "Toward the Year 2000: Work in Progress," *Daedalus* 96 (Summer 1967). (Daniel Bell, as Chairman of the American Academy of Arts and Sciences Commission on the Year 2000, acted as chairman and moderator for the working sessions of the Commission and as general editor for the transcripts of those sessions and the papers on specific problems brought together in this issue of *Daedalus*. (In addition, in consultation with the Commission's planning group, Bell set forth the agenda for the Commission's work in a "preliminary memorandum" to its members. *Ibid.*, pp. 652-55.) This fairly representative collection of papers deals mostly with probable future developments in the areas of institutional and community change; changing social values, character, and psychology; technological forecasting; world industrialization and national output, etc., which tend to center around the themes of technological contributions to national power and probable future adaptations of institutions, community, and character to the "technological society." Nowhere, however, do they enter into any detailed examination of probable changes in class structure in this society. In their overriding interest in the meritocratic elite which they view as guiding development in the "technological society" of the twenty-first century, the questions of class differences, deprivations, and conflicts seem to have been expunged from the agenda of these technocratic futurists, though not because they believe Technopolis will be classless. Thus, the only essay touching in any way on the matter of class structure, David Riesman's "Notes on Meritocracy," introduces some stylistic qualifications to the current "metrical" *criteria*

for entry to the meritocracy, but does not discuss the resulting class structure, except to emphasize that it would not be "classless," and winds up extolling the *principle* of meritocracy itself: "Even though meritocracy brings heightened standards of performance everywhere, [!] in a country as large as the United States, resistance movements based on local pride and even local paranoia will persist." (*Ibid.*, p. 908 our emphasis.) (Riesman presents no data, "metrical" or otherwise, to support this rather sweeping statement.)

23. Cf. Harvey Cox, *The Secular City* (New York: Macmillan, 1965), for the description of a highly advanced society with a complex combination of qualities which are just now emerging in postindustrial society. The symbol which Cox employs is the term "Technopolis," appropriately representing a "fusion of technological and political components into the base on which a new cultural style has appeared." (*Ibid.*, pp. 1-6.) The cultural style is a sophisticated antitraditional pluralism, based on the wide freedom of choice offered by the diversity and social differentiation of the contemporary metropolis.

24. Brzezinski, "America in the Technetronic Age," p. 21.

25. Kerr, *et al., Industrialism and Industrial Man*, p. 295.

26. Kerr, *The Uses of the University* (Cambridge, Mass.: Harvard University Press, 1964), pp. 91-94.

27. David E. Apter, ed., *Ideology and Discontent* (London: Collier-Macmillan Ltd., Free Press of Glencoe, 1964).

28. *Ibid.*, p. 31.

29. *Ibid.*, p. 38.

30. *Ibid.*, p. 37.

31. *Ibid.*

32. *Ibid.*

33. *Ibid.*, pp. 32-33.

34. *Ibid.*, p. 36; emphasis added.

35. Cf. Nieburg, *In The Name of Science*, pp. 103-16: ch. VI, "Science: Process and Ideology."

36. Brzezinski, "America in the Technetronic Age," pp. 16-18, 21-23, for an attempt to articulate a model of a self-transcending society. Cf. Bell, *End of Ideology*, for some early suggestions in this direction; for example, Bell's comments that America today is probably the world's most rapidly changing society because it "is probably the first society to have change and innovation 'built into' its culture. . . ." (*Ibid.*, p. 37.)

37. Cf. Charles E. Silberman, *The Myths of Automation* (New York: Harper & Row, 1966). It is interesting to note that Daniel Bell aligned himself with a position similar to this in a number of articles on the automation controversy in the *New York Review of Books*, August 21 and November 25, 1965. See Ben B. Seligman's critique of Bell's position and use of data in "On Theories of Automation, A Polemic Against Daniel Bell and Others," *Dissent* 13 (May-June 1966): 243-64, esp. pp. 248-49. See also Ben B. Seligman, *Most Notorious Victory* (New York: Free Press, 1966); and Charles R. Dechert, ed., *The Social Impact of Cybernetics* (New York: Clarion Books, 1967).

38. John J. Corson, *Business in the Humane Society*, p. 216, table 10.1.

39. *Monthly Labor Review,* 93 (May 1970): 97, cited in Robert Perucci, "Work in the Cybernetic State," in Perrucci and Pilisuk, eds., *The Triple Revolution Emerging* (Boston: Little, Brown, 1971), p. 177.

40. Corson, *Business in Humane Society*, p. 216.

41. *Ibid.*, p. 222, table 10.3. From 1947 to 1970 the total number of white-collar jobs increased by almost 18 million to about 38 million jobs, while the number of blue-collar jobs increased by little more than 4.5 million to about 28 million; the effect was to increase the white-collar share of employment about 12.5 percent to almost 47.5 percent of total employment, while

the blue-collar share actually dropped by almost 5 percent to approximately 36 percent of the total. Estimates for 1975 predict a further expansion of white-collar employment to almost half of total employment (48.5 percent) and a further decline in the blue-collar share to about one-third (34 percent).

42. Donald N. Michael, *Cybernation: The Silent Conquest* (Santa Barbara: Center for the Study of Democratic Institutions, 1962); Charles R. Dechert, ed., *The Social Impact of Cybernetics* (New York: Clarion Books, 1967).

43. See Ida R. Hoos, "When the Computer Takes Over the Office," *Harvard Business Review* 38 (July-August 1960): 102-12, on possible impacts of cybernation on office employment patterns.

44. Cf. Dennis H. Wrong, "Social Inequality Without Social Stratification," in Dennis H. Wrong and Harry L. Gracey, eds., *Readings in Introductory Sociology* (New York: Macmillan, 1967), pp. 498-507.

45. Perrucci, "Work in the Cybernetic State," p. 181. As Perrucci notes, thus far automation has tended mainly to involve less than totally automated production systems, owing to costs which are currently prohibitive. Nonetheless, even on this limited basis, its effects are already clearly discernible. Cf. Michael Harrington, "Automation: A Revolution That Is," *New York Times*, April 24, 1966, Section 11: "The Computer and Society, Six Viewpoints," pp. 6-7; Charles C. Killingworth, "The New Technology Is Shaping a New Labor Force," *ibid.*, pp. 8-9, and Michael, *Cybernation*, pp. 20-25.

46. Some theorists have argued that a new working class consisting of the majority of the scientific and professionally trained work force is currently in the process of emerging, or even well on its way to crystallization. (Cf. Andre Gorz, *Strategy for Labor* [Boston: Beacon Press, 1967]; Serge Mallet *La Nouvelle Classe Ouviere* [Paris: Anthropos, 1969]; Martin Oppenheimer, "The New White Collar Working Class," *Social Policy* 1, No. 2, July-August 1970; Bogdan Denitch, "Is There a New Working Class?" *Dissent* 17, No. 4, July-August 1970.) The further implication is that this college-educated class of technical and social service functionaries constitutes the essential work force of the technological society promising to act as a radical political stratum in its own right and possibly as a vanguard to segments of the more traditional working classes. In our view, that definition is premature, though useful as a heuristic concept against which to measure future class developments in technological society. Our own understanding of the current role of this class is that its members constitute a technocratic staff of experts and advisors whose skills are essentially at the service of the upper executive-managerial class in the society today, and whose level of financial and status rewards still remains considerably higher than that enjoyed by the blue- and white-collar "middle mass." The technocratic staff is thus currently still best described as a stratum that stands between the contemporary working class and the executive-managerial ruling class. Any significant emergence of a "new working class" from the contemporary technocratic staff of scientifically and professionally trained employees would first require a serious reduction in status of the bulk of this class. This could conceivably be one important outcome of major growth in the proportion of this class to the total work force, accelerated by widening automation. Nevertheless this still appears to lie at some distance in the future, and intervening events, including the very politicization of the technocratic staff which the "new working class" theorists forecast, could possibly forestall it.

47. Ad Hoc Committee, "The Triple Revolution," *Liberation*, April 1964, pp. 9-15.

48. *Ibid.*, p. 13.

49. Cf. Robert Theobald, *The Guaranteed Income* (New York: Doubleday, 1967).

50. Robert Lekachman, "The Automation Report," in Perrucci and Pilisuk, eds., *The Triple Revolution*, pp. 178-90.

51. *Ibid.*, p. 187.

52. *Ibid.*, p. 190.

Chapter XI

1. Clifford Geertz, "Ideology as a Cultural System," in David E. Apter, ed., *Ideology and Discontent* (London: Collier-Macmillan Ltd., 1964), p. 58.
2. *Ibid.*, pp. 58-59.
3. Cf. Harold L. Wilensky, *Organizational Intelligence, Knowledge and Policy in Government and Industry* (New York: Basic Books, 1967), pp. 24-34.
4. Michael Young, *The Rise of the Meritocracy: 1870-2033* (London: Thames and Hudson, 1958).
5. Michael, *Cybernation.*
6. Brzezinski, "America in the Technetronic Age," p. 21.
7. Cf. William Connolly, *Political Science and Ideology* (New York: Atherton, 1967), for useful comments on the analysis of ideological thought. In this regard, see esp. chap. 5: "Toward Responsible Ideology," pp. 117-55.
8. Cf. Mason Drukman, *Community and Purpose in America: An Analysis of American Political Thought* (New York: McGraw-Hill, 1971).
9. Richard Titmuss, "Social Welfare and the Art of Giving," in Erich Fromm, *Socialist Humanism: An International Symposium* (Garden City, N.Y.: Doubleday, 1966), p. 384.

Index